Freedom From Psychiatric Drugs:

A Psychiatric Survivors Handbook, Manual and Workbook

by Chaya Grossberg

© 2018
All Rights Reserved.
No part of this book can be reproduced without written permission from the author.

Cover photos by
Kata Gomeztagle-Johann

Book Layout by
Sheena M Hamilton
www.lynxcreatively.com

Acknowledgments

My gratitudes are many. Rather than naming individuals and inevitably leaving some out, I will name the groups of people who have helped. Thank you to everyone at the original Freedom Center in Northampton, who were there for me when I was coming off psychiatric drugs.

Thank you to my parents for supporting me in that process and for encouraging me throughout my life as a writer, reader and seeker of knowledge and truth. Thank you to those at Windhorse Associates, who were there for me spiritually and in so many other ways while I was coming off psych drugs.

Thank you to my high school English teachers of poetry, creative writing and metaphysics, who encouraged and inspired me to write and saw the writer in me, as well as all of my writer friends as a teenager who wrote poetry alongside me, went to open mics with me and had writing groups with me.

Thank you to the Western Massachusetts Recovery Learning Community for supporting my work when I started teaching yoga and leading other support groups. Thank you to the director and staff at the Alternative to Meds Center. Thank you to the Mental Health Association of Portland, Portland Hearing Voices.

Thank you to the organizers of conferences where I spoke including NARPA, INTAR and Alternatives. Thank you to everyone who housed me during my times of transience, when I was first building my business.

Thank you to all of the staff at Mad In America who have published my blogs over the past 5 years (some of the content in this book was first published on Mad In America). Thank you everyone in the film Coming Off Psych Drugs by Daniel Mackler.

Thank you everyone who helped with my Indiegogo fundraising campaign. Thank you to all of the donors of money, rewards, advice and time from that campaign. Thank you to the networking communities in Olympia, Washington where I now live, and all who have helped with and attended the events I've hosted here.

Thank you to everyone at Mindfreedom Seattle for supporting my work. Thank you to the Twitter chronic illness community.

Thank you to every one of my friends and relatives who has been there for a phone call, a walk, a talk or a distant prayer over the years. Thank you to everyone who has read my work, and given me encouraging feedback.

Thank you to the few but valuable therapists I have had over the years who did not diagnose me (except for insurance purposes) or suggest drugs at all. They listened well, trusted me and supported me to find my own wisdom and healing. Thank you to my current therapist who tried to contain her excitement about this book.

Thank you to all of the clients who have trusted me with their vulnerability in some of their darkest times and shared their stories, struggles and dreams with me. Thank you so much.

Disclaimer

This book is a compilation of the best information and insights I've gathered over the past 15 years of working professionally with people coming off of psych drugs and living without them.

My perspectives are also constantly changing and I am always learning. Much of what I share here is time tested, but not all of it is relevant and true to everyone.

I'm aware many people do not like to be identified by the term "differently abled". I identify with this term myself because I am disabled in some ways but not others. I talk more about this later in the book.

Please know that I mention this term not to identify anyone with it who does not choose to, but to include my own choice of a phrase for describing my own abilities and disabilities.

We are each on a different path and have many blind spots to what is and is not relevant to others.

Please keep in mind that I am not perfect, this book is not perfect. In fact I am intentionally publishing an imperfect book because my own instinct is telling me it is more important to share it now than to polish it further or obsess over every single detail.

Use your own judgement. Trust your gut and your body and your own knowing. That will always be your best teacher. My goal with this book is to express what wisdom has come to me and what I have learned. I hope it will inspire you and that whatever does not resonate with you, you will let go of.

I am not a doctor and nothing in this book or that I say or write is ever any kind of standard medical advice. Please use your intuition and resources to find medical or other support that best suits YOU.

Psychiatric drugs should generally be tapered carefully and with support from knowledgeable and kind doctors and those with healing presences who also have good boundaries and know how to take good care of themselves.

Please research to make your own best decisions. I believe in you!

Forwards

"My name is Tariq Jalal. I live in San Francisco and I am Engineer. I have known Chaya for 3 years and I would say this is a great book by a person who has been through personal journey on psychiatric drugs and has been through the process of eliminating the drugs."

"This is a positive step for Chaya, a sense of healing and helping others who are on psychiatric drugs. The first couple of chapters are Chaya's personal journey and how she got into psychiatric drugs; her story."

"The chapters next I really enjoyed. They talk about the useful tools for finding the right information on supporting the body, connecting to people who are like minded. They discuss how not to be ashamed of who you are and how to say that publicly when and if you choose to."

"The chapters related to suicide and surviving suicide of a loved one are nicely written and I feel Chaya's presence in them. At the end, Chaya makes the reader at ease and makes a case for having fun moving away from psychiatric drugs if one chooses to do so."

- **Tariq Jalal**

"When Chaya asked me to write a forward for this book I was honored. Her personal story is both tragic and triumphant, with a strong dose of spiritual awakening tossed in."

"She uses all she has learned and experienced to help others find ways to heal outside of the psychiatric paradigm of diagnose and drug. A paradigm led by doctors who almost killed her."

"We are all human, and we all suffer. Chaya teaches that mind-body-spirit is connected and all need to be addressed when a crisis is experienced that gets labeled as mental illness. She focuses on all aspects of healing to help others live authentic lives, free of psych meds. A very inspirational and admirable woman."

- **Molly McHugh, author of "Bipolar 1 Disorder - How to Survive and Thrive"**

Contents

	Introduction	7
1.	My Story	11
2.	Understanding The System	25
3.	Alternatives	89
4.	Gathering Resources and Support	103
5.	Withdrawal	109
6.	After Un-Diagnosis: Finding Your Own Language For Your Suffering	125
7.	Turning Trauma Into Medicine	139
8.	Supporting The Body	151
9.	Connecting with the Worldwide Movement	167
10.	Finding Meaningful Work (or creating your own)	175
11.	Going Public, Being Known	195
12.	Suicidal Thoughts and Feelings	207
13.	Surviving the Suicide of a Loved One	217
14.	Surviving Deaths of Comrades	229
15.	Supporting Others Without Interfering, Accepting Others Where They Are, and Leading By Example	237
16.	Therapy?	245
17.	Having Fun Again	257
18.	Freedom From Psychiatric Drugs Workbook	263
	About the Author	265

INTRODUCTION

Psychiatric drugs and electroshock, the main treatments used in psychiatric medical practice, are rough on the body. While some people like the effects on their mind (and others find them to simply "not work" or to be terrible or even agonizing), they never have a good long-term effect on the body. This is a problem for disabled/differently abled individuals.

For those with very strong kidney/adrenal, liver, digestive and other organ function, the stress of psychiatric pharmaceuticals can be fielded for quite some time before fatigue sets in.

Maybe these folks can take psychiatric drugs for many years and still work at a job, maintain relationships and keep a solid sleep schedule and basic motivation. These are often the people who find the drugs to "work." Their bodies are able to easily release the toxins and continue functioning alright.

But for those who already have any kidney/adrenal, liver, digestive or other organ weakness, damage or dysfunction, it is another story. The psychiatric chemicals do not detox easily, the kidneys and adrenals are further weakened by the stress of having to work so hard to detoxify them and the digestive system is vulnerable to getting sluggish.

Of course, there are some people who are physically damaged by the drugs to the point of losing their basic health and motivation, but still feel that they need them, that the drugs are better than not taking them. Is it fair to leave disabled people with so few choices, though? To only offer treatments that make their physical disabilities or chronic illness worse?

There's a large range of tolerance of these drugs, with those with the strongest physical constitution more likely to tolerate the meds for a longer period of time. Those with more fragile, sensitive or weak bodies are more likely to be damaged, even permanently, by the stress of taking these drugs every day, especially if they are on multiple drugs or on them for years on end.

That's why it is gaslighting to criticize people for seeking alternative treatments, or for opting to go about their lives in ways that don't rely on psychiatric pharmaceuticals.

Gaslighting, or manipulating people into questioning their own sanity, applies here as people are often ridiculed, put down, ostracized or abandoned for trying alternative treatments. This is usually after psychiatric drugs made them too sick to engage with life.

I was told by a doctor once, "Herbs don't work. If they worked people would use them." He then put me on a drug that didn't work, and I now use herbs for sleep, relaxation, nutrients, adrenal nourishment, hormonal balancing, and physical healing with great success. The psychiatric meds I was subsequently put on, because none of my doctors knew about safe and effective alternative treatments, ended up making me bedridden for a couple of years and with neuroleptic malignant syndrome for three months.

For disabled and differently abled bodies, treatments for the mind and emotions MUST support the physical body as well, or we will only get sick physically, which is not exactly a cure for anxiety, loneliness or grief.

Many differently abled people are not aware of how vulnerable their bodies may be to these drugs, and doctors are unlikely to tell them. If doctors were doing a full physical before putting people on psych drugs to make sure it was safe for that person's health, the process would take longer and many people would find nutritional deficiencies, hormonal imbalances and other issues to correct before even going on them.

Cautions about the health dangers of psych meds for disabled and chronically ill folks are less effective than they should be. Even with the long lists of possible side effects, black box warnings, commercials that list all the side effects out loud, magazine ads with almost an entire page full of them, many people still think of these drugs as basically safe and medicinal, even as "good for their mental health."

This is due to (mostly indirect) pharmaceutical marketing that implies they are safe and effective, the stigma associated with "not taking your meds" if you've received a psychiatric label, and other agendas to control people such as family and social pressure.

Ableism is when able bodied people are seen as more relevant, valuable and somehow intrinsically mattering more than those with disabilities. The entire field of psychiatry is ableist, in offering medication that can only be tolerated by the extremely able bodied.

Those who are already physically ill or disabled will be made more and more ill by psychiatry over time, and the field of medicine marginalizes disabled folks by not addressing these issues or warning them sufficiently about these concerns from the beginning. Disabled folks are not given options that are sustainable and effective for them.

The fact that psychiatric drugs will make a tired person more tired (eventually if not right away), a sick person more sick, a weak organ system weaker, shows an inherent discrimination against differently abled bodies. It shows that people with physical health concerns are being completely marginalized by psychiatry.

A field of medicine that was friendly to differently abled folks would strive to ensure that all treatments and procedures were designed to strengthen both the body and mind. Some alternative and holistic modalities do this.

This is called the nourishment model and includes things like nature therapy, person-centered nutrition that takes individual constitution into account, adaptive exercise, creative arts, herbalism, and hands-on healing.

Then there are alternative treatments that can help build the body such as vitamin, mineral and supplement therapy. Disabled folks will often have better success with these, if they can tailor a program to their own specific nutrient needs and deficiencies to support their bodies.

Psychiatric drugs completely ignore the body and what it might be asking for. This is ableist. This is why the disability rate keeps rising as more and more people are being put on meds.This is why the disability community should never be gaslit, or told they are crazy for seeking and researching alternative treatments.

Of course we need to be cautious. Alternative and holistic treatments can cause harm to disabled bodies as well (none have ever caused me as much harm as psychiatric drugs though, not even close). There are very expensive products that aren't covered by insurance that may have minimal effect or make things worse.

Most vitamins and supplements are not covered by insurance, regardless of whether they have been proven to work. This again is ableist, because it makes the treatments people with disabilities and chronic illness need inaccessible and even stigmatized.

Some nourishing methods of healing can be free or very low cost such as foraging wild weeds which have more nutrition than store bought vegetables (but this isn't REAL medicine). Some issues of accessibility can be overcome with knowledge of plants and nutrition, community support and grassroots organizing.

This is why education and stigma reduction about the need for alternatives to psychiatry for disabled and differently abled people is crucial.

Any one-size-fits-all medical system will be ableist. Alternative treatments and approaches can be much more helpful to less able bodied folks if they are catered to each individual and their specific needs, preferences, beliefs, sensitivities and health challenges.

Psychiatric drugs, on the other hand, have been shown to harm the body. They have been thoroughly researched by their own funding and have still been found to cause extreme harm.

Every psychiatric drug advertisement and prescription insert must list these potential health dangers because they are serious risks. And guess who they are more serious risks to? Yes, those who are more physically vulnerable, who are less able bodied.

Ableism says it's okay to have insurance only cover the harshest treatments, which only the most able bodied people can tolerate. Models inclusive of disabled folks would cover a wide range of options so that more people could access safer options that support their bodies, mind and emotions.

Non-Medical Consultation

It's been over 5 years since I started offering non-medical consultations to people in the process of coming off or hoping to come off psych drugs. I have also worked with families of people looking for alternatives and seeking to get out of the hospital/medication runaround.

Before I started this consulting business, I had gained a decade of professional experience with various organizations using different approaches to support people seeking alternatives to psychiatry.

Working for these different groups and businesses helped me to learn about models of peer support, nutritional and herbal/supplemental support for the body, detox strategies, tapering methods, and the common challenges people face when withdrawing from substances their doctors told them were safe and medicinal.

I also had my own experience of getting off of 7 different psychiatric pharmaceuticals. I knew I would have died if I hadn't been able to safely withdraw (and the story would have been that I died of mental illness).

None of the people I have worked with have had an easy time. People don't hire a private non-medical consultant to help them get off of a prescription medication because it's easy and straightforward. If there was a simple step-by-step process that could be written in a book or blog, we wouldn't have this epidemic and I wouldn't get despairing emails and messages almost daily.

The workbook sections at the end of each chapter are designed to help you process all of the content in this book. If you answer all of them, you will have your own book, so this is a good template if you'd like to write a book (or some blogs/articles).

CHAPTER 1

MY STORY

When I was 5, an author came to my elementary school in Brooklyn and my classmates and I sat on stage and listened to her read some of her book to us. Then there was a question/answer period and I asked, "How did you feel when you got your first book published?"

I remember few details and conversations from that age in such vivid detail, but that stage and question are among them. I don't remember who the author was or what she responded. It was a time before the internet, before self-publishing broke loose on a large scale, a time when your words basically had to be published by someone else, some important out of reach company, and your ideas had to be likely to sell.

I spent a long time writing poetry and publishing my own books on a very small scale before social media and blogs became options for sharing my words. I took my passion for language mostly into the ethereal, magical world of my imagination, since nothing I said had much possibility of making societal impact-only my chosen friends and people I encountered at open mics would hear them anyway.

And there weren't many open mics for short essays, or autobiographically influenced political commentary. The small audience I had, at times, felt so limited and frustrating compared with how much writing meant to me.

When I was 22 I told an older friend of mine, "I want to write about every single thing that has ever happened to me. I want to publish TONS." He said, "Well you'd better get writing, you're creating a huge backlog right now." At this time, as well as the instance when I was 5, I had no idea what would be possible with blogs, social media and self publishing. No idea.

I thought my dreams were far-fetched, yet something in me still dreamed them and knew they were real. They were possible.

They were also without a doubt what got me labeled psychotic and forced onto psychiatric drugs. If I'd been more "realistic" I never would have devoted my life to something impractical like writing. I never would have brought boxes of my handmade books too heavy for me to even lift on a train from Massachusetts to New York.

I never would have devoted a season to living with my father and putting together books with a hole puncher and screws and snail mailing them to 30 of my closest friends. I never would have demanded, in my less lucid moments, that my dad try to get them on display at the Brooklyn Museum. I was, without realizing it, in withdrawal from a neuroleptic at the time, so at least I have that to blame, in part, for my display of delusional thinking.

At the same time I was daydreaming of writing everything and publishing TONS (and actually writing quite a bit), there were likely millions of people around the world fantasizing about creating media of some form and sharing it with the masses in various states of "delusion."

The structures in place at that time could never have supported all of us, but we all dreamed. Without most of us knowing each other, we dreamed new possibilities into being, and now they exist full force, anyone can publish anything and we're just getting started. We're just sensing, many of us, how much possibility there is.

We're just learning what it is to be this free and starting to even wonder what is the most responsible and effective way to use our power and voice. These aren't concerns most of us were privileged to have a decade ago.

There is another dream individuals are having now, masses of us, and that is a dream of vibrant health. Just as there was a crisis of voice until this past decade, where mainstream media projected only a sliver of the many important voices in need of being heard, there is a crisis of health and health care that is reaching its peak now.

Most people I know are quietly hoping for access to all the resources, circumstances, practitioners and methods they need to be healthy. They are all out there in abundance, in fact there are more underemployed health care practitioners and thrown away organic foods, herbs and natural medicines than we can imagine, with incredible capacity for healing our bodies and beings in integrative ways.

At the same time as my dreams of sharing my writing with the world widely were seen as unrealistic, my dreams about health were ridiculed too. I remember feeling very very alone in 2000 when I wanted to use non-conventional methods for healing my body and mind.

I had some kindred spirits at my hippie college, but no practitioners who I trusted. I was seen and talked about as "not believing in science or 'real' medicine." It took this 'real medicine' (psychiatric drugs) nearly killing me, for my family to begin to trust that maybe I knew what was best for me.

Luckily my strong minded, dreamy nature prevailed (after being subdued for a couple of years with psych drugs) and I started to encounter many opportunities for the kind of medicine that felt healing to me.

I see this collective dream of health being the next one to surprise humanity. We will soon see it is actually possible for us to get massages and acupuncture as often as we'd like (just one example of a possible health care desire), have our choice of health care practitioners we actually resonate with, who speak our language and have things to teach us (not just us to them) about our health (not just our illness).

Most of all we will have thriving communities that support health so well, we will rarely have to look outside of them for supplementary, anonymous "care." We are already seeing some of this with free/donation based alternative health clinics of various types and many versions of health care bartering and trading.

My massage therapist friend trades massages for dental care. Some forms of healthcare, especially mental health services are illegal to barter for, but people are thinking outside the box and finding ways to get around these laws.

Peer counseling is one example, and most mental health approaches can be converted into forms that can be practiced peer to peer. (See wisdomnet.com for an example). Thinking outside the box is indeed the key to resolving the crisis of health we are experiencing.

The democratizations of media and health care are far from 2 separate issues. In many cases, having a voice and expressing oneself to masses is the best medicine fathomable. We are already seeing some steps taken toward health care accessibility and options for all. Many of them have been made possible through free media online.

We now have access to information about any form of health care we choose, as well as abundant free advice and testimonials from nearly infinite others. Using social media, we can also quickly get information we trust from people we trust.

Lack of Informed Consent

Lack of informed consent, one of the major pitfalls in Western medicine, is no longer a valid excuse in most cases (thought there's still forced treatment, lack of access to alternatives and the expectation a doctor will give us all the info we need and wouldn't prescribe something dangerous or addictive).

In many cases all we need to have true informed consent is the desire for such. Most of the issues currently blocking people are lack of access to alternatives, poverty, not enough time for self care, and lack of support. And the biggest one I see is all of those combined with already being on pharmaceuticals for such a long time that they are nearly impossible to safely come off of.

Still, with all the resources we could have available to support those coming off addictive or dependency creating drugs, I believe it is more than possible in many cases.

There are related socio-economic and political discussions that are beyond the scope of this particular essay, but integral to the conversation of access. I recommend Charles Eisenstein's work for a discussion on how our economic system can improve to create a healthier world.

The more we learn, the better (no, I didn't listen to the doctor who told me not to read, it would "only confuse me"), yet right where we stand we can dream of the health care we'd like to have.

Many people didn't know anything about computer engineering and website development, and still don't, despite how necessary these things are for our new media we are successfully utilizing.

Right now, a healthy society is a pipe dream, as publishing our media to the masses so easily and readily at any moment was just over 10 years ago. Soon we will see quality health care and abundant health for all or most of us will be easily accessible. Until then, keep dreaming and envisioning, knowing you are far, far from alone in your fantasies.

Prozac and Psychiatric Hospitalizations

As a teenager, I was labeled with depression and given Prozac. I took it for about a year and it made me manic, less sensitive to others, more impulsive, more of a social butterfly, less able to be still and calm. It also gave me acne. One day I just stopped taking it.

In college, I had a spiritual opening and went into somewhat of a spiritual retreat state for awhile. Childhood trauma, physical health issues, religious confusion, genuine spiritual experiences and many other things played a part in my "meltdown."

In a way, I love meltdowns. I love that people have them. I want us to all be safe to have them. My meltdown(s) from the ages of 18-21 did not feel safe, except for the spiritual aspects. I was force drugged, shot with tranquilizers against my will, and hospitalized.

The drugs and "treatments" given to me made me much sicker, physically and mentally. I went from being a bright, smart, energetic young woman (with a lot of trauma), to being lethargic, sick, unable to think, drugged into oblivion, emotionally flat. I was on the lowest doses of most drugs that I was prescribed, but they still made me exhausted, dull, and sick.

When I was 20, I faced involuntary outpatient commitment, which is an encrypted way of saying court ordered forced psychiatric drugging. My life had 2 possible paths before me. One was freedom to live my life and learn from my struggles and the other was mental health treatment.

It was 2001 and I didn't know much about the mental health system except that I didn't trust it.

I sat in a psychiatrist's office at Four Winds hospital in Katonah, New York, where I was told I could find a place to be discharged to or go to court against two doctors and a judge to decide that I'd be mandated to take the psychiatric pharmaceuticals that had already caused me panic attacks, non stop eating, obsessive compulsive behaviors, strange thoughts and violent actions. Four Winds was a better hospital than most, the kind with a yard you can walk around in, decent meals, an exercise room and a nice looking campus with trees, fields, frogs and bunny rabbits.

I was a hopeful girl with a gleam in my eye and I had big dreams-dreams of sharing my words and art so big I'd transported them in boxes too heavy for me to lift from Amherst, Massachusetts to Brooklyn, New York by Amtrak.

When my mom heard the news that I'd be put on trial to decide if I'd be forced drugged (involuntarily committed as an outpatient) or locked in a state hospital, her maternal instinct led her to drive up to get me. On the drive home she was shaking and so anxious I was scared to be in the car with her. A lot of things about the world I was living in were deeply wrong. A girl who already felt such supreme purpose she would sacrifice anything for her dreams and ideals was nearly robbed of her life, liberty and pursuit of happiness by psychiatry and the systems of law that support it.

Sure, I had grandiose thoughts, anxieties, fears, and overwhelming bubbling up of sadness at times. I had anger, hope, excitement, vision and all of the tears, smiles and love that make a full life as a full person.

What you should know is that even the psychiatrist and therapists at Four Winds didn't think I needed to be force drugged. After I honestly answered his standard questions, the psychiatrist there said these words exactly, "When in Rome, do as the Romans. Get your ass to a freaking ashram." He flat out acknowledged I was in the wrong place with the wrong system of thought, medicine, belief and practice for me. Yet the law allowed him to do 2 things: have me force drugged or find another place for me. If there was no easy and obvious place to send me, forced treatment would be inflicted on me-not because any doctor thought I needed it, but because there was no category for me, no protocol that suited my situation.

And let me tell you from having been in that hospital and spoken to many thousands of people in a similar place, my situation or "category" was not uncommon. There were and are many people who have been traumatized, misunderstood, labeled mentally ill and force drugged, not because they have an illness of any sort, but because someone has a job and only 2 legal options-lock them up or have them involuntarily committed as an outpatient.

Helping People Come Off Psych Meds

I work with people coming off these drugs, or who hope to someday, who were never involuntarily committed, and it's terribly hard even for them. It was also terribly hard for me.

I wasn't sent to a psychiatric hospital, where I was forced drugged, because my family had no other options. They had resources and plenty of choices, and were well educated, but chose psychiatric "care" because they perceived it to be the safest and most trustworthy form of care for me. They thought it was the only legitimate form of medicine in a crisis. And at a moment of panic, everyone knows the 3 digits.

Preventing involuntary outpatient commitment can be tackled at different levels, all of which change the cultural narratives we hear. Most states already have IOC laws that go by different names in each state. We need to address the laws, public perception, and most of all to equate funding for non-violent alternatives since we all know, deep down, medicine should not be harmful, damaging or life destroying. It should not isolate us, make us permanently numb, sick, or stupid and it certainly should not make us die early or become violent or suicidal, all of which psychiatric pharmaceuticals do regularly.

There are many types of medicine and support that are gentle, restorative, nourishing, healthy, holistic and based around love, connection and community. These are the ones that have allowed me and so many other trauma survivors to rebuild our lives and take back our voice. They have provided us with opportunities to give back to the world in ways we'd always dreamed possible and to inspire others. They have lifted us up out of oppression, at times, and healed us rather than brought us deeper into despair and disconnection. Why aren't our dollars going towards those? Why aren't our laws protecting those? Why isn't there funding to research those? Psychiatric Medications Nearly Killed Me

Many people in my life including parents, doctors, and friends, thought these drugs would be helpful. Few guessed that it was the drugs that were making me much sicker. I experienced myself becoming mentally ill as a result of the drugs. I could hardly think at all.

Others saw me as becoming more and more mentally ill, but they didn't know why. I had a fever with no infection, for 3 months. I took many antibiotics, and many tests, but they never found the cause of the fever. A doctor later suggested it was a drug fever, caused by all of the medications I was on.

During this time, I had many other worldly experiences. It was like a long near death experience. I felt close to my grandparents and others who had died, but little if any connection to anyone or anything on Earth. I ate the same foods everyday and didn't leave my apartment at all for those 3 months.

Songs and poems came to me from beyond; they certainly could not have come for my own brain, which was barely functioning! This time was a shamanic opening for me-I certainly have never felt the same since.

After the fever went away, on December 25th, 2002, I decided to try coming off one of the drugs I was on, a neuroleptic called Risperdal. Reducing the drug gave me panic attacks and made me feel truly insane in a way I had never felt before. So I got back on it by my psychiatrists suggestion.

Then I had a dream guiding me to reduce Risperdal by even less so I tried again. I was on 6 or so other drugs at the same time including sleeping pills, antidepressants, anti-anxiety drugs, and thyroid medication (even though no thyroid problem had ever been determined).

Coming off Risperdal was probably one of the hardest things I've done. Risperdal was one of the most difficult psychiatric drugs I ever withdrew from. Even though it was over a decade ago, I can still remember a lot of the withdrawal effects. I told a friend I felt like I was "slipping off the edge of reality". I had never felt that psychotic before, and I had done hallucinogens and had many spiritual experiences/ meltdowns.

Coming off Risperdal can be so scary that some people don't want to try again after having a hard time with it once.

While I was on Risperdal, the drug caused major blood sugar issues and I had to severely limit my diet, even though I was a thin 21 year old. After I got off I was eventually able to eat a diet that was normal to me again.

While I was coming off Risperdal, I needed to make sure I kept eating regularly even though sometimes I didn't feel like it. Sometimes I didn't even feel connected to physical reality, but I stuck with a basic meal schedule and that helped get me through it.

Risperdal Withdrawal Symptoms

The main withdrawal symptoms I experienced when I was coming off Risperdal were extreme psychosis, panic and anxiety. I couldn't sit still and sometimes needed to walk around all day, even if I was pacing or walking around the block. Akathisia is when you literally can't sit still and that's what I experienced on Risperdal and in withdrawal.

I also started to feel my emotions coming back when I was coming off Risperdal. As a friend said about getting off Risperdal, "I could feel music again".

Coming off Risperdal was hard and I needed to go slower and taper by smaller amounts than I expected. After each taper I would wait a couple of weeks, but some people may need to wait much longer and reduce by miniscule amounts at a time.

Another strange withdrawal symptom I experienced was a type of twitch where I would involuntarily bring my arm up to my chest and extend it out. It was so weird and I couldn't control it, but I only experienced that during acute withdrawal and thankfully it went away.

Sleep was also an issue when coming off Risperdal, as it can be during most psychiatric drug withdrawal. My best advice for Risperdal withdrawal is to go slowly, get plenty of rest, eat a high protein, low sugar diet with ample fat, and go for walks when possible.

Going very slowly I tapered one drug after another, seeing my energy, aliveness, health and strength rapidly return with each reduction. It still took me a long time to fully recover from the toxicity and damage done during the 2 years I was on all those drugs, and there may have been some permanent damage as well.

During this time, I went back to college and finished my degree. it seemed like magic to me since I had not known if I would ever re-enter the outside world. Part of me knew I would recover from the whole experience and live to tell about it, but I had no idea how.

The Freedom Center

It was during this reduction period that I was introduced to Freedom Center (freedom-center.org). The Freedom Center is a group of people who identify as psychiatric survivors and I worked with them for about 7 years to provide alternative treatments for those experiencing extreme states of consciousness.

I taught yoga, meditation and creative writing and shared my personal story to audiences large and small. Telling my story felt like the most meaningful thing I could do and every time I did it I felt so full of purpose, love, and spiritual guidance.

Having the support of Freedom Center during my transitional period was invaluable. I got so much information from the other survivors than i ever got from doctors or therapists. I wish for everyone to have this type of communal support and hope I can be a voice of reason and confidence in all who need a perspective from someone who has been through it.

Notebooks Instead of Psychiatry?

Notebooks are better than psychiatrists because our world isn't always a safe place to reach out for comfort. I remember reaching out for comfort at Hampshire College Health Services, from the counselor, and she responded with fear, escorting me to Umass Health Services to have a consultation with a psychiatrist.

That psychiatrist didn't want to hear about my sexual trauma or spiritual awakening. He gave me a Celexa prescription and sent me on my way. He said I wasn't ready for the spiritual energy-he understood these things, as he had practiced Chi Gong.

It was around Spring- wet, damp, humid, rainy. I learned my notebook is more comforting than people, paper is softer than skin, the hug of my hand around a pen is always real and safe, while a human to human hug can be insincere or dangerous.

Words are safer when expressed silently and edited later, if need be, than spoken to someone who may be unable to hear. The spiral binding of my notebook is a guaranteed listener while the spirals in the ears of others are not.

The lines on the page are a clear path for my outbursts of feeling while the lines of the law make my humanness unsafe. The margin of the page is merely a guideline; I don't ever have to use it. The limitations of psychiatrists and others are real regardless of how much I may want things to be different.

The three holes in the pages are benign-they don't affect me, I ignore them. The holes in psychiatric thinking and societal structures deeply damage me no matter how much I want to break free, ignore it or say it doesn't need to affect me.

Workbook
Questions for Reflection:

- What is your story?

- Write a timeline of what happened, including the major turning points.

- Who did you meet that impacted your life greatly?

- Have you had a chance to tell it?

- Can you tell it in different forms such as writing, photography, art, music, theater?

- Would others benefit from knowing your story? How?

- When were you/was your loved one first diagnosed?

  _____
  _____
  _____
  _____
  _____

- Who benefited?

  _____
  _____
  _____
  _____
  _____

- What were you going through?

  _____
  _____
  _____
  _____
  _____

- Were you given other options? What were they?

  _____
  _____
  _____
  _____
  _____
  _____

- What do you wish had happened?

  _____
  _____
  _____
  _____
  _____

- What can you learn looking back?

  _____
  _____
  _____
  _____
  _____
  _____

CHAPTER 2

UNDERSTANDING THE SYSTEM

Ten Things I've Learned In My 6 Years Of Consulting

I wanted to share here some things I have learned in this process, which is of course ongoing. Despite how far I/we have come, we have a long way to go in the quest to liberate all who wish to be liberated from psychiatry.

Despite the emails I've gotten from people telling me that my blog has completely changed their outlook on life and even some that say my writing saved their life, there are many more people for whom all of these ideas are great but the reality of actually going through withdrawal feels impossible.

1. Informed Consent Doesn't Happen

No one gets on psychiatric drugs with informed consent. No one is given lots of accessible, safe options and honesty about where their diagnosis came from and how arbitrary it is, with a good serving of social criticism mixed in, and still chooses to take psychiatric drugs.

People take them out of desperation. It's an inherently manipulative process that doesn't offer alternatives that are accessible and socially acceptable.

2. The Withdrawal Process Can Be Excruciatingly Difficult

The process of withdrawal and all of the physical, emotional, mental and spiritual healing that go along with it takes a lot longer than most people expect or want it to. It is bootcamp on all levels.

For those who come through to the other side, there can be a sense of death and rebirth of a whole new self.

3. Resources Are Needed to Attempt Withdrawal

Many people don't have the resources to pay out of pocket for the support they need to go through this extensive and expensive process. The pharmaceutical companies should be liable for this as they create this high cost for recovery from their harm and medical malpractice.

Since they don't take responsibility for their harm, the extra burden is on the rest of us. I've been criticized by people on the internet who don't know me for charging too much when I was scraping by myself and spending my free time voluntarily sharing the best of my knowledge and awareness to help those in this struggle.

This is the poor logic of criticizing down the social totem pole rather than up. Of course those whose health and lives have been destroyed by psychiatry and don't have the resources and support they need to get off psych drugs are rightfully angry and upset.

4. Lack of Energy and Motivation

Many people don't have the energy and motivation to change their health habits while in the throes of psychiatric harm and withdrawal. Changing one's diet and lifestyle and adding in herbs, supplements and/or other supportive practices can be confusing and just too much to manage for many.

Those who do have more money and social resources as well as knowledge about alternative health are most likely to succeed in coming off and staying off psychiatric drugs.

5. Younger Healthier People May Be More Resilient

Younger and healthier people with stronger constitutions have it a bit easier and may be more resilient. They may experience fewer damaging side effects and may have an easier time withdrawing from psychiatric medication.

6. It's Still Possible

It's still possible for those with the decks seemingly stacked against them, and having a strong conviction can make the difference. "Where there's a will, there's a way." This does not mean that if someone is struggling it is their fault or due to a lack of will.

Unfortunately psychiatric drugs have a way of dampening the will. The will for some has to come from something beyond themselves, like a higher calling. Sometimes things like destiny and mystery are at play and we can't claim to always understand or scientifically evaluate why one person can get off and another can't.

We all have different life paths and to deny the mystery in that or try to define everything in linear cause and effect terms is a modern day control mechanism similar to psychiatry itself. Like life itself, there are disparities and unfair things we can't always explain.

7. Those Who Come Off Psychiatric Drugs Want to Help Others

Those who have come off psychiatric drugs tend to want to help others do the same. Almost all of the people I've worked with over the years have expressed this. Coming off, we gain so much knowledge about what helps that we have to share with others.

It becomes a calling.

8. Liability Risk is Low

You won't necessarily get into liability issues for doing what I do. The first question most people ask me when I tell them what I do is about liability. I haven't been sued or come even close to this.

By not claiming to give medical advice and being clear that I am offering consultation based on personal and professional experience, the person I am talking to is free to do what they choose, including their own research and talking to doctors, naturopaths, etc. before making a decision.

Maybe I am lucky to have never been sued, but I also believe that by being genuine and honest about what I do and don't offer and listening to people, respecting their wishes and choices, the chances of being sued are pretty slim. If I had a lot more to lose, I might be more concerned.

9. We Need More People Helping Others Withdraw

We need a lot more people doing this at different price points and with different business models, including grant funding and public funding as long as it can be done without loss of integrity. My business model is a simple fee per hour of consulting and then I offer tons of blogs, videos, audios, talks, a newsletter and an e-book for free on my website.

Because I put in so much unpaid work behind the scenes and don't have other consistent funding, my price for consultations isn't super cheap. I do have substantially discounted packages and can sometimes offer sliding scale. I'm sure there are more efficient business models than the one I use, and I am always learning more.

Just like drug withdrawal takes time, discovering a way to work takes time to develop. In both cases we are reinventing the wheel and doing the best we know at any given time within a broken system.

10. Many Others Help With Psychiatric Medication Withdrawal

There are many many people out there who can do things similar to what I do, and many more are needed. We need at least as many people helping those who want to come off psychiatric drugs as we have casually putting them on.

I've started to train people in non-medically supporting those coming off psych drugs so I can list other practitioners on my website: www.chayagrossberg.com, Or they can create their own way of working. This is something I have started to do locally.

There's also an online training course in the works. Please contact me via my website if you are interested in one-on-one mentorship to learn how to do this or sign up for my newsletter to be informed when the online course is ready.

I hope some of what I've learned and shared here can be useful to those coming off or supporting others in coming off psychiatric meds. The biggest thing I have learned and continue to learn is how much this is an unmet need for so many.

And this need is only going to get greater as both prescribing and knowledge about psychiatric drug dangers increase.

There's a huge toolkit for alternatives to psychiatric drugs that work! Nutrition and health guidance, yoga and meditation for mental health, personalized herbal remedies, reiki and distance reiki for energy balancing,

Emotional Freedom Technique and massage for healing trauma, creativity coaching, spiritual exploration, redefining terms, and help accessing community to bring your unique gifts into the world.

From the very first time I heard the term depression, and learned what Prozac was, I felt a sense of darkness and a mission to bring light to it. I have been studying nutrition, wellness, meditation and yoga for mental health for over 15 years.

I have taught yoga, meditation, nutrition, wellness, intuition, creative writing, improv and art to psychiatric survivors individually and in groups since 2003. For the past decade, I have refined my knowledge of herbal healing, wild and medicinal plants and balancing brain chemistry through nutrition and supplements.

I have spoken at many conferences, sharing my own story of complete recovery from many labels of mental illnesses and being on almost all classes of psychiatric drugs. I know firsthand about the process of coming off psychiatric drugs and staying off.

I worked at Alternative to Meds Center, Western Mass Recovery Learning Community, Windhorse Associates and Freedom Center, bringing my passion for healing, and sharing love to many experiencing extreme states of consciousness.

In 2002 I was on a number of psychiatric drugs that messed with my physical and mental health. Getting off of them was not easy for me and it took time. But once I made the decision to do so, my conviction grew. Each time I lowered my dose of a drug, new energy, vitality, strength, wisdom and intelligence returned to me.

It was quite a magical (and tedious) time. I know there are many who feel they can never come off psychiatric drugs, or have tried but the challenges have been too intense. I totally get this, for I felt that way too. My challenges included extreme panic attacks, feeling like I was on speed, feeling completely insane (like I was "slipping off the edge of reality"), insomnia, other people pressuring me or not understanding, and so many more.

Deciding to Withdraw From Psychiatric Medication

If you do decide to withdraw, remember that the effects you feel initially are withdrawal effects. You are/were on a powerful substance and it takes time to detox. It is similar to withdrawing from cigarettes, alcohol, speed, or any other intense substance that your system gets used to. This is common sense, but in some cases the mental health system and the drugs rob us of our common sense. They certainly did for me!

Here's what helped me:

Supplements. I took lots of vitamins, minerals , superfoods and herbs while I withdrew. Much more than I need to take now. These can be expensive, especially high quality ones, but well worth it if you have the means. Omegas (flax, chia, hemp, walnuts, fish) are important and regulate mood, B vitamins, calcium and magnesium help with relaxation, Vitamin C helps with immunity and recovery.

Nutrition. When I was on psych drugs, I let my nutrition go a lot because I didn't care and didn't have the energy to cook. Plus I was so toxic and like attracts like, so I sought out toxic low-nutrition foods. Fish helped me a lot when I was withdrawing. You know the basics about fruit, vegetables, whole grains, proteins, etc, so be willing to spend a little extra money for higher quality items if you have it.

Food stamps are a great resource if you need more money to afford high quality food. Eating enough good fat is also very important. Olive oil and coconut oil are the best and will help keep you calm and prevent you from overeating sugar and carbs which can cause anxiety and mood swings.

Walking. Walking outdoors was one of my main pastimes when I was withdrawing. It helped me get exercise, and breathe fresh air. Time in nature and near water is balancing and healing.

Dance, yoga, weight lifting, whatever exercise you like. Creative expression and releasing energy is important since as you withdraw you will have more. More vigorous exercise may be necessary, just make sure you get enough rest too.

You are detoxing a lot of chemicals and exercise is necessary to do so. Yoga can help relax your muscles, balance your brain, regulate blood pressure and improve your mood.

Sleep and rest. Sleep as much as you need to/can during this time. Your body, brain and consciousness need time outs. Sometimes I stayed in bed all day. Having trouble sleeping was one of the hardest withdrawal symptoms I experienced. Melatonin, Valerian, and other herbs can help with sleep. Acupuncture also works wonders.

Journaling. Journaling helped me feel more grounded, keep track of my withdrawal reactions and note what was helping. It also helped me tune into my intuition and think of ideas (and still does)! You may be more drawn to drawing or other expressive arts.

After having my consciousness suppressed from drugs, I needed to express A LOT, and often in my own private space before I was ready to share with others. Being harmed and violated by the mental health system can lower your trust in the world and other people, so taking time alone to rebuild your relationship with yourself first is very important.

Meditation. Taking quiet time to tune in, listen to my intuitions and relax helped.

Massage / Hands on Healing / Touch. Touch is important for regulating hormones and improving mood. Asking trusted friends to hold my hand, hug me, etc. were safe ways to get touch in addition to massages, and reiki. This touch can come through animals and nature too.

Community. Having friends to talk to, especially by phone, was necessary for me. Having friends in other times zones or who I could call in the middle of the night was good. People who would listen and not give too much advice or judgement tended to help me the most. A lot of the time when I called someone in crisis, I needed them to just listen and be there with me. An invaluable class of friends are those who have gone through or are going through something similar.

Trust and Intuition

A large part of my journey of living free of psychiatric drugs has been about learning to trust and develop my intuition. This intuition extends to my body, brain chemistry, moods, relationships, and basically every aspect of life, including money. All of us are born with some intuition that can be built upon and developed.

Would embracing a slower lifestyle eliminate the need for psychiatric drugs?

When I was on 7 or so psychiatric drugs, I had a near death-like experience where I went through a dark tunnel, saw a white light, and received a message of my purpose in life. The message I received was threefold.

My purpose is :

1. To write without getting attached to it.

2. To Love.

3. To slow people down.

I didn't quite understand the part about slowing people down until today, ten years later! While I have questions about #1, it makes perfect sense. Writing feeds me like nothing else. "To Love," seems obvious, like #1, 2 or 3 on everyone's life purpose list. But the last one, to slow people down, sounds unique and like it's for me personally.

I live a slow paced life. I meditate every morning, refuse to get a smartphone (yet), and it takes me generous amounts of time to do things. This isn't because I am "stupid" or slow to get things. Sometimes I wonder how others get so much done each day-yet the quality and vibration of what I do is unique.

It needs time. It's fermented, then slow cooked; it comes about from a slower paced life. My writing and teaching require me to live in the slow lane, as does my body, my mind, everything about me and the structure of my life. I basically can't be rushed.

So I go slow, but it only occurred to me today how, of course, by going slowly, those around me are sometimes slowed down too. I don't respond to messages/emails/phone calls right away most of the time. My phone is frequently on airplane mode.

Emergencies need to go through my slow pace filter and often aren't responded to the way many others would. Meditation, writing and other forms of quiet reflection are my primary urgencies. Ha.

By not being able to relate with me on Type A timetables, people who are in my world are sometimes inadvertently slowed down. I also often gravitate towards slow friends who listen slowly and who I can listen to slowly, making sure nothing is missed or misunderstood.

Of course we talk quickly sometimes (I am from New York and actually talk and think very fast) and I certainly write longhand faster than anyone else I've ever witnessed- but there's a deep, thorough processing going on in the conversations and writing that doesn't often happen in the average chat or article I am aware of.

How does this relate with psychiatric drugs?

Psych drugs are rooted in impatience, urgency, emergency. Sure, there are real emergencies that have their time and place, but the psychiatric system rushes situations to a place of emergency and encourages emergency mentality, when oftentimes slowing down and seeing more clearly are the best medicines.

The chronic crisis consciousness in the mental health system is the "short long way" because it usually takes longer to recover from the trauma of being rushed/forced/coerced, not being given informed consent or options, and from the damage of the drugs than it would to slowly and patiently work with whatever is going on to begin with.

The psych drug withdrawal process can take a very long time too.

Take it Slow

Going slowly from the beginning might mean taking a few months or longer to sit with our challenging, even torturous, feelings, and to reach out to people willing to slow down and listen without diagnosing. This requires patiently processing our feelings, thoughts, memories, symbols, fears and longings.

All of this requires time, air, breathing, going slowly and having others who can appreciate the slow pace, the right now; who can accept the stuckness, are okay with boredom, monotony, feelings and intensity. Slow pace is required for the "long short way," where things actually, ironically, happen faster because we aren't trying to force them to, we aren't resisting life or pushing the river.

Going slowly is my new/old medicinal offering to myself and others. I offer it as my very being so you know there is someone out there going slowly, waiting to respond. Whatever the pace our souls move at is what it is; it cannot be altered by drugs. In the words of Robyn Posin: You can leap forward and slide back as many times as you need to. Or you can just take smaller steps.

What an "aha" for me to realize that going so slowly, the thing I've been criticizing myself for, is a big part of my life purpose, not only for myself, but to slow others down as well.

When we have a health problem of any sort, Western medicine and our current culture (which many of us are stepping away from) tell us, "There's no time for this. How can we eradicate it as quickly and easily as possible?"

Perhaps the real question is, "Do we have time for that view?" Do we have time to ignore our body/mind messages? Do we have time to deal with the long term ramifications of rushing, crashing and being inundated with a whole new set of problems?

Even more pertinent, what does slowing down look like? How do we listen to our symptoms? My ways are through writing, meditation, time in nature, and other practices that fine tune my intuition. These include connecting with others in the slow lane, others who are exploring life as a mystery, a process, an opportunity for communication.

As I slow down and practice being honest with myself first, I begin to see the fears I have that keep me stuck in symptoms. Does this make it easy to overcome them? Sometimes, but not necessarily. It does make it easier to connect with others and attract people I can connect with deeply and genuinely. By slowing down enough (externally) to find self communication that is honest, it becomes easier to express myself to others and to intuit who will get it.

Eradicate Fear

As for fear based symptom eradication, which I still find myself knee jerking towards, good luck. Take as long as you need to, try as many quick fixes as you can find. When you're done and ready to return to the slow path of soul, I'll meet you on the dirt road, unpaved, picking berries in the sunshine, or being poured on in the rain.

Sure there's a time and place for efficiencies- for raincoats, cars, airplanes, the internet- no doubt. But mostly, we're headed for the unpaved road in the country, the slow path of our souls, the unavoidable, undeniable underbelly of life. It's unpredictable, unmapped and undocumented until we take the time to document and map our own course.

When we live there, rushing through to eradicate our "problems" becomes less and less of an option, and life is actually worth living and learning from-slowly, kindly, with heart.

Workbook
Questions for Reflection:

- If you got off psychiatric drugs, how did you do it?

- Have you shared your methods with others?

- How did you learn?

_____
_____
_____
_____

- Who helped you?

_____
_____
_____
_____
_____

- What made things worse?

_____
_____
_____
_____
_____

- If you haven't gotten off psychiatric drugs yet, how have you tried?

_____
_____
_____
_____
_____
_____

- What research have you done?

- What has supported your efforts?

- What dangers are you now aware of?

- How do you hope to go about it in the future?

_____

_____

_____

_____

_____

On this birthday morning in my bedroom in San Francisco with the sun shining in so strong on my face I need to duck out of it, after a day of the strongest winds, still in my layered pajamas, and after many prayers, some tears roll down my face. I have no idea what I'm about to write, but it's like that sometimes.

I'm glad I'm crying, that something can make me cry and I don't know how to put words to what it is. This has been one of the strangest years of my life; I've been a stranger in a strange land over and over. Over and over being stripped of comforts and grounds, to be blessed with new ones.

The loss of friends and family and colleagues and the finding of new ones has happened more times than I care to count. Home after home after home after home. The coldest Winter of daily snow in Brooklyn in February. A hot summer like Spring in Portland Oregon in May.

A half a year of sunny weatherlessness in San Francisco. Friends lost, reconnected with, composted, recycled. People moving through my life like a stream or cyclone, ocean waves crashing and a still quiet pond.

This morning I woke up and gave thanks for everything I have, out loud, to whoever God is, and I asked them that everyone have at least what I have. At least this much of everything: friendship, love, health, good food, kindness, family, money, home, because right now I have all of these things to varying degrees.

I'm not extremely close with most of my family, I often feel lonely, I worry about money, my health is not perfect, I will need to find a new home soon, yet again, but right now I have what I need, and far more than many.

Our world is so very full of lonely people, severely unhealthy people, and those who have no family or friends, some without a home that feels good, or without a home at all and most without access to or knowledge of good real food. For these folks, the "safety net" is a mental health care system that has abundant drugs on offer with the promise of making lives happier and easier somehow.

I listened to these folks one after another after another working on a warm line this year for 40 hours a week. I heard their stories about their lives and often heard along with it a diagnosis and medication as a side note, such as, "and I'm bipolar and I take Lamictal."

I feel hopeful only because the sun shines on my face, warming an otherwise cold December morning, and because writing this is curing my own down in the dump lonely feelings, which can come even when we have everything.

I can't "have everything" if others out there "have nothing." I can't dream of a future for myself without wanting healing for every being on earth, and without crying at the impossibility this strikes me with. No one "has everything" if they don't sit down some mornings and cry at how disconnected our world is for so many.

The sadness in me salutes the sadness in you. We are real, we care, we are NOT broken machines that need chemicals to run more efficiently, to be faster on the assembly line. We may as well give up now- and by give up I mean give up the idea we are isolated entities with some kind of objective mental health status.

We're a bit more like a stroke in a huge, messy, sometimes beautiful painting, inter-meshed with trillions of other strokes of life, never as alone as we may think.

Question: Do you think I should go on antidepressants? I'm going through a really hard time.

My Answer: It depends on your goals. Is your goal to be authentic or to fit in with a certain part of society? (I do have a bias towards authenticity, as you might have guessed). The thing is, you never know how the drug will affect you-it could make you feel better for awhile, then worse. It could make you tired, manic, suicidal or cause health problems or insomnia-you really don't know. There's no guarantee of anything if you go on antidepressants; it's not like going on will guarantee you a happier or better life, despite what the ads want you to believe.

Being true to ourselves is a "slower" process, sometimes feels tedious and is hardly without pain or hardship, but it yields better tasting fruit in the end. It can take years to grow the kind of fruit that develops naturally from a life lived with self- honesty.

It's like the difference between large scale corporate agriculture and growing food in your backyard or foraging berries and greens.Big Agriculture yields fruit that is lacking in flavor and nutrients; it's the same with Big Pharma.

A Life Without Psych Meds

A life without psych drugs requires tending, self study, learning and practicing, growing your garden year after year after year and learning from your mistakes, and yields authentic delicious fruit that can't be compared to a life on a maintenance drug for mood or personality.

Yes this is a controversial thing to say and may offend you. Yet, it hurt me so much that when I was nearly killed by psych drugs, no one wanted to "offend me" with the truth of what was going on, why I was losing my health and personality in bucketfuls.

I recently saw an example of this in my own life, as I think we all do cyclically. We work hard at a certain discipline and sometimes feel deprived of certain things in life while doing so. But then one day, those things return to us even better than ever before.

For the past couple of years I have had a lot of hardship in certain areas of life between constant moving, financial ups and downs, health problems, loneliness, living in undesirable places without security.

The answers to these problems came in living the questions themselves, as the poet Rilke noted, patiently, and taking the opportunities to grow my garden, wherever I was, however humble, however transient, knowing well I would have to tear it up in a few months so was any of this even worth it? Was life a cruel joke?

I wouldn't say I'm out of the woods on any of these questions, but I do feel a sense that progress has been made by taking the slow and honest path. For me there is no other way.

What No One Is Saying

It hasn't been easy. I have had extreme mental states of every single kind. I could have been diagnosed with absolutely every single mental disorder without exception in the past few years, and given every single psych drug.

Well that's pretty cool.

It's joyful to know you could be diagnosed with a mental disorder but to opt out, to say yes to yourself instead, to have the patience and care to resist the label that never got you anywhere before, that was voted into existence as an illness, that simply isn't helpful in looking at your life.

Nothing tastes sweeter than inching toward self mastery, self intimacy, the progress that comes slowly over a long period of taking good care of yourself, the very best way you know how to, and very imperfectly at that.

Nothing is more satisfying than meeting kindred spirits that are more aligned and connected than ever before after long periods of solitude and loneliness, even extreme isolation.

I know I should say something about everyone having their own unique path, some people benefiting from psych drugs and diagnoses yada yada yada. But everyone else is saying that, so it's getting boring and overstated. It's not even whether I agree with it or not, I just find it a boring line of thought, yet a diplomatic one that has value in some circumstances.

There are so many saying it though, and I've always wanted to say what no one is saying.

Question: I was telling someone about your work and she asked about the people whose mental illness makes them violent. She did not believe it would be good for these people to go off their psych meds. I did not know how to respond to her. What are your thoughts? How would you respond?

My Answer: Thanks for asking. This question is complicated because it involves certain assumptions and interpretations that have never been proven to be true.

It isn't "someone's mental illness" that makes them violent since people can be violent whether or not they've received a psychiatric label. It is a matter of many factors that get someone labeled with a mental illness, but none are objective.

Some psychiatric drugs cause violence (it is fairly well known that most of the mass murderers in schools in recent years have been on psych drugs). The other complication is that psych drugs, like all toxic substances, have withdrawal effects which might lead to violence. So someone in withdrawal might be more likely to be violent.

Violence is mostly a learned behavior and is generally perpetuated by victims of violence and trauma.

I think focusing on healing from abuse and trauma would be more direct than labeling and drugging. There may be cases where drugs are chosen to sedate someone and make them less likely to be aggressive (if they are really tired) but I see this as a short term emergency "solution" and certainly not a resolution.

Psychiatric Drugging is a Form of Violence

Psychiatric drugging and other mental health "treatments" are also a form of violence. So we must ask ourselves if this repression of emotions is in fact acceptable as an approach if we strive for non-violence.

It has never been shown that persons labeled with a mental illness are more likely to be violent than others though. I know violent people who have never been to a therapist or psychiatrist and the gentlest people in the world who have many psych labels.

In fact, Thomas Insel, director of the National Institute of Mental Health, recently stated that all DSM labels lack validity and are not scientific. So it's important to admit and acknowledge that these labels are arbitrary and can be given to anyone in a crisis at any time.

- I think people watch meteor showers to remind themselves anything's possible.
- I think people have kids to remind themselves anything's possible.
- I think people become doctors or healers to remind themselves anything's possible.
- I think people go to sleep at night to remind themselves anything's possible.
- I think people get out of bed in the morning to remind themselves anything's possible.
- I think people read, listen to music, view art, to remind themselves anything's possible.
- I think people rebel against the norm to remind themselves anything's possible.

People cook to remind themselves anything's possible. People opt to live without psych drugs or go off them to affirm their suspicions: Anything's possible.

Anything's possible if I slow down, if I water my garden, if I wake up in the morning, if I open my eyes.

- I think people take photos to remind themselves anything's possible.
- People write down what's happened to them to affirm anything's possible.
- People put their life story in their own words to assert: Anything's possible.

People rage against the police, government, psychiatry, the Man, the system, patriarchy and all other oppression because they know anything's possible and it's killing them.

Knowing anything's possible isn't vague or airy fairy, it's deep within, sad, real, it's a wild bear, a big snake, a shooting star, a baby, an unexpected feeling, uncontrollable, unwilling to be silenced, shut down, quieted, pushed under, told, "That's impossible."

Anything's possible won't stop, won't quit, won't ever accept our efforts to limit it, so we may as well create with it. We may as well join its team, fight for its rights, for if we're not with it we're against it, drugging and drugging and drugging feelings and fears and creativity,

love, imagination, rightful rage, begging the world to confirm that we are inherently limited, which it will not, even once we die, especially once we die, so we remind ourselves, affirm, assert, anything's possible today!

84 Capacities That Can Return When Getting Off Psychiatric Meds

In order for an experience to create a life mission and strong sense of purpose, it has to affect you to the core. Though I was only on psychiatric drugs for a few years of my life (and the very lowest "clinical" doses available), they affected me so strongly and took away so much that I could never forget or simply leave that experience behind me.

I've seen getting off psychiatric meds give so many other people their lives back as well.

I share this list, not to torture people who are on them or struggling with getting off psychiatric meds, reminding them of how much is being taken away (or could be taken away), but rather to validate the desire that many have to not take these substances and to be supported in better ways.

I share this to validate how very necessary it is to create better systems for being with trauma and to facilitate the process of getting off psychiatric meds for those who would like to come off in every way we possibly can.

When I was on a psychiatric drug cocktail at age 21-22, I lost the abilities to do the things on this list with any regularity. Many of these things I could not do at all.

Once I was done getting off psychiatric meds, slowly and carefully, which was quite tedious and difficult, all of these capacities returned to me.

1. Reading (there were times when psychiatric drugs made me unable to focus on reading)
2. Thinking clearly
3. Communicating my thoughts with others directly (for some reason psych meds made me very passive aggressive and it was really hard to ask directly for what I wanted to needed)
4. Night vision (my vision would get super blurry at night but once I recovered from psychiatric meds the vision issues went away)
5. 20/20 vision during the day
6. Eating all kinds of foods (psychiatric drugs messed with my blood sugar and caused a lot of food intolerances that I had

never had before and haven't had since)
7. Traveling (this was too overwhelming while I was on psych drugs)
8. School work
9. Graduating college
10. Writing
11. Developing friendships
12. Developing romantic relationships
13. Walking more than one block
14. Aerobic exercise
15. Weight lifting (I was able to lift more weight immediately after withdrawing from "anti-anxiety" meds)
16. Discernment about what to eat and which supplements to take
17. Being attractive to others (these drugs made me look horrible)
18. Showering regularly (I was too tired and apathetic to shower a lot of the time)
19. Brushing my teeth twice a day
20. Changing my clothes (why bother when I wasn't leaving the house?)
21. Dressing nicely (this never occurred to me while on meds)
22. Understanding my own experiences and being able to communicate them
23. Empathy for others
24. Intuition (with a few exceptions)
25. Grasping and formulating complex concepts
26. Teaching others from my experiences
27. Yoga
28. Doing artwork
29. Dancing
30. Singing
31. Computer skills
32. Awareness of some current events (while on psych drugs world events did not occur to me as significant in the slightest)
33. Appreciation of music
34. Sexuality (I lost all capacity while on psych drugs for some time

and it came back "too strong" after withdrawal but eventually normalized)
35. Leaving the house and socializing
36. Meeting new people
37. Trying new things
38. Seeing a future
39. Caring about people
40. Caring about principles
41. Feeling sad
42. Feeling excited
43. Feeling calm
44. Being awake during most of the day (i stayed in bed for most of the day)
45. Researching topics and discerning accurately what is relevant to me
46. Working for money
47. Committing to regular activities/classes/meetings
48. Falling in love
49. Having creative goals
50. Learning
51. Grocery shopping (I needed to have others do this for me even though there was a grocery store a block away)
52. Detangling my hair (my hair turned into a big dreadlock)
53. Expressing my feelings
54. Doing my dishes
55. Cleaning (absolutely never did this while on meds)
56. Being able to benefit from subtler health treatments like acupuncture, homeopathy and organic herbs
57. Eating healthy
58. Loving people
59. Attracting friends
60. Engaging socially and feeling (somewhat) "normal"
61. Caring what's going on in the world/my city
62. Caring about other people's needs and acknowledging them
63. Being able to talk about my life without using unproven "mental

health" pseudoscience jargon (I would talk about my "mental illness" as if it were a chronic permanent disability while on psych drugs but never before or after)

64. Being able to see fact from fiction
65. Writing down and finding meaning in my dreams
66. Smiling for real
67. Wanting to help others
68. Caring about my life, health and future
69. Praying
70. Believing in God/Higher Power/Angels/Being guided (I actually lost a connection to the God of of my lived experience (not a religious concept) which I have had my whole life before and after.
71. Having faith in myself and my life
72. Inspiring trust in others
73. Inspiring creativity in others
74. Typing fast
75. Journaling
76. Shaving
77. Wearing deodorant
78. Regular menstruation(this was the only time in my life where my menstrual cycles weren't completely regular and sometimes I went months without menstruating at all)
79. Awareness of moon cycles
80. Sexual arousal
81. Normal hair growth (my hair fell out excessively)
82. Immunity
83. Cooking (I only ate things out of a can or a box or frozen food which required minimal thought and effort and I ate the same things every day)
84. Staying out of the house all day

May all beings be free to choose, and to choose with true informed consent, which cannot be expected from a doctor or medical care provider, but must be gotten with a combination of research, self study, intuition, personal accounts and fierce, unbiased logical analysis.

We must take back science from under the fist of commercials and indirect advertising (who tell us getting off psychiatric meds is irresponsible or wrong).

Workbook
Questions for Reflection:

- Why did you/do you want to go off psych drugs?

- What harm did they cause/are they causing?

- Do your doctors believe you?

- Are your doctors competent in withdrawal?

- What skills and experiences do you want to get back?

　

- What parts of your physical health and mind do you want back?

　

- Would you prefer to have your difficult emotional experiences or not?

　

- Do you have mixed feelings?

- Write a pro/con list:

_____
_____
_____
_____
_____
_____
_____
_____
_____

Most people sense there is something up with the increase in psychiatric drugging correlating with more suicides, school shootings, health problems and disability. You may sense there's more to the story that the mainstream media often hides. Here are some sources that might be helpful in putting together the pieces of the puzzle.

General Principles:

1. "Mental illnesses," even severe ones, are relational. Psychiatry, by focusing almost exclusively on biology, is making itself increasingly irrelevant.
2. Psychoactive substances provide at best, temporary relief, but always make things worse in the long run. They make things worse directly (chemically) and indirectly by distracting from the real issues.
3. All psychoactive substances have rebound and withdrawal-related problems. "Relapse" rates, in general, during withdrawal from psychiatric drugs, are about 10 times higher than would be expected if the drug had never been taken.
4. "All biopsychiatric treatments share a common mode of action — the disruption of normal brain function" (Peter Breggin, M.D., Brain Disabling Treatments in Psychiatry, Springer Pub. Co., 1997, p. 3). Drugs never correct imbalances.

They never improve the brain. They "work" by impairing the brain and dampening feelings in various ways.

http://www.alternet.org/story/153634/7_reasons_america%27s_mental_health_industry_is_a_threat_to_our_sanity

"A generation ago, psychiatrists admitted that their diagnoses were unreliable and agreed that this was a major scientific problem. So in 1980, in an attempt to eliminate this embarrassment, they created the DSM-III with concrete behavioral checklists and formal decision-making rules, but they failed to correct the problem.

Psychiatric diagnoses remain unreliable, but now psychiatry no longer talks about the unreliability problem."

http://www.washingtonpost.com/blogs/wonkblog/wp/2012/12/17/seven-facts-about-americas-mental-health-care-system/

1. The United States spends $113 billion on mental health treatment. That works out to about 5.6 percent of the national health-care spending, according to a 2011 paper in the journal Health Affairs.
2. Mental health dollars mostly go toward prescription drugs and outpatient treatment.

http://healthcareforamericanow.org/2013/04/08/pharma-711-billion-profits-price-gouging-seniors/

Big Pharma Pockets $711 Billion in Profits by Price-Gouging Taxpayers and Seniors

Drug makers charge customers in the U.S. – especially the government – vastly more for the same drugs than they do in places like Canada and Europe, where government health plans bargain with the drug companies to protect their citizens. Per capita drug spending in the U.S. is about 40 percent higher than in Canada, 75 percent greater than in Japan and nearly triple the amount spent in Denmark.

The drug companies say they must impose higher prices in the U.S. to pay for research that enables them to innovate and develop new drugs that save our lives. But that's not true. Half of the scientifically innovative drugs approved in the U.S. from 1998 to 2007 resulted from research at universities and biotech firms, not big drug companies, research shows.

And despite their rhetoric, drug companies spend 19 times more on marketing than on research and development." http://www.bbc.com/news/business-28212223

In one recent year, US giant Pfizer, the world's largest drug company by pharmaceutical revenue, made an eye-watering 42% profit margin. As one industry veteran understandably says: "I wouldn't be able to justify [those kinds of margins]."
http://www.rethinkingpsychiatry.org/wasting-the-taxpayers-medic-aid-dollars-on-psychiatric-drugs/

"There have been double-digit increases in yearly Medicaid drug spending with psychiatric drugs representing the largest percentage of that cost. [i]

Psychiatric medications are among Medicaid's most costly and commonly prescribed drugs. [ii]

While Medicaid officials (many former pharmaceutical industry employees) reported concerns about the effects of restricting access to drugs for those with serious mental illnesses, such as schizophrenia, but these officials do not seem adequately concerned about the growing numbers of adverse effects, episodes of violence, fatalities and suicides on these medications.

Side effects of psychiatric medications can include seizures, low blood pressure, irregular heartbeat, diabetes, tardive dyskinesia (a neurological disorder characterized by involuntary movement), and other extrapyramidal symptoms (neurological side effects)."

Psychiatric drugs have the capacity to biologically cause all of the experiences that get labeled as mental illness; we need look no further than the lists of "side effects" provided by the drug companies themselves to know this.

Psychiatric drugs have been known to frequently cause depression, anxiety, suicide, violent behavior, trouble focusing, psychosis, hallucinations, insomnia and delusions to name a few. How else do psych drugs cause the very illnesses they presume to treat?

For one thing, historically, mental illness has risen exponentially with the creation of psych drugs and the rise in prescriptions.

The very shift from "mental illness" being a religious or personal problem in most cultures (not a medical illness at all) to an illness presumed to be caused by brain malfunction, directly coincides with there being some sort of medical treatment administered in the name of "legitimate medicine" as opposed to witchcraft/shamanism/occult practices, religious rituals or even basic common sense activities.

Most research indicates this shift started in the 5th century BC with Hippocrates defining mental illness as a problem in the brain to be treated as an isolated physical condition. In contrast to witch hunts and vague mystical practices that couldn't be officially quantified or qualified, this idea was perhaps a relief to the masses.

Hippocrates used certain substances to treat these "brain problems" which were, perhaps the first notions of mental illness similar to the ones we so readily accept today, with names, symptom lists and specialized substances to treat each one.

Mental illness did not even exist as this type of phenomenon until there were substances or drugs to treat it. The religious or personal problems they were seen as earlier were not in the category of medicine, but rather issues of the soul, moral issues or other phenomenon considered to be outside of the self entirely such as demon possession.

There was never a biological brain disease until there were "medications" purported to correct chemical imbalances.

Is it safe to say psychiatric drugs themselves created mental illness and sustain the phenomenon?

Let's break this question down by pretending, for just a moment, that my wet dream came true and psychiatric medications ceased to exist (as FDA approved medicine. The drugs themselves could still exist as drugs).

That's right, no ads in magazines suggesting you ask your doctor about Abilify if your anti-depressant alone isn't enough, no TV commercials to laugh at because they pay millions of dollars to tell you their drugs cause impotence, trouble breathing, diabetes and sudden death.

No doctors, therapists or psychiatrists suggesting or prescribing any psychiatric pharmaceuticals whatsoever.

Let's keep imagining this world.

You are having an extreme time in life. You feel exasperatingly alone, freaked out, your heart is racing, you are having an out of body experience, a threatening voice in demanding you do something dangerous, and you wish there was something, anything that would take the edge off.

Even a pill.

Okay, so you figure something out-you ask for help- you drink some vodka or eat something or you smoke a joint or go for a run or cry into someone's arms. There are infinite things you can do at that moment. Infinite.

The only option you don't have is to go to a doctor covered by your insurance company and get free or cost-subsidized drugs and a mental illness diagnosis.

Every other option is available to you.

You can even get drugs similar to benzos or other psych drugs (in this utopia all drugs and substances are legal for consenting adults), but you have to pay for them, and they don't cost a lot. Let's say they cost a few dollars per pill (the street cost of most of them now, though it could be far lower).

You are choosing to take them, if you do, over the glass of vodka, the joint of marijuana, the herbal supplement, the community acupuncture, the hug, whatever. Or you are taking them in addition to one or many of these things.

You're treating yourself as a respectable adult and making a conscious choice. You are viewing all of the substances and practices or "treatments," if you will, as equal before "god".

None are intrinsically more or less "medicine" in the eyes of the law or in terms of resources sponsored by social services. If anything, benign or nourishing, life giving treatments are funded by social services.

So, let's say you opted to buy a benzo for a few dollars. You take it, it calms you down, you assess what's going on from a less panicked place. Maybe you decide it's worth the investment to take benzos everyday and you become addicted, but just like a cigarette smoker or alcoholic, or soda drinker for that matter, you pay for your intake based on how much you use (plus tax).

You are still harming your body and the ecosystem to some degree, and you may argue (and perhaps rightly so) this is harm reduction, keeping you alive until you can find a less harmful way.

And maybe you will save the ecosystem someday, or have an important role in it, so it is important to keep you alive.

Or maybe staying alive is intrinsically better than dying. In any case, mental illness has not been mentioned yet.

And the reason? We are in an imaginary world where there are no psychiatric drugs prescribed as medicine.

The other thing to consider is what sorts of things would not be taking place in this post-psychiatry utopia of sorts. Polypharmacy, for one, would taper or cease to exist.

Anyone taking multiple psych drugs in this imaginary reality would be seen as having a problem, similar to a person in our current culture who uses 3 different types of synthetic street drugs on a daily basis, even in small to moderate doses, or who uses several different forms of one each day.

There would also be far far far less people taking psych drugs for daily "maintenance" of mood or with hopes and illusions of drug-induced emotional stability with a hefty price tag of good health.

Why? Because these drugs would not be labeled medicine, therefore few people would go beyond the initial week or two of delirium.

Psych drugs meant for daily use (excluding stimulants and sleeping pills) don't "work" right away the way benzos do. Benzos, like opiates, are designed to be a quick emergency fix of relief.

Other psych drugs like SSRIs, neuroleptics, and anticonvulsant drugs start off with a week or two of making the substance user feel disoriented, sick, confused and nauseous in many cases. Few people would bother to take them beyond that trial period (or at all) without a doctor coaching them along.

Recreational and Addictive Use of Psych Drugs

People take stimulants, benzos, sleeping pills and opiates recreationally and/or addictively, but other classes of drugs give no immediate good feeling or relief beyond the placebo effect.

Doctors routinely execute the placebo effect and encourage their patients to wait out the first few weeks. They give their clients hope by saying, "The drugs take a little while to work."

All of this is very well supported by a system that covers or highly subsidizes doctors visits and drugs under the heading of medical need.

If someone were to try to sell you a drug that would take a few weeks before possibly making you feel happier, would make you feel bad first, had lots of side effects and health risks and had not been shown to work better than placebo, AND you had to pay a few dollars per day for a months supply to start out, would you try it? It just sounds like a scam.

Without the dishonest medical validation of drug use for a non-medical situation that has never been shown to have a biological basis that can be diagnosed, treated, cured, or prevented (despite FDA approval) with any medical procedure, people would not become psychiatric patients for life.

We may become substance abusers or drugs addicts, and many of us currently are.

These issues would surely need to be addressed, as would, of course, the needs of the millions of psychiatric substance users who already exist and whose substances are called medicine to treat a mental illness because a doctor diagnosed them based on unproven theory and speculation.

Medicine is not the track. It's not Vegas. It's not, and should not be, a cheap scratch card.

Millions of lives are being gambled on with these unproven theories. The drugs we are gambling with cause violent behavior, suicides, diabetes, early death, obesity, birth defects and so much more.

For those fully covered by insurance, they can be cheaper than a lottery ticket, cheaper than a game of poker. What will it take to remind the American public (and other countries Western Psychiatry has infiltrated) these are not safe substances, these are not medical necessities?

Psychiatry has grown rampant not only out of greed, but out of imbalances in our lifestyles, the loss of the arts of listening, both to ourselves and others, which are two sides of the same coin (not two sides of the same pill).

A pill or drug does the opposite of what listening does. It instead silences the voices that want to speak, or mutes them somehow. As someone who felt most at home writing, I couldn't fathom taking drugs on a daily basis that would alter my perceptions of myself and the world and change my feeling states.

My thoughts, perceptions and feelings were my ground. How would I have any ground at all if they were consistently altered? This grounding has saved me from believing in certain fables and psychiatric mythology consistently throughout my life. I feel lucky.

Despite being often lonely, stressed, overwhelmed, and sometimes despairing and lost, I am married to my perceptions. I'm loyal to them and that is what being an artist and a listener means to me. I love them no matter how screwed up they are, no matter how traumatized, frozen, hypocritical, selfish, cruel, vengeful, you name it – I'm sticking with being me.

I'm going to listen to myself until the end, for as long as I can.

I'm never bored or tired with what I have to say when I'm writing, which is my listening practice. It's true I've never been even close to married to another person, but I won't cheat on myself with a doctor who has lost the capacity to listen. And it's the best thing I can imagine being able to say for myself. It's my self-definition of success, another thing we all need, to escape and stay free of psychiatry.

Psychiatric Medications Increase Suicide Risk

In light of recent research on psychiatry increasing suicide risk, I would conclude psychiatric "care" increases suicides because it decreases listening, or the kind of listening that can give one a sense of meaning and a reason to live.

Being lied to and told you have an incurable brain disease and will need to ingest toxic, brain disabling and health compromising drugs every day for the rest of your life, would lead the average intelligent person to feel paranoid, suspicious and unhappy—as if someone is messing with their head.

If the structures we have set up to comfort and relieve people in their darkest hour are drug pushers disguised as experts on neurobiology, but can't even explain or justify their own theories when questioned further, what are we left with? And more importantly, how could these structures not lead a clear thinking, clear seeing, breathing, feeling, sensing and intuiting human being to paranoia and upset as their breath rises and falls?

Psychiatry is like the parent who says, "I'll give you something to cry about," and abuses a child who is already feeling powerless. Hitting a child while she's crying will either make her cry worse, or silence her. In either case, the parent has "given the child something to cry about" when perhaps the initial apparent reason for tears was a fallen cracker.

Similarly, whatever one is upset about when seeking psychiatric "care" (the loss of a loved one, loneliness, abuse, injustice, or a bad mood or hard set of days feeling 'off'), psychiatry will clearly give that person something to more justifiably cry about: that in the darkest hour of human loss and misery, our fellow humans are motivated by one thing: profit, in an industry that is already overstuffing the pockets of wealthy CEOs to the point of having a larger share of the economic pie than any industry or person deserves.

This reality, that some men are getting filthy rich off of lying to people about the cause of their suffering, and paying groups of people in all sections of life (government, politics, law, medicine, education, activism, housing, beauty, entertainment, news, insurance, etc.) to call these lies science, is something worse than anything I can think of anyone bringing to a psychiatrist.

These interventions can be likened to being sold on any other theory to sell any other product, but with Pharma money corrupting public opinion in so many facets of life by paying for a place in science, we must also ask ourselves whether we believe science is something that can be bought with money.

Are the basic things you believe about yourself and what you call reality, actually being bid on by men in suits?

We love the safety of "seek medical advice" and "ask your doctor," but would we be so confident if we brought to mind the fact that this so-called medical advice won its title as science by being bought?

First being hit with this truth, a psychiatric patient is bound to become more paranoid, "delusional" and "schizophrenic," as anyone would, after hearing such stark news about a system they expected they could trust.

The Good News is Many Recover

The good news is many people go on to recover from psychiatrically-induced delusions. Many people move from, "Psychiatry gave me something to cry about" to "Psychiatry gave me something to yell about," and then on to, "Fighting this propaganda connected me to other human beings who also sought authentic human love and gave us a shared purpose in the mystery of life."

By considering or falling prey to psychiatric bubble theories that pop as soon as you look at them rising, we are afforded the opportunity to examine our human condition and that of our fellows, and perhaps appreciate that we were initially upset by something.

I've come to find meaning in all states: panic, anxiety, despair, and even "delusional thinking," for in having these human experiences without imposing any bid-upon pseudo-science onto my reality, I am expressing my fight. I am expressing social resistance.

And instead of being alone with this expression, lost in taglines of "I am mentally ill/mentally challenged/have a chemical imbalance or a brain disease," I am rooted in the community and collective healing that comes with an alternative perspective that no one paid anyone to lobby: we have a society in need of repair.

Silenced Voices Need to Be Heard

We have silenced voices that need to speak. An epidemic of pill-pushing over the past 40 years has not repaired us, brought us closer together or happier and it certainly hasn't cured us of any mass delusions. In fact it's given us all new delusions to contend with, ones that are easy to spot if our minds and hearts are set on progress.

I was at a meditation gathering of a specific Indian tradition one night where I happened to be the only female present. Disclaimer: the purpose of this is not to "genderalize" or specifically focus on gender differences, but rather to use socialization differences (which are not solid or permanent) as an example.

I noticed at the end of the evening when people were talking casually, some of the guys got into "name dropping" spiritual books, teachers and traditions (all men, written by men and conceived of by men alone) in a similar way I've seen people talk about sports stars, celebrities, politicians, cars, history and current events, with an empty-of-substance naming of things. This, of course, can happen in any group of people regardless of gender ratio.

There's comfort, I suppose, regardless of gender, race or class in sharing common celebrities, priests, psychiatric labels, medical jargon, language, and tradition of any sort-but if it's simply about naming books, traditions, "illnesses" and teachers to show you know of them, it becomes empty trivia.

Trivia sounds like trivial and becomes not only trivial but harmful if used as a social lubricant without exploring these books/people/labels in more depth and being sure to contrast male written books, theories and traditions with the voices of women and other minority viewpoints.

Trivia for its own sake is a subtle but powerful form of hierarchy (and usually patriarchy) whether it is about celebrities, sports stars and pop culture or the celebrity priests and pop culture of a specific religious tradition. It's not inclusive and can hurt those who are not in the know, or outsiders for any reason whether gender, race, class or something else.

When I first got to college I met a boy I was enamored with and started dating immediately. He was into obscure songs from very popular Broadway musicals. As a musician and sincere music appreciator, which he was, this was fine except that he made fun of me for only knowing the hit songs from these shows.

His trivia was more elaborate than mine (in this area), yet the game he initiated was about seeing how many of these songs you could name.

Whoever decides the rules of the game can, of course, design it so they will win, if it's trivia. In mainstream trivia, many are allowing and accepting of the fact that the trivia games they play have rules that have been decided by someone they have little in common with.

When our lives feel empty, these trivial games can "fill the emptiness" in countless cult-like ways whether through gossip or fetishes of memorization (of any group of characters/labels/"facts" etc).

There may be many real reasons for our interests, but reducing them to trivia (guess what) trivializes them.

All Cults and Subculture Has Trivia

Realizing that every cult or sub-culture has its form of trivia (including spiritual traditions, branches of medicine, academic subjects, groups of friends, families, etc) can point us back in the direction of real life, which is about not only digging deeper into that which has been trivialized, but studying the things that don't make it into the trivial sphere.

Whatever group of people you are in, notice what and who the trivia includes and does not include. This will point you in the direction of social justice and personal integration.

If any race, gender or class predominates the trivia you discuss with your friends or cohorts, challenge your group to study other groups.

Trivia topics aren't empty until they become trivia-at which point we are no longer thinking for ourselves, but rather regurgitating back what we've been told similarly to how we did it in school. Knowing the names of people, places, songs, movies, actors, gurus, writers or diagnoses does not equal an understanding of their meaning and if you fill your mind with the accumulation of "facts" that have been told to you by a trivializing culture, of course that culture will tell you you are very smart.

Liberating Ourselves

In order to liberate ourselves from this rat race to "know," we must as individuals retreat from the cult to some degree, at some point, and find our own answers. Knowing trivia can help connect us with others and the basic concepts they hold, but this should be a stepping stone rather than a tired destination.

When it becomes a destination, we become very boring people, so bored we have an insatiable addiction to more trivia. And this boredom that trivializes (out of shame and fear) is at the root of all addictions.

Psychiatry and Psychology use Trivia in Their Cult

When human experiences become categorical diagnoses to study and memorize, they are boring trivia, as well as harmful.

I once went to a Smith College School of Social Work classroom with 2 other members of the Freedom Center to teach on our activist work and share our experiences in the mental health system. We waited out in the hallway for them to finish playing "Mood Disorder Jeopardy," where you can probably guess they had to name the disorder label that went with an oversimplified, medicalised and stigmatizing description of normal human experience.

This is a perfect example of our most meaningful, vulnerable and important life experiences being literally trivialized.

The benefit of this awareness whether in psychological, spiritual or mainstream circles is that seeing through this trivialization brings relief. Every one of us experiences suffering due to trivialization, and seeing it for what it is brings us directly back to what matters, our actual experiences, especially the ones that don't fit into the Jeopardy squares.

All trivia is in jeopardy, as our stories, idols, gurus, diagnoses and mythologies are constantly changing. If it doesn't fit into a Jeopardy square, it might have a chance of providing meaning to the evolution of our communities.

If feelings aren't socially acceptable, discussing trivia may be one of the only socially acceptable options. I get a painfully bored, left out, marginalized feeling when I'm the only female and the males around me go into "trivia talk."

I get this feeling even if I'm not the only female, but in a different way. It brings up feelings from my childhood of experiencing this with my father and brother, but I am not feeling my pain alone.

There's a great deal of pain in the need to escape from feelings and into trivia all the time. This can happen with any gender ratio or group of people, though each gender has been more conditioned out of different types of feelings, in many cases.

There are exceptions to this and my purpose isn't to say that this is a problem that exists because of men or their conditioning. It exists in all of us in different ways. If you look at any group that is especially focused on trivia, you will also see that feelings are not safe or acceptable in that demographic.

Trivia is marginalizing and hurtful (and of course we all participate in it). If our lives are REDUCED to trivia, there is no choice but to check out and take a drug or develop an addiction, which is why the trivia of psychiatric labels continues to create drug dependence and increase other addictions.

Being true to ourselves is the only way out of the maze of trivia.

Studying names, diagnoses and "facts" becomes a procrastination, protection, numbing out technique to avoid the pain, triumph and challenges of living our real lives which are messy and unable to be jeopardized. All people can take the risk to be vulnerable and real, to take a few baby steps away from trivia, away from procrastination of their deepest desires.

There was a time in history (not even too long ago) when trivia had more practical value, but we're mostly past it now that we have technology that affords us the luxury of not needing to memorize facts. Western medicine is an entire medical system almost entirely of trivia- NAMES of illnesses, body processes, pills. To go beyond trivia in medicine would require looking at the whole person, environment and community in all health issues-otherwise it will continue to be primarily a band-aid medicine, perhaps lengthening human lives in the short term, but drastically decreasing the health, natural wealth and sustainability of the planet and its inhabitants in the long run.

This is how trivia harms us, only looking the names and titles of things.

The challenge we face is that knowledge of trivia is still seen as expertise, while true expertise is having experienced something. Experience is the opposite of trivia-it's not boring, nor is it about memorization, rote repetition or outside "experts" who know more. Instead it's about real life, the one thing we lose when trivia is the sole focus of affairs, such as in the DSM, psychiatry's rule book for their game of Trivial Pursuit (where they pursue explanations which have no meaning and make the rules of their own game).

Creating a system of trivia that is accepted on a grand scale has been a good way to "win" in our current economy since trivia is still widely revered and humans have imbued it with so much power that could be better used to advance our own meaning.

Myths About Psych Drugs

3. Psych drugs are prescribed by a doctor so they're safe.
4. You can stop taking psych drugs easily if they don't help.
5. Psych drugs correct a chemical imbalance.
6. Psych drugs stabilize people.
7. Psych drugs are medicine to treat an illness.
8. Psych drugs don't do harm.
9. The "side effects" of psych drugs aren't so bad.
10. Psych drugs make relationships function better.
11. Psych drugs reduce violence.
12. Psych drugs make it easier for people to work through trauma.
13. Psych drugs have been tested for long term use.
14. Doctors know how psych drugs work.
15. Psych drugs save more lives than they kill.
16. Psych drugs increase functionality.
17. Psych drugs get people out of bed more than they flatten people in bed.

18. Psych drugs reduce disability rates.
19. Psych drugs make people feel like themselves again (by altering emotional responses).
20. Psych drugs help children learn better.
21. The main problem is the stigma against taking psych drugs.
22. It's kind and caring to suggest psych drugs to family and friends.
23. Forcing psych drugs on someone against their will is compassionate.
24. Psych drugs should be used preventively in children and pregnant women.
25. Psych drugs are safer than illicit drugs

I was at a Twelve Step meeting recently and heard several references to the "mentally ill." One was a woman who said she had a mentally ill sister and that was one reason she didn't like to have friends over as a kid.

Another was a man who said on his block growing up there was alcoholism, mental illness and incest (just like that, in that order) in the families of his friends, so he didn't want them at his house but didn't want to go to their houses either.

The last was a woman struggling with having grown up in an alcoholic home and having an alcoholic boyfriend and she listed taking anti-depressant meds and going to therapy as things she was doing to try to improve her situation.

For her, it seemed, nothing was helping her feel good enough to get out of bed or do the things she cared about, including the meds and therapy, but she was doing the things society had prescribed for "people like her." Psychiatric drugs and therapy are protocol even though they haven't proven to have better results than, say, cooking and eating a meal with friends, playing tennis, or singing in a choir.

Well, I doubt they've ever been statistically compared.

The Meaning of the Term Mental Illness

When people call someone in their family "mentally ill," what does it mean? The term mental illness has gotten out of control vague. There is no way to prove someone does or doesn't have a mental illness in the way it is referred to, so why don't we hear people say, "There's someone in my family who's extremely challenging for me (and others perhaps)"?

Why don't we hear descriptions of the behavior, how people feel in response to it, and what concerns it brings up in an honest way where the speaker owns their own experience?

Using the term mental illness might seem like a quick and easy way to reach common ground with other people, for some, but it doesn't give accurate detail, so people don't know what is being referred to. Since things like nail biting, leg shaking and restlessness are now becoming mental illnesses, it's more important than ever to be specific in speech or writing about what we are referring to.

Not long ago, homosexuality was a mental illness and currently premenstrual cramps and moodiness, gender non-conformity, and children or teens not obeying authority are all mental illnesses. When someone describes a mentally ill sister, all we know about her is that her behavior has been stigmatized. She is probably taking the label for the family (and society).

The other reason it's problematic to use the term mental illness is that most people by now have been labeled with one (or more). So those listening or reading are likely to feel alienated by the term.

People are questioning what it means more and more and it's starting to sound old-fashioned to those with more multicultural awareness and understanding of mental diversity. People are starting to see the political and socioeconomic factors that go into who gets that label, and who doesn't.

In order to get insurance coverage for therapy, one needs a diagnosis of a mental illness. Some may say, "But I'm talking about MAJOR mental illness. My sister is schizophrenic/psychotic." For one thing, "anti-psychotic" drugs have been some of the top selling of ANY pharmaceuticals in this country, so it's important not to underestimate how many people have MAJOR mental illness labels.

Most importantly, though, even in cases of extreme diagnoses, and extreme behaviors and situations, people will not know what you mean unless you describe it. Using a label is stigmatizing, so it is more powerful and clear to say what is actually going on; then others can understand, connect and empathize with a unique situation.

Talking Myself Down

When I hear labels used, I have to talk myself down, remind myself that not everyone has been studying mental diversity for the past 15 years and not everyone investigates the language they use.

This talking myself down takes time and during that time there is a disconnect between me and the one using a label. It's similar to if you are listening to a white person make racist comments or use the word "nigger" or a heterosexual use the word "faggot" or a man "bitch."

A close family member has struggled with substance addictions and extreme mood swings for as long as I can remember. Another family member once said to me, "I think your (family member) is bipolar."

I was in my mid-20's and it had never occurred to me to label this family member. This could be because she was high on the social totem pole: she owned a nice house, made plenty of money, was very active in life and had an extroverted, yang personality.

Perhaps I had never thought to label her since she had labeled me and I was the one in the family to be stigmatized for awhile.

The Bipolar Label is Stigmatizing

The term bipolar would have served to stigmatize her but not clarify, heal or deeply explain any of her behavior, its roots or how it affected me (or others). Since I experienced and still experience a lot of agony, pain and fear (as well as joy, love, nurturance and comfort) in response to her behavior, labeling her might feel like retaliation, or it might give me a chance to put the stigmatizing lens on her after she'd (unfairly I'd say) put it on me.

But it wouldn't be honest. She could get that diagnosis as readily as most people who've gotten it, but it's a low blow. It's dehumanizing and lacking love and empathy to resort to a label.

I recently asked a friend who hears voices (and has gone through quite a bit in the mental health system, gotten diagnoses and taken psychiatric drugs in the past) if her parents label her. She replied, "They love me too much to label me." Enough said.

The Label Schizophrenia

The first time I heard someone labeled schizophrenic I was at Prospect Park, on a walk with my mom. I was about 10 years old. A man was talking to himself and appeared to be homeless and perhaps on drugs. My mom, a very good teacher and explainer of things to me, said, "That man is schizophrenic.

That means he can't tell the difference between what's inside of himself and what's outside." In retrospect, as many of the things my mom said to me as a child, this seems like a relatively sophisticated and sensitive explanation. I can appreciate her intention, looking back.

My mom studied psychology in the 70's and gave me a version

of the description she had learned. She, like many, assumed herself qualified to diagnose someone schizophrenic after less than a minute of observation.

There is no blood test, brain scan or any other reliable diagnostic procedure to diagnose what we call "schizophrenia." While, of course, anyone who sets foot into a psychiatrist's office is likely to be suffering in extreme ways, schizophrenia, in fact, does not exist. Meanwhile, it is the mental health label that many people, even skeptics, think is the only real one.

Often times when I mention that it does not exist, I see the light bulbs go on in people's minds and they become visibly awakened. Their eyes light up, they look relieved, and they have a lot to say! The truth about the man we saw in the park 20 years ago: if he had been given a home, good food and help sobering up, he likely could have seemed "normal."

Anatomy of A Schizophrenia Diagnosis

The truth about getting an actual schizophrenia diagnosis from a psychiatrist is that many people get it either after or during a recreational drug experience or spiritual breakthrough/psychic opening.

People who tell a psychiatrist they "hear voices" can get the label, regardless of what hearing voices means to them. Prophets, religious people, mediums, and ordinary folk have been hearing voices from beyond since the beginning of recorded history. Nearly all religions document these experiences.

Hearing threatening voices is often a result of trauma. In either/any case, there is no cookie cutter "schizophrenia"-everyone who gets the label has a different experience and needs to be seen as an individual-not as a category. This is obvious for nearly every other diagnosis, so why does society, even those radically inclined, have a blind spot about this one?

Since there is no uniform physical basis for this label, giving everyone who receives it a similar class of brain damaging drugs -neuroleptics- is wrong, and fails to help most people. What it does do, if someone identifies with the label, and their community identifies them with it, is makes them a lifelong outcast and sick person- both from the debilitating effects of the drug, and the identification with a label that scares people.

Please, for the sake of humanity, don't use the word schizophrenic to describe anyone. Tell us what you mean instead-and if you don't know enough about someone to say what you mean, please just admit it. If you had a bad drug experience or a trauma or heard a voice from beyond, would you want to be ostracized as a schizophrenic?

Would you want to be made sick for life?

If we go back to my mothers definition (which is one of many vague definitions of schizophrenia)-not knowing the difference between what's inside of ourselves and what's outside, and look at the things that make life worth living, they all put us in that category.

Falling in love, hearing music that enters our heart, having children/giving birth, connecting powerfully with another person in a meeting of the minds, feeling empathy, deeply caring about something, experiencing oneness with nature, are all examples of times when the line between inner and outer reality is blurred.

This is how we achieve what we value most in life-connection.

There are extreme cases where the blur between external and internal reality can be torturous, or so strong that one may shut down and disconnect. Let's remember, though, that everything starts as an impulse to connect, which requires inner and outer realities to merge in our hearts.

Hearing Voices is the Source of Every Success I've Had

Hearing voices from beyond is cornerstone in my life and is the source of nearly every success I've ever had!

Another question that arises is: Why do we often glorify recreational drugs use but not what we call "schizophrenia?" People often take recreational drugs, whether occasionally or regularly, to experience a more extreme version of merging inner and outer realities-and sometimes receive profound insights from these experiences.

I'd venture to guess that we view the "schizophrenic" as alone, dysfunctional, and unable to relate with others. We see how s/he has been ostracized, yet the ostracizing takes place mostly after the diagnosis is given.

The diagnosis, in essence, creates the disease. It allows us to simplify the questions in someone's life and say, "Now we know what's wrong with them." Recreational drug use, on the other hand is more likely to be associated with social life, community and togetherness.

But when we use the label schizophrenic, do we know any more than before? If curiosity about a person closes off, we know less. We also have no potential to learn more. Intelligence is a responsibility and a gift. Using mental health labels puts a dam in the flow of that river and its power to heal and transform us all.

An Anti-Anti-Stigma Campaign

The whole anti-stigma campaign is something of a joke. Google the word "stigma," see for yourself. Mental health labels are inherently stigmatizing, yet the industry that was responsible for creating and perpetuating them, simultaneously pours money into anti-stigma campaigns which will come up right away on your search.

They tell us not to stigmatize people who take psychiatric drugs for these labels. While I agree, as a politically correct (sometimes), compassionate (sometimes) person who aspires to be humble (mostly), stigmatizing anyone for anything can be hurtful, there is a fine line between an anti-stigma campaign and repressing discernment in the general public.

Is it possible to stigmatize actions but not the people who take those actions? In theory, yes. In practice, inconclusive, but we must not allow the anti-stigma campaigns to cloud our judgment, silence us, or tell us to accept everything, every behavior, everyone being on psych drugs, etc.

It is fishy that the same people who created the stigma to sell their products are now demanding we not stigmatize people for using their products. They are basically saying, "Don't stigmatize people who are bringing us such immense profits. We must protect the oblivion (in some cases) of our customers so they will continue to generate income for us." In this case, perhaps a bit of stigma (or better words: discernment, non-acceptance, intolerance) is better than repressing those things.

What if cigarette companies/Big Tobacco ran anti stigma campaigns? Much of advertisement is actually some form of an anti-stigma campaign. Advertisements for all things unhealthy have beautiful, healthy looking people in their ads to promote their products and give the message that by using them (even cigarettes, alcohol, candy, etc) you will also be beautiful, healthy and stay forever young.

Pharmaceutical companies, of course, do this too, featuring happy looking people to sell their products. The irony is this creates stigma against being human and having sadness, difficult emotions and grief.

Having natural emotional reactions to life is stigmatized but if you get a mental health label and "take your medication" you suddenly have a whole group of comrades to defend this anti-stigma campaign with. You have a place in society now, that is being guarded by those who profit.

At least there are guard dogs fending off the stigmatizers. At least you're not that sad, "depressed" person in black and white in the anti-depressant ad. We can stigmatize her in our ad-until she takes our drugs. Then she's safe from scrutiny. Then we'll shame you for suggesting there may be a better way and the drugs may be doing more harm than good. Is stigma, in this context, a dirty word for caring?

Let's all stop being so intelligent and stop using our brains! Let's sit in front of TV all day smoking cigarettes, eating GMO snacks, drinking Pepsi, popping Benzos and let our party line and dying words be "End the stigma," when the real stigma was the initial one.

The Real Stigma

The real stigma is the stigmatization of our humanity-unlabeled, free and wild. The real stigma is against sensitivity, intelligence, introversion, feelings, grief, creativity, uniqueness, brilliance and pain.

How's that for politically correct? People who commit to accepting their feelings and nature make far worse consumers. They are much less likely to buy or get addicted to your products. So you'd better keep stigmatizing them if you want to stay afloat Pharma!

Whoever decides the rules of the game can, of course, design it so they will win, if it's trivia. In mainstream trivia, many are allowing and accepting of the fact that the trivia games they play have rules that have been decided by someone they have little in common with.

When our lives feel empty, these trivial games can "fill the emptiness" in countless cult-like ways whether through gossip or fetishes of memorization (of any group of characters/labels/"facts" etc). There may be many real reasons for our interests, but reducing them to trivia (guess what) trivializes them.

Realizing that every cult or sub-culture has its form of trivia (including spiritual traditions, branches of medicine, academic subjects, groups of friends, families, etc) can point us back in the direction of real life, which is about not only digging deeper into that which has been trivialized, but studying the things that don't make it into the trivial sphere.

Whatever group of people you are in, notice what and who the trivia includes and does not include. This will point you in the direction of social justice and personal integration.

If any race, gender or class predominates the trivia you discuss with your friends or cohorts, challenge your group to study other groups.

Trivia topics aren't empty until they become trivia-at which point we are no longer thinking for ourselves, but rather regurgitating back what we've been told similarly to how we did it in school. Knowing the names of people, places, songs, movies, actors, gurus, writers or diagnoses does not equal an understanding of their meaning and if you fill your mind with the accumulation of "facts" that have been told to you by a trivializing culture, of course that culture will tell you you are very smart.

In order to liberate ourselves from this rat race to "know," we must as individuals retreat from the cult to some degree, at some point, and find our own answers.

Knowing trivia can help connect us with others and the basic concepts they hold, but this should be a stepping stone rather than a tired destination. When it becomes a destination, we become very boring people, so bored we have an insatiable addiction to more trivia.

And this boredom that trivializes (out of shame and fear) is at the root of all addictions.

Common Disorders Psychiatrists May Have

Over the past 30 years, an epidemic of new disorders has been on the rise in psychiatrists. Some have only recently been discovered and fully understood. Remember, psychiatrists need our love and compassionate understanding to heal from these.

Compulsive Labeling Disorder (CLD): This is a common one that requires early intervention. If a psychiatrist does well on her/his exams in school, initial treatments of extra love may be indicated.

Symptoms include finding a DSM (Diagnostic and Statistical Manual of Mental Disorders) category for the majority of persons who enter his/her office, looking up DSM categories while a patient is talking, inability to concentrate on things other than diagnostic categories, boiling a person's life-concerns down to a label, thinking about most life experiences of others in terms of a disorder.

More education in multicultural history and spirituality are indicated as well as extra love and heart opening. Many psychiatrists with this disorder do not understand themselves very well but spiritual growth is sure to improve symptoms over time.

Obsessive Pill Pushing Disorder (OPPD): This shows up frequently and is characterized by suggesting psychiatric drugs to most patients before considering other options. It's a very serious disorder and many psychiatrists don't realize how serious their condition is. Many with this illness suffer from self-hatred so it is important to give them love, while protecting yourself from their dangerous behavior.

It's very easy to spot and the best antidote is abstinence. If the psychiatrist can go a month without prescribing pills, usually they will be able to find more effective and harm-free solutions. If not, it would be best to stop practicing psychiatry until the desire to engage in this behavior has entirely ceased. Heal the psychiatrist with love.

Fickle Trial and Error Disorder (FTED): This is seen when a patient is tried out on numerous different drugs one after another, or simultaneously. The psychiatrists will often get heady and forget about the humanity of the patients when getting caught up in this behavior. It is necessary to take away prescription pad and protect patients from this illness, reminding them that their psychiatrist has a flawed mind and needs love to heal.

Poly-pharmacy Mania (PPM): Doctor gives patient numerous drugs at once, often for the same label or condition. In cases becoming more common, doctors have been known to give 13 or more drugs at once! This is one of the most dangerous of all disorders and prescription pad must be confiscated immediately and permanently.

If doctor does not comply, the only answer is to have them take every single drug they've prescribed. After a few days of this, they will not argue and can be tapered off and treated with love.

Love Lacking Disorder (LLD): This occurs when the psychiatrist forgets to treat patients with love, believing that pills and other techniques are more powerful. The Psychiatrist will always be always deprived of love him/herself and self-love intensives can be helpful.

Inability to Recognize Side Effects Syndrome (IRSES): It is common for Doctors with this illness to forget that drugs have unwelcome effects and to attribute these harmful effects to the original label they gave their client. This creates a lot of confusion for patients. Studying DSM exacerbates this condition.

This syndrome can be healed with the same antidote as that for PPM.

Money Clouding Eyes Disorder (MCED): Symptoms include accepting money from pharmaceutical companies. Minor symptoms include lack of compassion and seeing interactions as transactions only.

Can also show up in the form of a sort of mania, squeezing in as many clients as possible into a day, giving them each less time. Another majors sign is the impulsive acceptance of vacations, cruises and other escapes from pharmaceutical companies without checking in with their conscience.

Can deteriorate into complete loss of conscience if not treated early. Early intervention is necessary. Persons with this disorder should be disallowed from medical school. New screening methods are being developed to prevent this very serious mental illness.

Love is the answer!

Breaking Down Serious Mental Disorders

Some Journalists criticize the peer movement for focusing primarily on the "worried well" and neglecting those with serious mental disorders. This distinction is vague and unfounded. There is no evidence base to support this supposedly clear distinction used to mock efforts to treat all people as human beings on a human spectrum, regardless of how serious a label they've been given.

Let's break down these serious mental disorders starting with the first word: serious. What does it mean and who decides what is serious and what isn't? If something, anything, is presented as solely serious it sounds one sided and manipulative to me.

Sure, death, violence and oppression are serious but let's get more honest than that-everything has a heavy side and a light side. No individuals life ought be damned SERIOUS. Just thinking about the word serious and facing it head on makes me feel light and like laughing.

Condemning someone to a sentence of seriousness is dishonest and limits that person's potential.

While I do take many things seriously, the only way I can be effective is by combining serious commitment to a cause with some lightness, some letting go. Nothing of value has ever been accomplished by being sanctioned as a "serious matter" only. In the darkest hour and starkest tragedy, it is humor, love, friendship and lightness (combined with respect for the weight of things) that bring relief to suffering people.

And what friendship or love is all serious?

We see this manipulation of public sentiment with the word serious in all aspects of Western medicine and politics as it's a way to use people's fears of the Ultimate Serious Problem to garner support for a large variety of business and corporate interests.

When you hear or read the word serious, ask yourself who is making money from calling this situation serious. It's complicated, of course, because there are genuine concerns that fall under the "serious" umbrella, yet I've never met a person, cause, business or movement I trust that can't laugh, and laugh at itself.

Wise People Have a Funny Bone

All wise people have a funny bone underneath their solemn and steadfast efforts, so let's not let the serious in "serious mental disorders" derail us or blind-sight us from seeing that all people and their lives have some lightness, some joy, some laughter even- or from seeing that even someone with a completely different mind than you might not see their mental state as serious.

As for violence, sure it's serious, AND it is everywhere. In all of our media, politics, medicine, families, within ourselves, and in every corner of society there is some form of violence. Protecting ourselves and our loved ones, especially children and those without the ability to protect themselves is important and serious, if you will, but does this indicate serious mental disorders?

To tackle this question, let's move to mental disorders and what they are.

What Are Mental Disorders?

Mental indicates of the mind or brain and disorders are situations perceived to be chaotic, but what exactly is a disorder? The word disorder isn't used with any individual part of the body (besides the brain) such as a liver disorder, kidney disorder, lung disorder, etc.

We do hear about speech, behavioral, personality and brain disorders. Disorder isn't a scientific term, though Western Medicine has accepted it as such. There is no official brain, speech, personality or behavioral order that humans are "supposed" to have.

In fact, just the idea that our personalities, minds, brains, speech and behavior should follow a certain order sounds fascist, conformist and utterly non-human. It sounds like a serious problem. But instead, some are focused on the seriousness of those whose brains, personalities, speech and behaviors are seriously not in "order." Yet, what is this order?

If we are talking about violence, let's talk about violence, and stop mixing it up with these alleged serious mental disorders and treating people labeled with them violently. You know something is wrong when the same group of people preaching the seriousness of the risk of violence are pushing an agenda to "treat" these mentally disordered folks with serious, life threatening and violent drugs.

Let's ask ourselves what's serious and what's humorous about all this. The Value of Disability For Everyone

"There's a crack in everything. That's how the light gets in." – Leonard Cohen

The word disability gets tossed around a lot when discussing mental health law and advocacy. It looks like our movement is far from ditching the word entirely, I think it is time to reclaim the word disability. Disability needs to be appreciated.

To the extent we value community over isolation, anything anyone cannot do, or needs help with, builds community. In a society that truly values community, anything that would be labeled a mental illness in our culture would be seen as a community building opportunity, a situation ripe for fostering connection.

When everything is going along fine and everyone is "functioning" "efficiently" in their cubicles, what is there to connect on? Who needs community? When there is a problem, disability, or lack of ordinary functioning of any kind, community is needed and therefore built. True connections are made based on need.

Having a family life that overwhelmed me as a child caused me to need to rely on friends. I became very good at creating friendships and fostering community because I needed to — because I was "broken" and in a "dysfunctional" family. If I had not developed powerful friendships

I would have likely become suicidal; but instead my disability and deficit (having a torturous family life) led to stronger connections with friends. I experience that making and developing friendships is still one of my strongest points and others tell me this, too. It's because I am disabled without others. (Top secret: we all are.)

Relating With Others

Relating with others is as much about what we can't do as what we can, for anything one person can't do gives another person a reason for existing! If I need someone to talk to, someone who cares to listen has a reason to be alive.

If someone else needs someone to talk to and I can be that for them, I have a purpose. I can fill a need. A disability is basically an unfilled need, waiting to be filled. Feeling a lack of purpose in life can easily translate into a DSM diagnosis, therefore, we are all disabled individuals until our needs are matched with those who can meet them and others needs are matched with something we can do to help.

We don't always stop to think about the indisputable fact that every single thing we do in life that has any meaning whatsoever is dependent on someone else being disabled in some way. It can be as simple as serving food to people who are too tired at that moment to make their own or protecting someone who is unable to protect themselves or sharing ideas and inspiration with those who feel demoralized.

There are infinite examples in every career and walk of life of how necessary "disability" (since we're calling it that) is for connection, service and meaning in life. Without it we'd have absolutely no need for each other. And the fastest way to despair is to feel unnecessary.

Someone once said to me, "The best things in life have come to me out of desperation." The most profound connections in my life have resulted from my disabilities. They have come especially from those times where I would have easily been labeled mentally ill by psychiatry if I had not found meaningful connection in its place.

The most important relationships heal those parts of myself that would feel broken and lost without them. The schizophrenic, multiple personality, bipolar, dissociative identified, post traumatic stress and anxiety ridden person is none of those things with the right people around them to fill in the gaps with love and humor.

This is what makes life romantic — being unable to do everything alone or heal ourselves in isolation — and the love that comes to every single person who is willing to be "disabled," "imperfect," "broken,' "dysfunctional" or otherwise in need of companionship and caring.

A Speech I Gave to Protest The American Psychiatric Association

If you haven't been labeled mentally ill by the American Psychiatric Association, you have to ask yourself what's wrong. Perhaps you were ahead of the game: you knew not to reveal yourself to them, you knew how to avoid them, you found other social support, and if so, a big congratulations.

If not, what's wrong?

Why have you conformed? Why have you not gone, in their words, psychotic, yet? At least a few times. Why haven't you let the inequality and injustice in the world upset you enough to warrant a diagnosis of clinical depression?

Why haven't you allowed yourself to reach heights of ecstatic joy and celebration, so high you want to take off your clothes and run around the neighborhood, introducing yourself to strangers and giving away all of your possessions?

Have you conformed so much to consensual reality that you never experience the intense anxiety that comes along with challenging it?Perhaps you have felt or done all or most of these things, and if you are listening at all, it's likely. Maybe you have received a diagnosis and maybe you have even identified with it at times. Taken drugs for it. Allowed the APA into your living room and learned how hard it is to get them out once you did.

Now you keep them at arm's length. You rely on yourself and your close friends. You've developed good eating and exercise habits, you're committed to getting enough sleep. Maybe you even practice yoga, meditation or prayer. Please, though, for the rest of us, don't be afraid to go bonkers, don't deny your need to go to extremes sometimes.

Don't shut off your grief or tone down your ecstacy. Don't shut yourself up or shut yourself down.

I say all this because, to some degree, I have. I don't speak up as much as I did before I was invaded by the APA. I have a hell of a lot more impulse control and I'm a heck of a lot less free.

This is in small part due to my own traumatic experiences of psychiatric drugs being given to me against my will. I was on 7 pharmaceuticals at the age of 21, and bedridden for the greater part of 2 years due to the debilitating effects of these drugs.

It took me another year to withdraw from them, yet I don't feel the APA robbed me of those years. There was a part of me that got stronger, even as they robbed me of my physical and mental capacities against my will and coerced me into addiction to their products. Yet, my story is one in a million in that regard. I'm more of the haystack than the needle, and that's the primary reason I'm a lot less free.

Millions and millions more Americans and people worldwide have been, in effect, castrated and made impotent before and after me and the numbers are growing everyday. Let me assure you, the DSM 5 would have every single one of us on psychiatric pharmaceuticals, which is why grief, PMS and adult onset ADD are mental illnesses since May 18th 2013 when the DSM 5 was officially released.

When I say castrated and made impotent, I am not only referring to the loss of sexual potency that often come along with taking psychiatric drugs. I am talking just as much about other drives that are lost.

Other parts of you that end up going missing, such as your creativity, your voice, your rebellion, your desire to take risks, your ability to dream big, your sense of safety, and absolutely most importantly, your trust in yourself, and others; your sense of inner knowing and integrity.

As millions of people lose these parts of themselves all around me, everyday, in the hands of the APA, I am vicariously silenced. The mirror all around me reflects our patriarchal society's fears rather than mutual support towards authenticity and liberation, much of the time.

I hardly see happy people anywhere anymore. I hardly meet people who aren't on pharmaceuticals. More Americans take prescription drugs than vote. They are in our drinking water, we're all taking them. This issue affects absolutely everyone: those who are good at fitting into the patriarchy, those who successfully climb the social ladder, especially anyone who is not conscious of the fears the APA has implanted in them.

The primary thing I believe each of us can do, is break our own silence. Tell our own story. Make our own media. Spread our story as far and wide as it will go. The APA is a large scary body of social control, yet the primary power anyone has over me, is the power to silence me.

So I'd like to state my personal commitment to you: I will no longer be silenced. I will dig inside myself to find those things I'm still scared to say, and I'll keep saying them. Please, please commit to finding your own sense of safety to do the same for yourself.

A quote from Martha Graham: *"There is a vitality, a life force, an energy, a quickening that is translated through you into action, and because there is only one of you in all of time, this expression is unique."*

If you block it, it will never exist through any other medium and it will be lost. The world will not have it. It is not your business to determine how good it is nor how valuable nor how it compares with other expressions. It is your business to keep it yours clearly and directly, to keep the channel open.

You do not even have to believe in yourself or your work. You have to keep yourself open and aware to the urges that motivate you. Keep the channel open.

Choosing Psychiatric Meds: The Pro Choicers Dilemma

The dilemma of choosing psychiatric meds is in some ways like the omnivore's dilemma...

Yes, we all like to say people should be able to choose whether or not to take psychiatric drugs, and for the most part I say the same thing. It's politically correct and choosing psychiatric meds for oneself sounds diplomatic, it sounds like offering people respect and self-determination.

But is it really that simple anymore?

Now that psychiatric drugs, substances that are too dangerous to be sold over the counter, yet drugs that aren't actually medicines for any biological illness or condition with any valid scientific basis, have created a worldwide health crisis, more than tripling disability rates in the past couple of decades, is it as simple as a personal choice?

Public health standards (as poor as they are) in the United States acknowledge that we are affected by the behavior of others and the substances they use, with certain standards. For example, in the U.S, smoking is no longer allowed in public indoor spaces due to the health dangers of secondhand smoke and drunk driving is illegal due to the risk it imposes on other drivers and pedestrians.

Psychiatric drugs, while currently posing as prescription medications (to treat illnesses that have not yet been proven to exist by any scientific test or biological markers) also affect others, not only the individual consuming them. Some of them cause dizziness, drowsiness and problems with motor coordination as well.

For example, on the Stanford University medical website, they say "Depakote may cause drowsiness, dizziness, or blurred vision. Patients taking Depakote should not drive, use machinery, or do anything requiring mental alertness until the effects of this drug are known."

Also relevant, psychiatric drugs cause many cases of chronic disability and chronic poverty, which of course affects all of us financially and otherwise whether we have "chosen" to take them or not.

There is No Shame in Taking Psych Meds

I don't say any of this to scapegoat, blame, or otherwise insult those who are taking these substances for any reason, whether by force or choosing psychiatric meds or somewhere in the middle. Psychiatric drugs are harmful and we know that (the drugs companies themselves know that, which we see in their advertising), but this does not mean that people who take them, prescribe or advocate for them are bad or defective or anything else.

There is no choice, however, that we make for ourselves alone-absolutely none. Everything we do or don't do affects the whole.

So when we talk about self-determination and personal decision choosing psychiatric meds, it is a nuanced conversation. If psych drugs were on sale at the drugstore next to homeopathic remedies, herbs, hugs and song circles, for the same price, we could talk about choice, public safety and social impact.

I know that sounds extremely woo-woo, but even the idea that everything other than FDA approved drugs is witchcraft or New Age BS is one that has been sold to you by corporate media.

Mysterious Chemical Concoctions

I can't think of anything more woo-woo than prescribing mysterious chemical concoctions for illnesses that have never been found to exist medically, yet requiring a doctor's script and calling them medication. THAT my friends is witchcraft, but not in the good sense I have come to think of the (now reclaimed) term.

Depakote Ingredients (Depakote ER 250 and 500 mg tablets):

sodium valproate, valproic acid, FD&C Blue No. 1, hypromellose, lactose, microcrystalline cellulose, polyethylene glycol, potassium sorbate, propylene glycol, silicon dioxide, titanium dioxide, and triacetin.

So how can we talk more honestly about choosing psychiatric meds? How can we include social responsibility on both sides of the equation?

This includes social responsibility on the part of those presenting the "choice" (to vulnerable, suffering people) to offer other viable choices and make them accessible, affordable and socially acceptable (this responsibility falls largely on government and policy makers), and "choice" to take a drug that will not only affect you, your health and your personality, but everyone else you encounter and many people, plants, animals and ecosystems you will never encounter at all.

There is no simplicity in saying, "it's your choice" as if it's all up to your individual ego to self-determine and affect you alone.

There is a choice, however, that taps into a larger field, one that chooses in a way that benefits the whole. We know when we are making those choices. There's something about them that feels good, and actually simple. Those choices cannot be manipulated by advertisements or fraudulent "science."

The more we practice making those choices, the more easily they come to us, and the less need humanity will have for a "medicine" that fractures our personalities, ruins our health and destroys the planet.

Paradoxically, true Self-determination takes all things into account and acts from a place beyond the self. Ironically, psychiatry, which should be the the medicine FOR the psyche/soul, works against the Self by isolating it artificially from the interconnected web of reality, which results in irresponsible action when taken as a life path.

Psychotropic Medication Harm Reduction

How does this relate to Harm Reduction? Aren't there times when we need to isolate ourselves out and use psychiatry as a means to reduce even worse harm? This must be decided on a case by case basis.

Harm reduction has its place as long as it doesn't reduce us to fight or flight mode forever. I know very well the necessity of doing whatever it takes to get through the day or night sometimes. I've spent many years of my life living primarily in that mode. Yet building a life around sacrificing important parts of ourselves and choosing psychiatric meds for the sake of survival can ironically lead to more problems surviving.

By making choices from a larger field, beyond the self, we are guaranteed something even greater than survival-an interconnected, soulful journey, where we are part of something larger rather than always separate and acting out of "self" interest alone.

The individuals and families I work with are moving more and more into an expanded awareness of the "Self" in self-determination; it is inherent in aspiring to come off psych drugs, this desire to be more inclusive in our sense of self, less isolated, even though Psychiatry will tell us otherwise.

Psychiatry might twist the facts, try to convince us that choosing psychiatric meds will fix us so we can participate better in society, but this is where we must not be sold. We must hold to our essential knowing of ourselves that can't be broken or fixed, and that is so inherently connected to all of life, it finds strength and power in the collective field itself and overcomes oppression without excessive isolation of the self as a biochemical entity alone.

Teaching people how to move from chronic survival mode that psychiatry imposes, to a larger field where decisions can include other people, plants, animals, without sacrificing our health or life path, is the main focus of this book.

Intentional Peer Support Poems

Who you think you are
and who I think I am
is similar to wind and trees
we sing songs of sixpence
we table our woes
so we can find them again someday
on the same table, for we never moved them,
still we are surprised to see them in the same spot after all these years
of sorting pepper shakers and salt shakers,
cayenne and black,
sugar and cinnamon,
we thought we had it all figured out
yet felt so enlivened to know we didn't.
We were so alive once
when we knew nothing
of expert and student
doctor and patient
helper and helpee
even the very simple me and you.
The water streams down the rocks in any case
the wind blows the trees,

and then in an earthquake, perhaps,
the trees impact what we call wind.
Yet what we call wind is simply air and the forces that move it.
What I call me is a body and a spirit that moves it,
moves me to leap, to collapse,
to celebrate and mourn
all in the name of equality
whether it seems that way or not.
 All in the name of mutuality with every single particle of existence
there ever was and ever will be
and every particle of life that is screaming
for liberation right now–
for example, an ant crawling across a field of grass–
I might call that ant slow, but how will I connect with the ant?
By watching, suspending my agenda,
and knowing that the spirit of the ant has value
is a gift for its existence alone.
It is existence right now that
liberates some cells in my heart, some
ineffable parts of me–
etheric, ethereal, and for me the most real,
for the ether is more expansive than the earth and
doctor/patient
helper/helpee
expert student
are figments of our collective imagination
as we circle around our very own version of an ant farm,
or so it may look like from above or afar.
 I'm whispering all these secrets to you to move closer to now
to move closer to a we that is not you or me–
yet what troubles me is when I lose this very magic
when trauma takes over and grips me,
telling me there is no now,
telling me safety is in a bottle or a can
or a title or a billfold
or a binder or an embrace.
I cry sometimes because my safety always comes
in the form of an embrace or a feather,
something so far from the future
and indifferent to the past
yet there are things from the past that come back to save me
there are tears I have yet to cry,
for this love we moves towards,
it takes time.
 There's so much to unravel, even when at moments all is simple

and straight, blissful and heartfelt
there are more knots to untie
as we have all separated so much,
 the hierarchy can look so real
my tears get delayed
in the name of "sanity" or "reality" or
the honest word: conformity.
 I am a conformist like any other
yet when I cry, I cry for the piece of each of us
that is not.
 Connection is this,
this "insanity," this
wildness, madness if you will–
this love that will not stop at anything
and knows the "we" I yearn for when I play any role.
When I sing any song.
 II.
Tempting it can be to correct or deliver "peer run services"
yet peer once meant two individuals with a similar world view
and now it means nothing
and perhaps the word "peer" was never anything
but an assumption,
an evaluation,
an assessment that you are like me
and perhaps we are exactly alike in one way
and completely different in another.
 So peers must be all of us or none of us
so doctors are peers
teachers are peers
police officers are peers
ants, babies, blades of grass…
where do we draw the line if a line must be drawn?
 It's always all or nothing
 yet it's never all or nothing
 and reality can contradict itself
so many times it becomes madness
and we diagnose objective reality itself
as quite insane and schizophrenic
making the label holders closer
to the truth of all things
 that lies within all things
and is told in so many stories
felt in as many ways.
 To diagnose one person is to diagnose reality itself.
 To diagnose reality itself is honest

and beautiful
for if reality were not schizophrenic
or multiple personality
or bipolar
or anxious
or manic
there would be no us,
 no dynamic interplay of forces coming together
and apart,
there would be no beauty
no movement
no nothing.
 By splitting off and becoming mad, reality
has always been moving towards a diagnosis
of Love.
Or Love and Disorder as the DSM may have it.

Mental and Physical Diversity

The obvious flaws with the mental illness system point to similar but maybe less obvious issues in physical healthcare.

Both say that if you are suffering it is your responsibility to do whatever it takes to relieve your suffering, no matter how much it compromises your integrity.

Most of us don't enjoy physical pain and do want relief, but similar to emotional suffering, sometimes it can be nice to explore physical symptoms or simply experience them and accept them on one's own terms without seeing them as a mistake.

Like we advocate for mental diversity, why not physical diversity, such as some people are more tired and have less physical capacity in certain ways but that doesn't lower their value in society, especially because loss of certain abilities almost always increases others.

Maybe the abilities that are increased aren't socially valued, such as connecting, loving, even sleeping! There have been times when I've enjoyed being exhausted and sleeping a lot, not being able to keep working due to illness or injury, even though I had "less worth" to society. .

The illness itself helped me come back to myself.

The hardest part is often the isolation and lack of feeling worthy or of value when our bodies aren't capable of functioning at a level that others appreciate.

Also modern medicine creates this illusion that we should always be in control of our bodies (and minds, emotions), and if we're not it's because we aren't doing the right things or we aren't doing enough. But that's an illusion. We aren't meant to be in full control of everything and exert our will on everything and fix every problem in a linear fashion as quickly as possible. That would be the most boring and unimaginative reality ever with no room for real healing, real connection or honest meaning making in our lives.

Informed Consent

What is informed consent? Informed consent obviously means if you are being given drugs you should know the common and potential adverse affects, drug interactions, risk of dependency and addiction, and counter-indications with other substances, health conditions or health concerns.

This is the baseline of informed consent (which many people don't receive) but there is an incredible amount more that is included in what you deserve to know about any drug you are prescribed or medical system you are advised to subscribe to. Informed consent includes adequate, transparent knowledge of the following things:

1 When, where and how did the system of medicine begin and evolve? Who had a voice in the forming of the theories behind the system? In the field of psychiatry (or any Western Medical field) you might ask whether poor people, women and non-white people were part of the "discovery" (or invention) of these fields.

2 How does the medical field advertise (directly and indirectly)? This is your health and your life-financial transparency is required for there to be informed consent. You need to know if you believe in a system of medicine because they advertise in the magazines you read (and if their financial support blocks articles that would challenge their drugs efficacy), if their ads and financial clout affect your news and other media, and that of your friends, family and extended community, all of which make up your reality and affect your judgment. In the case of psychiatry (and other Western medicine), most funding goes to indirect advertising in the form of "consumer advocacy groups." "grassroots self help groups" like NAMI, and for true informed consent, you have to have a good idea of where pharmaceutical money is going before making a decision. As Americans we've been so abused by the patriarchal and violent medical system, we are like abused or neglected children who come to believe this is all we deserve.

3 Informed consent is knowing at least 20 other possible explanations for your experiences than the Western medical model so you are choosing which one to go with rather than accepting the one that pharmaceutical companies paid billions of dollars to put in

front of your face in every corner of your world. For true informed consent, study models from all different cultures and times in history before consenting.

4 Informed consent is having options that are affordable. For true informed consent you should have at least 20 choices of types of medicine, counseling or other healing modalities to choose from and they should all be affordable and accessible. If your insurance only covers one or 2 choices, you don't have access to informed consent since you may not be able to afford to try other models for comparison.

5 Informed consent is knowing what the financial ties are between drug companies, hospitals, doctors, insurance companies, the government, the media and educational institutions. (Ha!)

6 Informed consent is knowing the fears, motivations, history and trauma history of your doctor and anyone else who prescribes a system of medicine to you-officially or by suggestion.

Informed consent is the largest history book and encyclopedia you've ever seen and informed consent lies in the rising and falling of your own breath-it lies within you.

Informed consent is knowing what is on your food, water and air and why. Who profits?

Informed consent is the voice within you, quiet or loud, the feeling you get of trust or distrust about a person, place or decision.

Informed consent doesn't always have to be explained-sometimes it's something you just know.

Informed consent is knowing which questions to ask; it's withdrawing from mainstream media and pop culture enough to develop your own prescience. Once you develop that, informed consent become secondary to your inner wise self who is so much larger than a diagnostic medical system.

No one is going to give you complete informed consent. The best a doctor can do is give you the information they have, encourage you to do your own research, admit that their system has holes and encourage you to follow your own feelings, intuitions and to make your own decision.

Of course our decisions are biased and affected by the water we're swimming in, but no one will spoon feed you complete informed consent.

When we are healing ourselves, we are also healing the cultural narrative, the history, biology and medicine of many years and many other people. Being one person who finds what informed consent means for you and commits to it is a powerful force and source of healing for all beings. Healing is never isolated, never isolated in a person, a relationship, a time period, a system of medicine, a pill bottle or a doctors office.

Healing is big. It's about everything. It's as big as that history book and encyclopedia about informed consent and maybe a bit bigger.

Don't let psychiatry make you small, projecting its insecurities and inadequacies onto you. Of course a form of medicine that is so limited will tell you you are so limited too. It's a lie. You aren't.

Your voice and truth and fight for informed consent is huge and getting larger everyday. There's no turning back now.

Healing with informed consent is a state of expansion. It's all seeing, all knowing, all wise. It's light years larger than the DSM. It's you.

Workbook
Questions for Reflection:

- What lies were you told about yourself?

- What lies were you told about your health/illness?

- Have you researched the process of voting on diagnoses?

- How much do you know about the science behind psychiatric drugs and their long term use?

- What do you think the purpose of the mental health system is within our current economic system?

- How do you feel about any dishonest information you received?

- Do you feel inspired to educate others (via conversations, blogs, videos, public speaking, anonymous posts, sharing research etc.)?

- What do you hope will come out of learning the truth/hearing your own truth/trusting your intuition?

- What is YOUR system? What do you believe? Sit quietly and see what comes to you.

_____

_____

_____

_____

_____

_____

_____

_____

_____

_____

_____

CHAPTER
3

ALTERNATIVES

My friend Jake, in his words, experienced two decades of intense declining psychosis, terrifying and agonizing beyond comprehension. These states were triggered when he was in college and tried out a simple chakra meditation every day for one year. He describes the states of consciousness he couldn't understand that resulted from it as possibly kundalini energy and/or psychic attack.

During these 20 years of mental suffering Jake developed a practice in which he sits quietly for at least 3 hours a day doing nothing, that has been the primary source of him feeling substantially better.

JAM, or Jake's Anti Meditation is how he refers to it. He doesn't follow his breath or focus on anything, but rather sits and does nothing. If he misses JAMMING for a day his state of mind often becomes intolerable again.

This practice is one he can do almost anywhere: at home, on the bus, at a cafe, in the park, it doesn't have to be quiet or solitary or free from distractions but he needs to be doing nothing, not talking, typing, reading, watching TV or focusing on anything.

As a result of JAMMING, aka sitting and doing nothing, Jake put other pieces of his life back together. He has his own online business, is financially stable, has satisfying friendships and enjoys the simple life he's created using his own rules for what he needs to stay sane and happy by his own definition. The flexibility of his work allows him to take hours of JAM time everyday.

He has never taken psychiatric drugs for any extent of time and doesn't go to a therapist but does put some attention on his diet and exercise.

A lot of us have those little things we need to do to feel sane by our own definition that perhaps no else needs to do in quite the same way. Mine include writing with a pen and college ruled notebook 7 pages every day, sometimes about things of no interest to anyone but me.

Many need a certain amount of exercise, time in nature, certain foods and connection with certain people. Jake's main need is to do nothing for as many hours a day as he can squeeze in. If he weren't financially stable and socially adept, this need might be labeled as a mental illness in itself. It's all arbitrary.

From Jake's JAMMING, sometimes he gets clear intuitions and thoughts that guide him in his life, or ideas for other people. From my journals come the same type of thing.

Maybe you have a need to spend hours a day playing with clay, talking to yourself, singing to flowers, or staring into space. Something incredible could be born of your idle hours, and even if not you should be able to live in a way that allows you to thrive, however different it may be from your neighbor's way.

A World Without a Mental Health System

I envision a world where there is no need for a mental health field/system because communities are strong and we have a holistic understanding of health. Still, there are definite needs for support at times in life when there are transitions, spiritual breakthroughs and loss (amongst other things), and for some of us these times may be more frequent, even constant.

Since we are all unique individuals, the most important elements of a support system are personal choice and respect for diversity while keeping the needs of the community in mind.

Currently the system rarely acknowledges how mental diversity strengthens community. Instead it isolates individuals by labeling them with disorders, which is not a holistic or community strengthening practice.

Community strengthening needs to value all characters in a community, including the hermit, artist, visionary, or person whose strongest place is in solitude. History confirms that hermits, spiritual seekers and prophets return when it is the right time and have tremendous gifts that live on well beyond their lives and support the spiritual strength of future generations.

I like the Open Dialogue model, which brings the whole family and/or community into the conversation.

Choice is key in supporting someone since what will help one will harm another and vice versa. The old adage, "First Do No Harm" must be brought back as currently the first course of treatment is psychiatric drugs which do harm even if in some cases they suppress "symptoms." Harmful substances and behaviors (legal or illegal) might always be part of the picture but the system itself advocates practices that cause obvious harm (psychiatric drugs and electroshock therapy, among others) while criminalizing and pathologizing behaviors that cause less harm (other drugs, certain harmless extreme states like hearing voices that are positive, spiritual or supernatural).

These are the primary challenges in the system, a paradigm that focuses on pathology and not root cause, strength building or choice. There are also many tools in place that can and will be used to overcome these challenges such as peer support, WRAP plans, advanced directives, Open Dialogue and similar methods, holistic health care, and health insurance (access and coverage for wider options need to improve).

There is a need for centralized "top down" support and, just as important, a need for grassroots organizing and anarchistic change on a small scale. This means people connecting with their local communities in simple ways, going back to basics and common sense- sharing meals, connecting with the earth, valuing and making space for creativity and other simple things that make a big difference.

Perhaps the greatest cause of what we call mental illness is the mental health system itself, for our challenges are not respected as sacred passageways in this model. What I would like to do is continue to create bridges, roadways, bike paths, foot trails, and road maps between the alternative, life serving systems being developed on a large scale and the organic communities of neighbors, friends, families and co-workers. In this time of so much technology, we have challenges in reconnecting intimately with each other, as well as more hope than ever for learning across borders and advancing our capacities to learn from, grow with and value each other. And that means all of us.

Before You Take Psychiatric Drugs

Before you take psychiatric drugs a few things to consider:

1. Are you eating a reasonable diet? This doesn't mean you have to eat kale for breakfast lunch and dinner (which wouldn't be healthy for most people anyway), but before taking a drug for your state of mind, look at your nutritional habits. I know, a months supply of Paxil is cheaper than a fish dinner, but taking psych drugs on top of a poor diet is adding insult to injury. Before you even think about going on meds, make sure you're eating a good amount of protein, vegetables and healthy fats every day, and at least work to limit non-foods that you know are bad for you like Doritos, 7 Up and overly sweetened packaged foods. To some, this is second nature, to others the connection between food and how we feel has hardly been made and their basic diet consists of addictive drug-like non foods that cause emotional highs and lows, and consistent irritability or anxiety. These food-drugs, like any addictive substances may need to be reduced gradually in favor of nutrient dense, nourishing, real foods.

2. Get outside. Breathe some fresh air every day, preferably at a park or a on a quiet street with minimal traffic. Bonus points for getting into the woods or going to a body of water. If you're not getting enough oxygen, psychiatric drugs won't help you feel refreshed.

3. Express your creativity somehow everyday. This is essential. Everyday you must do something creative whether it's writing, art, dance, piano, cooking, constructing or singing. Try this everyday practice for a minimum of a half hour (an hour if you can) before getting on a maintenance drug. Most people find their creativity and expressive capacities are blocked considerably when on psych drugs.

What do you do as daily practices that keep you feeling healthy and strong? Exercise? Prayer? Meditation? Hugs? All these things have better long term outcomes than psychiatric pharmaceuticals by actually changing hormone and brain patterns in a positive way, and without adding toxins to someone who is already overwhelmed.

Five Ways Meditation Can Help Free People of Psychiatric Drugs

1. **Reduces anxiety.** Meditation of any sort induces the relaxation response.

2. **Reduces depression.** By focusing on the breath, you end up taking in more oxygen, even if it's only for 20 minutes a day. You also expand your lungs and diaphragm so you are more likely to take in more air all day long. This improves mood, similarly to how exercise does.

3. **Increases energy.** Unlike psychiatric drugs, which deplete the body of its energy, especially in the long term, by damaging organs and adding more toxins for the liver to deal with, meditation simply and naturally increases your energy. By focusing on your breath and tuning in with your feelings, you harness your own energy rather than squandering it on unnecessary things.

4. **Helps focus attention.** By taking 20 minutes or more per day to focus on your breath or another object of meditation, you train your mind to focus. You can then use that focus for other projects. Focusing also helps you prioritize what is most important, which reduces stress and adds to a sense of accomplishment.

5. **Slows you down, helps to control "mania" and fear.** Meditation slows the heart rate, blood pressure, breathing and thoughts. Slowing down lowers cortisol, reduces the fight or flight response and helps you feel more in control.

How To Manage Sensitivity In Current Times: 11 Tips Spend time alone and in low technology places, doing something focused, away from the screen, such as meditation, walking, writing in a notebook, drawing on paper, playing an unplugged instrument, singing, crafting, cooking, etc.

1. Spend time with people screen-free as much as possible. When with friends or socializing, resist the temptation to use your phone, text, look things up etc. You may need to socialize more and meet new people. Find people who will give you their attention, who don't need to be constantly on their screens.
2. More time in nature. Eat wild edible plants, sit in the sun, walk outside and do outdoor activity in non urban areas as much as possible.
3. Spend time with children, especially if you don't have any.
4. Watch wild animals. Sit and observe a bird for a few minutes or longer. Refrain from taking photos sometimes and simply observe.
5. Cook and prepare your own food whenever possible.
6. Allow yourself to take respite from cities, crowds, the public, technology, even parties, frequently. You may have less tolerance for these things. Recognize this is natural as the amount of EMFs, wifi and radiation have increased exponentially.
7. Turn your phone and other electronics of or onto airplane mode as frequently as possible.
8. Cultivate and value your sensitivity rather than trying to numb it out with addictions. Find outlets and ways to share your genuine self and creativity with the world. Keep searching if you haven't found them yet. A lot of people are needing to recreate their lives and surroundings to keep up with their actual needs in these times. Some things are easier to come by, like online "friends" and lots of emails, but some are harder, like quality time with friends in person, deep nature away from EMFs and mineral rich food. Make it a priority to meet your actual needs and the rest will flow from there.
9. Take really good care of your health. It's harder than ever to be passively healthy, but easier than ever to get personal health information, access all kinds of health foods and empower yourself to make good choices. You won't stay healthy unless you take an active role in making good health decisions.
10. Release addictive substances when possible. As a sensitive person, you have a great capacity for deep peace, without any substances, so seek to avoid, when possible, things that you tend to overdo such

as sugar, alcohol, pharmaceuticals and other toxins. It's absolutely okay to use these in small amounts as needed, if they uplift you or resolve some kind of emergency, but be wary of cycles of addiction as your sensitivity thrives on homeostasis, stability and health.

8 Tips For Anxiety

What to do first? Do I need to exercise more/less/differently?, Should I focus on physical tasks or mental ones first? Am I sharing too much of myself publicly? Too little?

Try to resolve this anxiety alone or call a friend or mentor?

Then came comparing myself to others, and feeling embarrassed/ashamed/jealous...

My mentor suggested it's adrenal exhaustion, which I've had for awhile. Being on 7 psychiatric drugs at once when I was younger completely shot my adrenals and they've been weak ever since.

As I started to work myself up, I made a few phone calls and did a few things. And I feel calmer now, so here's what helped:

1. Taking the pressure off. This is soooo important. When you start comparing yourself to others, telling yourself you should be better/doing more/cooler/smarter/healthier yada yada yada, just stop. Lie down, breathe, it's just one day, you can always go back to bed or spend all day in distraction, and it wouldn't be the end of the world. You also don't REALLY know what or how anyone else is doing, especially the ones you are comparing yourself to.

2. Once you stop the mean voices, replace them with something else. Find one sentence you can always replace self criticism with, and make it simple so you won't forget. Mine is "I love you Chaya." I repeat it over and over as many times as I need to to calm myself down when self-shaming thoughts arise.

3. Reach out. Call someone who will listen to you, if you have that kind of person. This can sometimes be hard and the right person isn't always there at the right time. Try at least 5 people before you give up. If you can't find anyone who is available by voice, or in person, texting or online chatting might tide you over.

4. Move your body very gently. When I'm super anxious, even thinking about a full yoga session can make me more anxious and go back into self scrutiny, indecisiveness and commitment-phobia. Don't do a full yoga session (unless you really feel like it). Don't even take out your mat. Lie in bed and do a few stretches and gentle movements. Hug your knees up to your chest. Rock your hips side to side. Circle your knees around.

5. Try EFT, the Emotional Freedom Technique. If you don't know how to do it, look up some tutorials, or simply tap of different parts of your body on both sides for now, while saying your feelings/fears and thoughts out loud. Then simply state out loud: "Even though I feel this way, I still deeply and completely love and accept myself" while tapping.

6. Take some calming herbs/supplements or drink herbal tea. I have a bunch of adrenal supportive herbs that my naturopath recommended (some of them I haven't actually bought yet), but I don't always remember to take them. The ones I took today (in tea) werelicorice root, nettleand chamomile. I also took extra magnesium and vitamin C.

7. Rescue Remedy. This is a homeopathic calming agent which comes in lozenges or a little spray bottle. I often forget to take this too when I'm anxious but when I do, it helps. I like the lozenges, because having them in my mouth for awhile comforts me.

8. Get into nature, if you can. If not, even holding a stone or looking at images of nature/water can help.

These are "emergency" toolkit items. There are a bunch of other things you can do daily or regularly to improve your body's ability to manage stress and anxiety like eating well, exercising hard and expressing yourself creatively.

Alternatives to psychiatric meds! This is the number one thing I get asked for when I tell people that I consult with those who have been harmed by psychiatry and psychiatric drugs. What are the alternatives to psychiatric meds?

A lot of people say psychiatric drugs are a last resort, or that everything else should be tried first. They don't even mention alternatives to psychiatric meds though! Even many doctors claim psychiatric drugs should only be a last resort if all other options have been exhausted.

Really? Are people trying everything or even close to all of the alternatives to psychiatric meds?

Some of these options might be prohibitive due to cost, beliefs, interest or access, and that's why I'm sharing a long list. Please look up any terms on this list you aren't familiar with and be sure to do enough research to give yourself the best shot at succeeding at these methods. Most require ongoing regular practice.

Some are self explanatory, others require instruction or even medical advice. Some of these alternatives to psychiatric meds won't work for you, but keep scrolling and a few will. If you're considering going on psych drugs (or planning to come off, or in the withdrawal process) here are some things that can help:

1. Acupuncture (community treatments are often $15-30, some areas have free group acupuncture.
2. Journaling. Writing my thoughts down every day has no doubt kept me out of the mental health system entirely for many years.
3. Art. Whatever kind you are drawn to can reframe your experiences so it no longer makes sense to see them as a mental illness.
4. Less refined sugar. Nutritional alternatives to psychiatric meds could be tried before taking "mood stabilizers" such as Lithium or Lamictal.
5. More protein, cooked vegetables and healthy fats
6. Massage from a friend/Self massage with oils
7. Professional massage
8. Magnesium- Some supplements can be great alternatives to psychiatric meds for anxiety and sleep!
9. Run/walk/hike most days- wonderful alternatives to psychiatric meds such as SSRIs and SNRIs that would be good to try.
10. Yoga/gentle stretching
11. Meditation-Quiet time, breathing, yoga and meditation are important alternatives to psychiatric meds for many people, myself included.
12. Prayer
13. More time in nature
14. Eating wild foods
15. Methyl folate-especially for people who have the MTHFR gene, methylated B vitamins are important alternatives to psychiatric meds to try first. They can help with anxiety and stress.
16. Methyl B12
17. Herbal teas- these are great alternatives to psychiatric meds and work best when loose leaf whole dried herbs are used.
18. Vitamin C
19. High quality food-based vitamins if you have any deficiencies (or working to get them met through dietary additions and adjustments)
20. Cod liver oil- this and other essential fatty acids are important alternatives to psychiatric meds as they have been found to help

with depression and anxiety as well as lowering inflammation in the body.

21. Flax seeds/chia seeds
22. Bone broth
23. Blogging
24. Peer counseling
25. Warm lines
26. Starting a business with your talents
27. Probiotics
28. Go organic
29. Go to the beach/ lake/ river more. Many people in cities might forget to consider these important alternatives to psychiatric meds. Negative ions in natural flowing water change brain waves and make people happier and more relaxed.
30. Plants
31. More hugs/cuddling
32. Music
33. Tracking the lunar cycles- these alternatives to psychiatric meds have been used to understand moods in relation to the fluids in the universe since before psychiatric drugs existed!
34. Astrology
35. Tarot
36. Get tested for all vitamin/mineral deficiencies- very important to try these alternatives to psychiatric meds before starting any.
37. Naturopathic advice- Many naturopaths can give you detailed information about a lot of the items on this list of alternatives to psychiatric meds.
38. Homeopathy
39. Flower essences
40. Crystals
41. Weight lifting
42. Sports
43. Date and/or join a women's group/men's group/gender queer group
44. Clean your closets
45. Hire/ask someone to help you do something you can't do your-

self
46. Peer support groups
47. rotests/activism- These alternatives to psychiatric meds that lets you use your emotions and integrate them into a greater purpose, while understanding more deeply where the issues come from. All emotions and states of mind are sociopolitical and none exist in a vacuum within an individual.
48. Helping others with your madness/genius- this is the best of all of the alternatives to psychiatric meds
49. Travel
50. Make more friends
51. Spend more time with your friends
52. Spend more time alone, in quiet
53. Let yourself stay in bed all day sometimes and let it be okay
54. Find friends you can have a meltdown with
55. Let yourself have meltdowns when needed
56. Avoid psychiatrists and people who believe in the medical model when you're in crisis
57. Martial arts
58. Express anger in a safe place
59. Write letters to family members that you don't send
60. Find someone who will just listen without judging or giving advice
61. Sing
62. Dance
63. Stick up for yourself
64. Avoid people who bring you down
65. Follow your inner guidance
66. Talk to yourself (vocal journaling)
67. Pray out loud
68. Get more sunlight
69. Avoid too much caffeine
70. Limit other addictions
71. Sex/masturbation
72. Bare feet on the earth

73. Garden
74. Find rock bottom faith in your life
75. Examine your beliefs either on paper or aloud, alone or with a friend
76. Join meetups/other groups
77. Play games
78. Theater-act out different parts of you safely
79. Self-trust-never give full authority away
80. Speak publicly about something that can help others
81. Make You Tube videos to reach out to others
82. Find more support people online via Facebook groups and other forums
83. Make online friends into phone friends and in person friends when possible
84. Connect with animals
85. Get more fresh air
86. Move somewhere with weather and culture that suits you
87. Do a fundraising campaign on Go Fund Me/Indiegogo/Kickstarter to raise money for a project, or just for your expenses/goals
88. Reach out more and ask for help directly (from people who won't label you)
89. Start a support group if you can't find the right one in your area
90. Listen to your voices; what is their message?
91. Reconnect with old friends
92. Find friends who understand difficult times
93. Allow all feelings and mental states to exist
94. Be patient when possible
95. Accept uncertainty
96. Talk to your loved ones who have passed on and see if they have a message for you
97. Go to a psychic
98. Lie on the Earth and ask it to hold your problems for you for awhile
99. Stay hydrated
100. Take Epsom Salt/baking soda baths regularly

101. Use Coconut Oil on your body; it helps detox metals
102. Exfoliate your skin
103. Floss regularly-it prevents blood stagnation
104. Unplug when you need to
105. Let yourself rest/sleep more
106. Oil pull
107. Make a list of things you can offer and things you need. See where you can barter.
108. Slow down
109. Spend an hour a day expressing your creativity
110. Let yourself go crazy sometimes and know it is part of the human condition
111. EFT/tapping

I have actually tried all of the alternatives to psychiatric meds on this list; these aren't random ideas I have heard of. Every single thing on this list is something that has kept me off psychiatric drugs! No joke.

Though I thought it would be hard to write such a long list, now I think there are many more things to add too. Please add your own ideas in your notes.

Workbook
Questions for reflection:

- What alternatives have worked for you?

- Which ones haven't?

- What support do you wish you have access to but don't?

- Is there a possibility of fundraising/asking for more help and support from family, friends and community?

_____
_____
_____
_____
_____
_____
_____
_____
_____

CHAPTER 4

GATHERING RESOURCES AND SUPPORT

Do It In a Group

The group can be on the phone, online, in person. If you're coming off psych drugs, hoping to someday, or staying off, do it in a group.

This doesn't mean you need to spend all of your time in a group while you're withdrawing (ha!). Most of us wouldn't want to do that.

It means you have a group of people who are on a similar journey and you meet regularly to check in.

When I was put on psych drugs, I didn't have a group of people who supported me to not take them, but when I came off I did and I attribute my success to this.

Even though I was young and had been on them for a short time, I was on 7 drugs and had lost all of my physical strength. I was too weak to even walk around the block. My withdrawal process was not easy.

I will forever be grateful for the Freedom Center in Northampton, Massachusetts, which held support groups and other events weekly for people who had been harmed by the mental health system and were looking for connection around that.

The strength to get through it came to me from others who had done so.

I went to those meetings every week while I was withdrawing. It was a unique group and there are few like it, but more similar types of support groups that advocate for self determination and informed choice are popping up.

Some are online and I made a list of Facebook groups where people are connecting and creating online meetings and weekly phone calls to support people in their withdrawal process among other things.

Information online can be hit or miss, so I recommend finding people you can talk to by phone or video chat with for peer support rather than simply trying to get medical information or advice. We need information and advice, yet this cannot take the place of personal connection, compassion and hope that is born from actually talking to people.

I recently participated in two webinars on other topics which were surprisingly healing.

Sometimes I have had doubts about whether online or telephone groups of people who don't know one another can be effective. I learned they can in fact be very powerful, and done from the comfort of your own home or even outside in a park or special nature spot. Facilitation in these groups is important.

Coming together with a shared intention is one of the most potent things we can do.

There are other types of support groups that could be helpful for coming off or staying off psych drugs, if this is your choice. Some include Hearing Voices groups and Alternative to Suicide groups. We definitely need more groups to specifically support people in withdrawal and here's a big thank you to all who are creating them.

Facebook Groups

There are an abundance of Facebook groups that speak to those who are coming off psychiatric drugs or already have and are supporting each other. These groups are also for those who never took psychiatric drugs in the first place and need support and allies for that. They are places for posting/reading the latest news articles and blogs (including your own).

Facebook groups are for networking with people and finding friends around the world who can be supporters and allies. Groups can help you keep up to date on upcoming opportunities and events that you might be able to participate in such as conferences, protests, speak outs, support groups, publishing opportunities and more. You also may get ideas for starting your own group (on Facebook or in person) or event. I started a group called Women Envisioning Change for women in the psychiatric survivor movement (and others) to share with one another about issues that affect us. By joining groups, you are voting for the message they represent as well.   Mad Pride
Society for Humanistic Psychology, Division 32
Psychiatric Drugs destroy Life
ALL AGAINST PSYCHIATRIST ABUSES
MENTAL HEALTH ACTION REFORM GROUP AUSTRALIA (MHARG)
Stop the psychiatric drugging of the elderly
Free Thinking About Psychiatric Drugs
Repealing Mental Health Laws

Mad Pride India
Psychs
Speak Out Against Psychiatry
OccuPsy: Critical Psychology for Decolonization
Recovering our Stories
Un-Diagnosing Emotional Distress

Note: When you join groups, you may get a lot of notifications if you don't adjust the settings. You can choose to be notified of all posts, only your friends posts or not at all. Click on "Notifications" in the upper right section of the group to make your choice.

Workbook
Questions for reflection:

- What types of support are most helpful to you? Least?

- Do you prefer text/phone/in person?

- Do you prefer anonymous support or not?

- Are you able to identify and ask for what you need such as just listening, no advice, or for someone to come over/talk on the phone instead of text/make you a meal/help you clean?

  _____

  _____

- Make a list of different types of support you need:

  _____

  _____

  _____

  _____

  _____

  _____

  _____

  _____

- Make a list of potential supporters under each category

  _____

  _____

  _____

  _____

  _____

  _____

  _____

  _____

  _____

  _____

- Where can you find friends of like mind who you can really talk to?

- Where can you find friends who won't freak out/pathologize you?

- Do you have any already?

- List all of your friends who may get it:

- Where did you find/meet each of them?

  _____
  _____
  _____
  _____
  _____
  _____

- Do you need more of a certain type of friend?

  _____
  _____
  _____
  _____
  _____

CHAPTER 5

WITHDRAWAL

The 4 Less Mentioned Obstacles in How to Come Off Psychiatric Drugs, and Overcoming Them

The most obvious obstacle to how to come off psychiatric drugs is unbearable withdrawal symptoms (or what some mistakenly call "return of symptoms")-panic attacks, extreme anxiety, nausea, insomnia, and many other effects.

These result from stopping use of a powerful mind altering chemical that was never healthy or safe to be taken on a daily basis in the first place.

Withdrawal effects are often the first things we think of when someone wants very badly to figure out how to come off psychiatric drugs but simply can't.

There are several other obstacles though in how to come off psychiatric drugs, that can be just as problematic, if not more so.

Not believing it is possible to live without them.

This lack of belief in the option of going off can stem from an idea that you are fundamentally mentally ill, that the diagnosis has validity (which even Thomas Insel, head of the NIMH says it doesn't) and fear of who you are without them if you've been on them for a long time.

This obstacle is huge, especially given how much harder it can be to have conviction in ones essence when the mind is being compromised by psych drugs.

The key to overcoming this obstacle to how to come off psychiatric drugs is to find your essence once again.

It is always there, intact, somewhere within you (the heart is a good place to look) and cannot truly be harmed, ultimately.

The key is, once you tap into your essence, to develop a rock bottom trust and belief in that larger Self to guide you.

This is the only thing that will ever be your Rock- a drug (or any one impermanent thing outside of yourself) is never the ultimate answer.

The belief that living without a psych drug is unsafe for you can make withdrawal symptoms far worse.

2 The second obstacle is fear from those around you-your family, friends, employers, and doctors. These people don't know how to come off psychiatric drugs and assume it's dangerous.

You may know very well that you would be better off without meds, but if most of those who love you think you need them, it is an obstacle, and it can heighten anxiety and withdrawal effects manifold.

The best way to overcome this obstacle is to gather a network of supporters, including many psychiatric survivors who know some things about how to come off psychiatric drugs and continue to reach out to them regularly.

(You can also try educating your skeptical loved ones, especially once you have more support).

Use internet forums and social networking sites and groups (as well as local groups if there are any near you) to expand your network of supporters and make sure to have some people on your list who have that rock solid knowing that their essence is gold, and so is yours.

Work with me as a consultant if you need another believer that You Can Do It.

3 The third obstacle in coming off psych drugs is fear of living so vulnerably.

Fear of feeling everything in a world that doesn't always honor feelings so well.

Fear of being powerful, of being unpopular, of losing control and a whole host of other legitimate fears.

This one requires a long term commitment to mastery.

Learning how to come off psychiatric drugs isn't for the faint of heart.

It's for those who are utterly and unwaveringly committed to facing big fears and moving through them on life's terms.

It becomes necessary to be more committed to the "god" of your higher Self, your larger purpose, your true unwavering essence than to the god of opinion, of "What will they think?" or even "How?" or "Why?"

This obstacle is overcome when your soul is so strong nothing can stop it.

The process of strengthening and growing your soul isn't something you can rush or force.

It's more powerful than your thinking mind questioning how to come off psychiatric drugs.

It's something you commit to and then surrender to and allow.

Fearlessness comes through the back door when you least expect it to.

There are practices you can do, however, to increase your chances of hitting the goldmine of soul growth, such as prayer (in your own authentic preferred way), meditation, connecting with nature, exercise, creative expression and time spent with others who are in close touch with their essences and committed to truth and honesty.

These things all lead you toward a deeper understanding of how to come off psychiatric drugs.

Being true to yourself as often as possible and sharing your honesty with chosen others, your journal, yourself, your Higher Power (your connection to something larger) can certainly expedite the process of soul growth, but there is no rushing it or getting around the alchemical and mystical process.

4 Health issues are the fourth obstacle figuring out how to come off off psychiatric drugs.

Any health issues make the withdrawal process that much harder.

When our bodies are compromised, it's harder to stand strong and integrated in our minds and emotions.

Really they are all so connected.

Focusing on health can help overcome this obstacle.

This means making yourself your priority and learning what works best for you nutritionally, exercise-wise and in all facets of life.

It's about no longer saying, "What's wrong with me?" or even "What illness do I have?" but rather, "What do I need to be my healthiest self?"

This can be frustrating at times in the withdrawal process if you don't have the resources or access to what you need to be healthy, but continue to list what you need.

In our modern society, few of us have what we need for optimal health but we can do our best with what resources we have and seek out the healthiest food, cleanest air and purest water, and most suitable lifestyle for our constitution.

I recommend spending a little time each day reading up on holistic approaches to whatever health issues you have.

Learn which foods, herbs, exercises and other lifestyle approaches have helped others with similar problems.

Learning how to come off psychiatric drugs and caring for your body holistically go hand in hand.

Seek out a community of inspiring friends who take good care of their health and try out their practices which appeal to you.

Having health conscious people around you can go a long way in improving your health since good habits are contagious.

People who have already figured out how to come off psychiatric drugs (or had the opportunity to) can be a great resource.

Psych drugs often perpetuate other addictions such as cigarettes, TV, sugar, caffeine and others.

So long term psych drug use often brings one's overall health down exponentially.

Don't despair though-return to your essence that has never been damaged.

"Health" also goes hand in hand with self-love, self-trust and soul growth.

Don't allow others or external manifestations to entirely define your health.

As you practice honesty with yourself and selected trusted others, your health will naturally improve and learning how to come off psychiatric drugs is part of that.

Those are the 4 main obstacles to figuring out how to come off psychiatric drugs (as well as withdrawal effects, of course).

The fruition to overcoming these is being free and living your dreams.

Every single one of us, whether on a lot of psych drugs or very little or just the amount in our drinking water, experiences these obstacles in our lives in one way or another.

There are other dependencies and addictions that come down to similar obstacles.

Keep plugging away at these 4 essentials, as we need you, we need your untamed essence, your true self, the you you are underneath any beliefs of there being anything wrong with you at all.

Question: I really would like to get off the psych meds I am on. What would you recommend doing to do that?

Answer: Hi there. I would recommend the following:

- Join internet forums where folks are talking about getting off psych meds.
- Find local support
- Eat really well and listen to your body.
- Get regular exercise and fresh air.
  Read as much as you can find about the process (check the resources list in the appendix)
  Once you have support, plan to go slowly and taper one drug at a time.
  Have a plan: What do you want those around you to do if you can't sleep during withdrawal, etc.
- Write a list of how people can support you and ask those around you if they are willing to do it, before you start to come off.
- Have alternatives to the hospital if you don't want to go (friends staying over with you, etc).
  Have a professional who can support you (if you want one).
- Keep a journal.
  Find some form of daily meditation.

Getting Off Lamictal

Recently a dear friend of mine went on Lamictal and her doctor told her getting off Lamictal would be easy because she was on a low dose.

I got worried because a number of my clients and colleagues have experienced hell (including seizures which they had never had before) getting off Lamictal (or trying to without success). It seems to be one of the harder drugs to withdraw from, so I wanted to make a post with the best info and resources I could find and ask you to post your own in the comments.

Here's a quote from a forum on Lamictal side effects:

"When I went on it around two years ago, I thought it was just the right med for me. Now I've started to struggle. My short term memory has gotten so bad, it's cost me two jobs. I'm always so dizzy, I feel as if I've had four or five beers. I've gone from the local Tabasco Kid to a diet so bland it would bore a baby. Go ahead and add in absentmindedness and clumsiness. Top it off with some plain old profound disorientation and major depression. In four or so months I'm a mess where I was a model."

Here's some info on breastfeeding while taking Lamictal:

"Lamotrigine (Lamictal) is being used with increasing frequency in childbearing women. We last reported on its use in of lamotrigine in breastfeeding women in 2005. At that time, several small studies indicated that lamotrigine was passed to infants through the breast milk in relatively high doses. Infant serum levels ranged from 23 to 50% of levels found in the mothers' serum.

The largest study comes from Dr. Jeffrey Newport and colleagues and includes a total of 30 women taking lamotrigine and their nursing infants. The authors reported that milk/plasma ratios were highly variable, ranging from 5.7% to 147.1%. The mean milk/plasma ratio was 41.3%. This type of variability has been reported in studies of antidepressants and other medications in nursing infants, indicating that milk/plasma ratios may of limited utility in estimating the extent of exposure in the nursing infant."

Here's what Monica Cassani of Beyond Meds had to say when she was going through Lamictal withdrawal:

"I started the second phase of my Lamictal withdrawal three days ago. I was on 400 mg of it for many years. Several months ago I went off 200 mg of it. It was rough, but only in that I was greatly fatigued. Today, three days after cutting 25 mg from my still remaining 200 mg I am going ape-shit."

Her post also has links to other forums and there are a lot of comments on her blog about Lamictal withdrawal, so I recommend checking it out.

Altostrata on the Surviving Antidepressants forum says this on her detailed page about getting off Lamictal:

"Like all psychoactive drugs, Lamotrigine can have withdrawal difficulties. Even doctors who are aware of withdrawal problems with other drugs can be surprised at how hard it is to go off Lamotrigine. As with other drugs, we recommend very gradual tapering at 10% per month, based on the current dosage (the amount of the decrease keeps getting smaller)."

Here'a another good quote that addresses how doctors often downplay the severity of Lamictal withdrawal:

"My pdoc was trying to scare me into staying medicated.

He then added if I really wanted to come off of my meds, I could "just stop."

WHAT?! My eyes flew open.

He stated he'd had patients who had stopped cold turkey without a problem. According to him, anticonvulsants don't have severe withdrawal effects.

WHAT?! His advice just flies in the face of what most doctors recommend. In fact, quitting Lamictal immediately increases the risk of seizures, which is exactly what I'm afraid of.

Philip's experience and Gianna's experience along with the comments on each blog are proof that many people have experienced tremendous withdrawal effects from decreasing Lamictal's dosage."

I never took it myself, but having a dear friend given this misinformation and a number of clients struggling with severe withdrawal or who feel they can't even try getting off Lamictal due to the risk of seizures (when they never had epilepsy before) inspired me to gather some resources and start this conversation.

Secretly I'm hoping my dear friend will come off of it asap, but I didn't want to belabor that point. We can't always know what's best for someone else or why they take psychiatric drugs that are dangerous. I can't even know for sure whether someone is best off taking them or not, but I am passionate about people having accurate information to make an informed decision.

This information is also relevant to send to friends and family who might be pressuring their loved ones to take psychiatric drugs, with the best of intentions but a lack of information about the dangers.

I realize she has access to the same search engines I do, and yet... some people don't necessarily know which keywords to look up to find the accurate information.

So this is a way for people (including my friend I care about) to have a bunch of information in one place, so they can hopefully make the best decisions possible.

Recently I learned from a holistic health coach a bit more about amino acids as an alternative. They can help with withdrawal as well and are used at the Alternative To Meds Center in Sedona. I worked there when they were in San Francisco. They have an elaborate supplement protocol for withdrawal which includes a lot of amino acids.

The health coach I spoke with also informed me that psychiatric drugs actually have amino acids in them (as well as harmful chemicals)!

Best of luck in finding the options that are best for you, as there is not one thing that will resonate with or "work" for everyone.

There are many things that have helped many of us withdraw from psychiatric drugs, and many things that can help you improve your life without them, if that is your preference.

For Those in Benzodiazepine Withdrawal,

such as those coming off Xanax, Ativan, Klonopin (or other psychiatric medications), Dr Charles Popper, director of psychiatry at Harvard regularly uses protein isolate with patients interested in tapering off. He especially recommends protein isolate for benzodiazepine withdrawal.

Dr. Popper makes it clear that when patients are using specialized treatments, "psychiatric drug doses need to be gradually and carefully lowered," and that "patients actually do better once the psychiatric medications are discontinued entirely."

I gleaned most of the following information from S P Hancock, MS, CRC @PsychRecovery on Twitter. She told me about protein isolate for benzodiazepine withdrawal.

Isolate can be from any non-seed protein source that is unfermented, unsprouted, unsweetened, unflavored & unenriched so as not to agitate the Central Nervous System (i.e. Rice, Pea, Whey, etc.). However, many find Whey isolate too constipating because it's required at such large amounts.

One Twitter user replied: "So grateful to find something that actually works! But it's only effective until the body needs more enzymatic support." Some (but not all) have found amino acid formulas helpful at this point.

Protein isolate for benzodiazepine withdrawal seems the safer route for some. If taken as described here, it is less likely to cause adverse reactions.

The naturally balanced amino acid profile of protein isolate for benzodiazepine withdrawal helps support your body's enzymatic process lessening withdrawal severity (A trick Dr. Charles Popper, head of psychiatry at Harvard teaches). Depending on deficit, it might initially require 4-6 shakes before you begin feeling relief but consistent use WORKS for some who report this!

Pea protein is often mentioned but it doesn't have to be pea protein; any protein isolate for benzodiazepine withdrawal can work.

Dr. Charles Popper, director of psychiatry at Harvard regularly uses it w/ patients interested in titrating off psychiatric medications.

It must say "protein isolate" in the ingredients. It can be from any protein source so long as it meets this criteria.

The isolate cannot be sprouted, because sprouted seeds have naturally occurring malt which is a sugar that feeds the gut's naturally occurring candida. As Candida grows it produces 20 alcohol byproducts which agitate the central nervous system. Receptors are essentially raw after having been damaged by psychoactive substances (prescribed or illicit) which makes them more susceptible to agitation—making withdrawal more severe.

Additionally many of the flavors are made from things which have been fermented (i.e. chocolate is made from fermented cacao beans & vanilla is made from fermented vanilla beans). Fermentation leaves behind fungal spores, Anything that feeds fungal spores will feed Candida—causing it to grow and generate those 20 alcohol byproducts, making withdrawal harder.

Fruit flavorings are generally made from the fruit & have the same ability to feed Candida. Nut flavorings are made from nuts—which are inherently moldy—leaving behind microscopic spores which can...you guessed it...feed Candida.

The sweeteners usually harm the gut's ability to absorb nutrition, which compromises the brain's ability to get the nutrition it requires to sustain the person through benzo or psychiatric drug withdrawal.

In a pinch, a person can use flavored, sprouted, fermented, sweetened isolates, but understand that Candida grows exponentially slower than bacteria, so the isolate will seem to make the person feel better, but 72 hours later when the byproducts are released, the person will feel worse.

So, it's best to be preventative and just get a non-sprouted, unflavored, unenriched, unfermented isolate from a cost-effective source you trust. It has to be unenriched, because Candida uses many of the same micronutrients that the human cell does—particularly B1, B3, B6 & Zinc, So you don't want to feed the Candida because those 20 alcohol byproducts will light up the withdrawal akathisia nastiness like a firework show.

Note: Special thanks to S P Hancock, MS, CRC (@PsychRecovery on Twitter) for sharing this information about protein isolate for benzodiazepine withdrawal. Most of this info is directly from her and others in conversation with us and I put it all together and edited it to bring it to people who aren't on Twitter.

Note 2: People with a certain genetic disorder have adverse reactions to protein powders. Those who are glutamine sensitive may experience anxiety when taking them and would do best using other withdrawal supports.

Coming Off Psych Drug Resources

These are some resources to start with and certainly not an exhaustive list. I have not vetted each of these resources, as some have come to me through others' recommendations. I do not vouch for everything in each of these, but this list can be a starting point.

BOOKS:

1) Dr. Peter Breggin
~ Drug Withdrawal: A Guide for Prescribers, Therapists, Patients & Their Families (2012)
~ Your Drug Might Be Your Problem: How & Why to Stop Taking Psychiatric Medications (2007)
~ Toxic Psychiatry: Why Therapy, Empathy & Love Must Replace the Drugs, Electroshock & Biochemical Theories of the "New Psychiatry" (1994)
~ Medication Madness: The Role of Psychiatric Drugs in Cases of Violence, Suicide & Crime (2009)
~ Brain Disabling Treatments in Psychiatry: Drugs, Electroshock & the Psychopharmaceutical Complex (2007)
~ Talking Back to Ritalin: What the Doctors Arn't Telling You About Stimulants & ADHD (2001)
~ Talking Back to Prozac: What Doctors Arn't Telling You About Today's Most Controversial Drug (1995)

2) Dr. Ann Blake Tracy
~ Prozac: Panacea or Pandora? The Rest of the Story of the New Class of SSRI Antidepressants: Prozac, Zoloft, Paxil & More (1991, 2001)
~ Help! I Cant Get Off My Anti-Depressant! (CD, 2010)~ drugawareness.org (her website)

3) Dr. Thomas Szasz

~ The Myth of Mental Illness (1984)
~ Antipsychiatry: Quackery Squared (2009)
~ Psychiatry: The Science of Lies (2008)

4) Gwen Olsen
~ Confessions of an Rx Drug Pusher (2009)

5) Robert Whitaker
~ Anatomy of an Epidemic: Magic Bullets, Psychiatric Drugs and the Rise of Mental Illness in America (2011)
~ Mad in America: Bad Science, Bad Medicine & the Enduring Mistreatment of the Mentally Ill (2010)

6) David Healy
~ Pharmageddon (2012)
~ Let Them Eat Prozac: The Unhealthy Relationship Between the Pharmaceutical Industry & Depression (2006)

7) Jack Hobson-Dupont
~ The Benzo Book: Getting Safely Off Tranquilizers (2006)

8) Bliss Johns
~ Recovery & Renewal: Your Essential Guide to Overcoming Dependancy & Withdrawal From Sleeping Pills, Other 'Benzo' Tranquilizers & Antidepressants (2012)
~ Benzo-Wise: A Recovery Companion (2010)

9) Matt Samet
~ Death Grip: A Climber's Escape From Benzo Madness (Feb, 2013)

10) Gary Null
~ Death By Medicine (2011)

11) Seth Farber
~ The Spiritual Gift of Madness: The Failure of Psychiatry & the Rise of the Mad Pride Movement (2012)

12) Jose Cardona
~ Psychiatry: An Industry of Greed, Misery & Death (2010) 13) E. Robert Mercer~ Worse Than Heroin (2008) 14) The Icarus Project~ Harm Reduction Guide to Coming Off Psychiatric Drugs (2012) 15) Joan Gadsby~ Addiction by Prescription (2001)

Documentaries:

1) Gary Null

~ Death By Medicine
~ War on Health: The FDA's Cult of Tyranny (2012)
~ The Drugging of Our Children

2) Kevin Miller
~ Generation Rx (2008)

3) Brian Baxter
~ Benzo Withdrawal Welcome to Hell (2009)

4) Daniel Mackler
~ Take These Broken Wings: Recovery From Schizophrenia Without Medication (2008)
~ Coming Off Psych Drugs: A Meeting Of the Minds (2013)
~ Open Dialogue: An Alternative Finnish Approach to Healing Psychosis (2011)
~ Healing Homes: A Swedish Approach to Healing Psychosis (2011)

5) Phil Lawrence
~ Numb: A Documentary (2011)

WEBSITES/Blogs:

~ mindfreedom.org
~ benzosupport.org
~ psych.healthwyze.org (International Center For Humane Psychiatry, Dr. Dan Edmunds)
~ drugawareness.org (International Coalition for Drug Awareness, Dr. Ann Blake Tracy)
~ breggin.com (Psychiatric Drug Facts, Dr. Peter Breggin)
~ Pharmalot
~ beyondmeds.com
~ survivingantidepresants.org
~ naturalnews.com (Mike Adams)
~ benzo.uk.org
~ theashtonmanual.com (Dr. Heather Ashton Benzo w/d schedules)~ paxilprogress.org~ Mad in America, Science, Psychiatry, and Community (madinamerica.com)~ kipcentral.com~proactiveplanning.us~ Alt_Mentalities (Blog)
~ Wild Truth: Healing From Trauma (wildtruth.net)

FACEBOOK ONLINE SUPPORT Pages/Support Groups:

~ Protracted Withdrawal Syndrome From Benzodiazepines & Anti Depressants
~ Benzodiazepine Withdrawal
~ Benzodiazepine (Benzo) Withdrawal Support Group
~ Speak Out Against Psychiatry
~ Psych Truth Seekers
~ Psychotic Psychiatry
~ Psych Drug Survivors
~ Speak Out Against Psychiatry
~ Benzo Withdrawal Christian Support Group
~ International Coalition for Drug Awareness
~ Benzodiazepine Addiction Needs Awareness (BANA)
~ Stop Psychiatric Diagnosis Harm
~ Un-Diagnosing Emotional Distress
~ Lives Destroyed by SSRI Antidepressants
~ 100, 000 Plus Who Realize the Great Harm That Psychiatry Does to People
~ Alternatives 2012
~ Stop the Psychiatric Drugging of Children
~ Mad in America
~ International Coalition for Drug Awareness
~ The Icarus Project
~ Free Thinking About Psychiatric Drugs
~ Madness Radio
~ Benzo & Psych Med Group
~ Occupy Psychiatry: Discussion Group
~ Benzodiazepine Recovery
~ Prescription Drug Dangers
~ Benzodiazepine & Psych Drug Withdrawal Video Group
~ Free Thinking About Psychiatric Drugs

Checklist of things to keep in mind:

1 It Gets Better. Most people find that after withdrawal symptoms subside, they feel much better. This is because a toxin is no longer hampering the bodily systems, so everything is easier from breathing, to exercise, to digestion, to thinking clearly, communication and memory.

2 Acute withdrawal is a time to lower your standards. Treat yourself as if you're recovering from surgery or someone close to you just died. Focus on the essentials, eating and sleeping; let anything

unnecessary wait.

3. Rest and sleep as much as possible. This will help your body recover.

4. Go as slow as you need to. If things get too intense, going back up a dose and tapering more gradually is kindness to yourself.

5. Keep it simple. Your mind may race, you may get really angry, you may have sudden bursts of energy, and crashes of fatigue. Listen to your body, keep commitments to others minimal and give yourself what you need whether it's a long walk, weight lifting, running, or staying in bed all day (or all week).

6. Eat regularly. If there's one thing you plan, it should be eating nutritious meals. Keep convenient, easy to prepare and nutritious foods on hand and avoid going more than 4 hours during the day without eating, unless you really aren't hungry. Include fat, protein and fiber of some kind with each meal. Now isn't the time to make drastic changes in your diet, but adding some extra nutrient rich herbs, vegetables, fruit and high quality fats like olive oil and coconut oil will calm your nerves.

7. Withdrawal is a process. Give it time. The process itself can be a coming back to yourself. It can be excruciating but also elating, liberating and thrilling. Practice not judging or labeling yourself but rather marveling at and loving the you who is emerging.

Often right after and even during withdrawal can be a romantic period of falling in love with yourself as you become reacquainted with parts that have been buried a long time.

As the sensitive, alive, awake to it all parts of you come back, you may feel celebratory or even ecstatic. Let yourself be thrilled too. Allow yourself the freedom to live beyond the labels, such as "manic" which existed to drug you.

Workbook
Questions for reflection:

- What is your withdrawal timeline?

_____

_____

_____

_____

- What do you need to do to prepare?

- What obstacles keep you from withdrawing?

- What do you most need in withdrawal?

- What are your biggest fears about withdrawal?

  _____
  _____
  _____
  _____
  _____

- What is your backup plan?

  _____
  _____
  _____
  _____

- Who can you trust to talk to about withdrawal and while in withdrawal?

  _____
  _____
  _____
  _____

- What daily routines will help?

  _____
  _____
  _____
  _____
  _____

CHAPTER 6

AFTER UN-DIAGNOSIS: FINDING YOUR OWN LANGUAGE FOR YOUR SUFFERING

Returning People Their Stuff

As a person who never celebrated Christmas, I quietly observe my friends each year as they anxiously search for Christmas presents for everyone on their list.

I imagine if I were to get a lot of presents, I might want to return some of the stuff I'd received. Similarly, I like to return stuff of any kind that feels excessive or like it isn't useful to me, or isn't mine to have.

Once I had art I'd borrowed from an ex-boyfriend hanging in my apartment for nearly a year after we'd separated before it occurred to me I wanted to return him his stuff.

Besides physical stuff to return, we also have emotional stuff to return or release. In relationships we often have an unspoken agreement: "I'll hold your stuff if you hold my stuff." This is not stuff that comes in a wrapped package with a bow on top, but in a way it is. It is stuff we can feel, and stuff underneath the "package" of the person we first met. This is why we don't always feel that sense of "holding someone's stuff" right away when we first meet.

But if we spend enough time with anyone, we will unwrap the gift and get to see the stuff, as well as hold it. When there is a lot of "stuff holding" people often get weighed down and sick. In any situation where someone is ill or in emotional turmoil, I'd be curious to ask that person, "Do you need to return someone their stuff?"

I once had a unique experience with a young acupuncturist/Chinese medicine doctor in training. He asked me a question that in my 31 years no doctor had ever asked me before. Yet it was a simple question. "What do you think your health issues are about?"

It instantly shook me out of my habitual thinking and "role" as a patient. In a sense he was "returning me my stuff." The doctor patient relationship is no exception; it has a contract of stuff holding. In the Western medical model the patient holds the doctor's stuff- her or his "sense of authority," while the doctor holds the patients stuff-her or his vulnerability in illness and fear of looking at root cause or deeper issues.

Together they hold societies "stuff"-being scared of change, revolution and the potent wild creative power that lies dormant in many of us. Medicalizing and drugging everything is a sure strategy for holding all this stuff. This is true in all fields of medicine, and in psychiatry it is more glaring. With all this "stuff holding" disguised as medicine, it's no wonder the medical system is failing to heal, connect and restore us.

The potency we fear has healing power. I took a breath feeling both present and a bit exposed before I even answered the young doctor. I thanked him for asking the question, such a simple and obvious shortcut to finding out the root cause of my health concerns. It was so much more common sense than I ever receive from doctors that it makes me laugh.

The answer felt heavy, however. I got quiet and listened for my truth as I wanted to accept this opportunity for mutual learning. This brave and wise young man in his 20s had wisdom beyond many doctors 2 or 3 times his age.

The answer I heard myself say was, "I am holding things for other people. My family and society."

Meditating one Christmas (there's time for that when you aren't running around buying knick-knacks) upon some recurring health issues and patterns in how I feel in relationships, I found myself wanting to give people back their stuff. I lay still in bed before falling asleep and visualized first each member of my immediate family, imagining myself giving each one back their stuff.

Other people followed, pretty much all people close to me or those I felt any conflict with or heaviness around. For some people, especially in my family, I noticed there was a lot of "stuff" to give back. I felt like I was carrying bags of sand and returning them in pails full. It took some time to return it all, but once I did, I felt lighter.

The kidneys, liver and other internal organs get bogged down, weak and stagnated when we hold these things, such as shame, guilt or fear. Everyday, or as often as I can remember, I intend to practice returning this stuff.

When we talk about an identified patient in the family or community, we are referring to somebody who is carrying other people's returnable stuff. If you find yourself ostracized or in that role, try this visualization: Imagine any heaviness you feel being returned to whoever it is coming from. If it feels heavy, it isn't yours.

That's not to say there is anything wrong with heavy feelings. Holding people's stuff is a natural, normal and inevitable part of coexisting with other humans. Yet the more sensitive, compassionate and empathic among us can become bogged down, overwhelmed and unable to take care of ourselves if we hold others' stuff for too long. So if you are reading this after receiving a lot of stuff-whether gifts or old family dynamics, or even feeling lonely because other people's stuff doesn't resonate or fit, I offer you this holiday gift. Return people their stuff. I feel much lighter after doing so and I think you will too.

Holding people's stuff is a coping mechanism we develop as children when our families and communities don't have enough support. I learned that holding family members' stuff when they didn't seem able to handle it made me feel safer. But these patterns are old and outdated. If we hold this stuff for too long we eventually fall down exhausted. When you feel light and at ease, free of fear, guilt or shame, you know you have done this practice successfully. It isn't about causing harm to others or dumping on them either, but giving them the opportunity to not hurt you. Health isn't heavy. It's light.

After this visualization, you can imagine returning it wrapped as a gift. That's how I want my stuff returned to me, because stuff is good, when it is in the right place, in the proper hands.

Am I a Loser?

It may be due to my introversion and need for lots of quiet alone time to write. It may be that my childhood traumas messed me up. It could have something to do with how the psychiatric system robbed me of ages 20-22, ripping me out of college for awhile and isolating and debilitating me. Or it could just be that I'm a loser.

Not that I believe in "losers," but my mind does go there and it has for as long as I can remember, even as a young child. I looked around and saw some others who were clearly (to me) "losers" and others who were obviously winners.

I imagine everyone who's been on psychiatric drugs has felt like one of the "losers" in life. It's a juvenile perspective, yet a commonplace one that has been perpetuated by the media in countless ways, to the point that most people who haven't thoroughly untrained their minds from mainstream thought, talk about others this way.

And if we're talking about others this way, there has been a day where we worried this loser archetype could be us. The Loser. Officially.

I remember expressing concern about being "that person no one likes" to my best friend in high school. I was going away to a new summer camp and had been, or felt like, one of "those people" at my previous camp. She reassured me, "You just aren't one of those people that no one likes." This soothed my ego, but something in me wasn't sure.

"The nerds now will be cool later," my father used to tell me when I talked about the nerds at my high school. The psychotic people today will be the prophets tomorrow. The depressed people today will be the rock stars tomorrow. This turnaround can be done for any psychiatric diagnosis.

On a walk today in Prospect Park with the same friend from high school who reassured me I wasn't one of "those people," I articulated something I hadn't said before in these words. "I think society is moving away from this dichotomy between the lowly and the triumphant, the crazy person and the shaman, the ignorant person and the expert." The gap is closing. We are realizing how much we LOSE by discarding one another.

I may still feel like a "loser" some days (and a winner others) but seeing through it, I release the fear of being officially discarded or rejected from the human race. Discarding, disliking and rejecting another is always temporary.

If you feel alone or like a Loser or Outcast or any other stigmatizing label, such as a mental health label, know that you aren't alone and that the illusion will pass. The feelings are real, yet in your essence, no label has significance.

The key to escaping the oppressive elements of the mental health system (and society) is to recognize them for what they are: collective illusions. Beneath them you are always you-breathing and bubbling up with the essential

Chemical Imbalance? (Real Talk)

Don't say you have a chemical imbalance. It's best to never say you have a chemical imbalance in your brain.

People hate to hear it because it sounds like an excuse to be inconsiderate of others. People also hate it because it isn't true or proven biologically. People say it without ever having their brain chemicals tested in any way whatsoever.

They might smile and nod, but most are really thinking "Yeah, whatever..." There's no established exact "right" balance of brain chemicals. They also might think you are falling for a scam and stupid for believing a theory that evolved to sell pharmaceuticals.

Don't say you have a chemical imbalance. It's best not to say you are "clinically depressed" or "chronically depressed". Clinically doesn't have any real meaning besides that a clinician determined you to have a non-medical condition. Thomas Insel of the NIMH publicly stated that no mental illnesses have any biomarkers or validity. So using the term clinical to describe your general state of mood makes people who know better think you've been duped. Same with "chronically depressed". It makes people think you will always be a downer forever, but you don't know that. You are better off saying you are going through loss or grief or a long period of difficulty.

Don't say you have a chemical imbalance. If you use unscientific psuedo-medical terms to describe your moods or states of mind people could either think you are duped by Pharma, or they could pity you but see you as having no value.

They are likely to stigmatize you and see you as having a permanent deficit, and attribute all of your shortcomings to that. They will probably be less likely to want to be your friend, date you, hire you or take you seriously. You are much better off describing your experiences in non-pathologizing, universal ways that more people can relate to. This way they will see you as one of them and not "other".

Don't say you have a chemical imbalance. Using medical language to describe non-medical experiences like moods puts you in the category of "other" in people's minds.

Even if your moods are affected by your biology, so what? Everyone's are. That doesn't mean telling people you have an (unproven) mental disorder will raise their opinion of you. They might pity you, but is that what you want?

Who Are You?

You know you aren't a mental health label, but have you ever asked yourself who you actually are? It may seem like the most simplistic of questions, yet pausing to answer it can be a protection from an inaccurate diagnosis.

For example, if you don't have a concept of "who you are", it's easier to fall for any number of diagnoses or other labels from society when you are feeling down and overwhelmed.

"Maybe I am crazy", "I think I am just different from everyone else", "There's something fundamentally wrong with me and that's why I'm not happy, can't seem to get along with people, no one likes me" yada yada yada. Or even, "I'm too sensitive".

If any of these phrases resonate as things you tell yourself on bad days or things others say or imply about you, there is a solution.

It's called the "Who are you? exercise". Try it. Sit quietly with a blank sheet of paper and a pen and ask yourself who you are. Allow all preconceptions to soften and relax and let yourself write whatever comes out.

Here's mine which I wrote on not a great day where I was feeling on top of the world or really inspired or anything. In fact the moment I took out my pen and paper to write it was one of the lowest points of my day. I was feeling cranky and overwhelmed, getting surprise a minute texts and emails from friends in crisis and feeling ready to scream myself. So you don't have to be feeling good or inspired to do this.

Who Are You?

I am a being on a spiritual journey crafted by mandala consciousness.

I am always loved and a being of love.

I am beyond all of the things that trouble me and capable of true ultimate freedom.

I have a destined journey nonetheless where I come in and out of awareness of this.

I am bigger than any health concerns and beyond hatred and fear.

I am here to express infinity many times over-infinite in fact.

I am un-damageable and unbreakable thought many times I will feel and have felt damaged and/or broken.

In the essence of me are infinite possibilities and I can be healthy and powerful if I chose, and if I am willing to release that which I am not and fear of judgement and criticism from others.

I am here to win actually. To win the love vs. fear game. To let my love go everywhere and not inhibit it one bit. I am a wellspring of love that is complete and never ending and reaches, touches all things.

Now...Who are you?

After you do this exercise, consider sharing your response somewhere or with someone. Sharing who you are increases its power and helps people overcome the limitations of diagnosis. By writing and speaking it, you become it. In voicing it, you are it. Say it and it is so.

This is why diagnosis is so powerful, and why it is effective in advertising and promoting drugs that are causing so many problems.

But you can change that for yourself. Rather than using a diagnosis to describe yourself, which focuses on the flaws needed to form a diagnosis, you can create a "positive diagnosis" replacement. This way there is something in place that is so much stronger than a diagnosis, it will be nearly impossible to believe in one as a core part of who you are.

You become invulnerable to advertising and propaganda when you KNOW who you are. So find out and try the exercise.

Being a Thought Leader

Being a thought leader you are also a thought follower, but you follow thoughts a lot farther, while leading them too. You are in devoted partnership with thoughts, working things through, talking them out, you are committed, you sit still and listen when something comes up, you see it through to its completion, for the time being. You actually care about your thoughts, which is strangely rare in our world, it seems.

Caring about your thoughts can result in asking, "Am I mentally ill?" more often because your focus is on exploring your thoughts.

You are exploring new terrain in your mind frequently, which is on a different frequency. If others don't understand, it can be uncomfortable or even scary.

The crisis we are looking at in "mental health" is one of too many thought followers and not enough thought leaders across the board in society.

Now, the truth is, everyone is a thought leader. Everyone who gets a mental health label is a thought leader. Everyone who asks themselves, "Am I mentally ill?" is a thought leader. Everyone diagnosed mentally ill is a thought leader; some are robbed of that position or scared of it, or a combination.

The current mental illness model reflects all of the challenges and resistances that thought leaders have in a world that seemingly would like to keep thought stagnant and still like a dirty pond, without movement. This system would like everyone to ask themselves, "Am I mentally ill?"

Leading thought changes reality; the more thought leaders we have the better. Whenever something is freed a zest goes around the world (Hortense Calisher quote), so if everyone were to free their thoughts consistently as thought leaders, life would be zesty all the time for all of us, like a crisp salad with delicious dressing.

Rather, we are drugging the minds of thought leaders. To call someone, or oneself, by a mental illness label, is to be a thought follower, yet there are many many reasons to shy away from leadership.

I could deny the complexity of my own mind and emotions and their relationship with a thought and feeling phobic culture and call myself schizophrenic, paranoid, anxious, depressed, or any other label, depending on the moment. I could constantly ask myself "Am I Mentally Ill?"

Or I can do the harder but far more rewarding task set out for me and synthesize all of my experiences and perceptions into a meal others can feast on when they are hungry.

Thoughts are like food. Many people only want the same old same old Burger King burger and fries with a cheap apple pie, only want the cheap, mass produced, bland or sugary sweet. If a cook makes a beautiful meal with home grown vegetables and an original recipe, many will reject it and say, "yuck," but those who are drawn to it will be sincerely nourished in all of their being.

The question "Am I mentally ill?" will then be the farthest thing from their minds.

Mental Health Perspectives

Interview by Emma Snyder Woodside, Evergreen State College student studying alternative health.

Emma: Could you talk about your mental health perspectives in general? What does it mean to be 'mentally healthy?'

Chaya: Here's something I wrote on that:

When someone uses the term mental health what do you assume they mean?
Someone who is happy most of the time?
Someone who lets others know and expresses it when they are sad or angry?
Someone who knows how to hide it well and keep on keeping on when they are grieving?
Someone who makes enough money to support themselves well?
Someone with a good brain?
Someone very intelligent who uses their mind creatively?
Someone who can think linearly and not get distracted with dreamy or "too creative" thinking?
Someone good at conforming to social norms?
Someone with a strong moral foundation who does what is right to them regardless of social norms?
Someone who can always keep a good balance between extremes?
Someone who never flies off the handle?
Someone who knows to break down and ask for help when things get hard?
Someone for whom things don't tend to get hard?
Someone who fits in well to society as a whole or at least some subset of it?
Someone willing to be true to themselves even when they don't conform with anything that already exists?

Someone who loves deeply and easily?
Deeply and with difficulty?
Cautiously?
Never, because love is destabilizing to the mind?
Mental health, a term that only psychiatrists and therapists should use?
Only people who self define as mentally ill should use?
Only self defined mentally healthy should use?
Only those with a relative or close friend they define as mentally ill should use?
Everyone should continue to use vaguely without definition and assume we all mean the same thing?

So yeah, I don't actually believe in defining what "mentally healthy" is. Mental health perspectives vary a lot from those who define the term rigidly to those who don't define it at all.

Emma: What are your perspectives on current mainstream practices (such as medications for ADHD, depression, anxiety)?

Chaya: There should be far more informed consent and options. Doctors should be honest about the science or lack thereof and about different approaches and perspectives. In most cases there are safer and more effective alternatives to medications that are healthy and don't create dependence, horrible side effects or withdrawal issues. They are also more affordable and sustainable (except that pharmaceutical companies, hospitals, insurance companies and the government have found ways to make pharmaceuticals the only accessible and socially acceptable resource for many).

Emma: What does your personal health routine look like?

Chaya: Daily meditation, journaling 3-7 pages (with pen and paper), eating regularly (every 3 hours), herbal infusions and tinctures, supplements, daily walks outside whenever possible, stretching, regular visits with my naturopath.

Emma: What is a typical session like with you? What techniques do you use to support people in getting off their meds?

Chaya: Typically the first thing I do is listen. Most of my clients have never been truly heard and believed, trusted about their own authority on their experiences. I listen, validate and ask questions such as "What is your passion?" and "What was going on in your life when you were first diagnosed?" and of course, "What is going on now, what are the challenges to withdrawal?"

Then we formulate a plan which may include a slow taper plan, some supplements, herbs, food choices and lifestyle choices. Some of my clients are ready to taper right away while others are not and it's important for me to respect them where they are.

If they need other referrals such as a local doctor/herbalist/naturopath/psychiatrist/support group etc, I do research for my clients in my network if necessary and make recommendations.

If the client needs a residential or semi residential but safe place to transition, we discuss ones that already exist or creating one.

I have created programs for clients that include a housemate, peer, therapist, herbalist and community connections to help get back on their feet after being isolated or hospitalized for a long time. These programs are very self directed and take all of the client's preferences/sensitivities into account.

Emma: What can support people with practices like yours?

Chaya: It would be awesome to have insurance coverage to help people safely withdraw from the drugs their doctors prescribed (often without enough information on withdrawal). Donations of money, herbs, supplements and other resources are always helpful. One of the main issues is accessibility.

The other is belief. One thing everyone can try on is to believe in others and not freak out when someone is different or going through trauma or spiritual emergence. People can refrain from telling someone else to take meds and encourage people to do lots of research and learn about their options, and different cultural ways of viewing tragic/extreme emotional experiences.

None of this is new and ancient cultures had different mental health perspectives and many ways of helping people through these things that we can learn from and incorporate them with modern science (but the real science).

Workbook
Questions for reflection:

- Which narratives make the most sense to you?

- How would you choose to describe your suffering?

- Do you have multiple stories/frameworks?

- How can you describe yourself/your experiences to others in non-stigmatizing language?

- If you do use a diagnostic label, how can you define it to describe your personal experience for those who don't know exactly what the diagnosis means to you?

- Do you feel a sense of choice in what you tell people about your life experiences?

  _____
  _____

- Do you have ways to change the subject or divert a conversation you don't want to have about your history?

  _____
  _____

- As a game, how would your story be told if you were a superhero?

  _____
  _____
  _____
  _____

- How would it be told if you were a normie?

  _____
  _____
  _____
  _____

- How would it be told if you were the most crazy, off the wall person ever to exist?

  _____
  _____
  _____
  _____

- Is there liberation in any of these stories?

- How can you share your narrative in ways that empower others to share their own?

- How can you shift from diagnostic to descriptive language?

- How does this make you feel?

- Where do you feel it in your body?

- What else do you have to say about this?

CHAPTER 7

TURNING TRAUMA INTO MEDICINE

Binaries and Spectrums

To voice experiences of oppression or inequality, there is sometimes an apparent need to speak in binaries or spectrums that might not be entirely fair or ultimately honest.

Yet these binaries such as white/black, rich/poor, and male/female have cultural relevance and reality. My purpose in naming and discussing a binary isn't to divide people further, but rather to bring them closer together in understanding, and to validate the experiences of the ones on the lower end of that particular pole.

Everyone has been on the top and bottom of some kind of social polarity in life. Using the knowledge of how each one feels, we can, I hope, topple the structures that tell us we need to be quiet when we are on the bottom, or that we need to put others down to pull ourselves up, or that we need to do things that aren't in alignment with who we are to "get ahead" or dominate others.

I suppose it is part of the human condition to think about the privileges we didn't have, and while we hear a lot about gender, race and class privilege, there are invisible types of privilege that are just as weighty, and one is the privilege of having grown up in a family where you felt safe.

In American culture and my generation I know several dozen people who were raised by parents who stayed happily together, weren't violent, didn't yell much and basically treated them with respect most of the time. These folks didn't have to take care of either of their parents, so they got the irreplaceable experience of being kids when they were kids. They got to be immature, bratty and out of control without severe repercussions. Their parents basically got along and supported each other, and when they didn't, they still were not violent with one another or their children.

This is really the bare minimum of what kids need to feel safe, yet few kids actually get it. Still, the ones that do often grow up with a better ability to handle stress, more capacity for complexities in intimate relationships and greater propensity for health and stability (see Adverse Childhood Experience studies).

Of course there are many factors that play into our wellbeing as adults and even the best possible family life won't shield us from other challenges in life. Sometimes people with a simple and safe home life go looking for danger elsewhere to fit in with the rest of us, or to experience the adrenaline that many of us didn't need to search for.

I know a number of people who had relatively ideal home lives and quickly found adventure by becoming addicted to hard drugs, alcohol or other adrenaline creating behaviors. They did things to their bodies that I'd never consider doing to mine (I have enough trauma induced health challenges, thank you) and often came out strong bodied and healthy nonetheless.

I do a lot for my health and still have quite a few major health challenges that are tied into emotions and trauma from my early life and not easy to untangle. Those who had less childhood trauma usually have a psychological advantage over those with more. (Like all things, this is a spectrum.) Without the knee jerk need to protect themselves from violence or manipulation, they tend to have a certain sophistication in relationships that I dream of- a sense of safety I've practiced many disciplines to attain, and still rarely have for long.

The reason I bring this up is because it goes unspoken too often, without any language for it. And, of course, like all forms of inequality and oppression, when it is named, those whose privilege is recognized may be quick to speak of their experiences and the challenges they did have. They might even become angry or deny this type of privilege exists.

One friend shared this:

Personally, I see I have privilege on this spectrum (non divorced parents who didn't hate each other and weren't alcoholics, for instance) AND the ways that the intense trauma I experienced and carried from my parents still is so hard for me to speak of/still believe myself (despite all the ways I do and have) because the worst parts happened pre-verbally (and then got echoed and energetically repeated during my whole childhood). It has taken years to unravel and still I have trouble "explaining."

And there is also the factor of being a highly empathic soul who was thus affected in a particular way (in a society that doesn't value empaths or empathy). There are certain kind of skills or safety that comes from having one's needs attended to/responded to that my family didn't offer in certain ways. Yet I also see my privilege in other ways and this made me think of other people in my life who had less stability/safety than I did in certain ways.

And basically all of us have a had a childhood that was more traumatic than some and less traumatic than others. I was not severely abused physically or sexually but experienced severe emotional abuse, guilt tripping and manipulation and witnessed regular physical violence and yelling in my home.

Many people who come from low trauma families attribute their personal and professional successes to therapy, spiritual growth or their own hard work. While these things likely play a part worth mentioning, it's necessary to acknowledge how hard or even impossible it is to trust a therapist or spiritual community when coming from extreme trauma in the formative years.

The ability to work hard at anything can also be compromised when there was little ease in childhood. Many who had to work so hard as children to take care of our parents and siblings (AND had that experience denied/invalidated) feel resentful and go through life secretly feeling like life owes us a break and the care and freedom we didn't get as kids.

My hope is that awareness will shine on this matter and humility will grow in those who had some form of this "functional family" privilege. Just as some whites, men and those of higher socioeconomic standing are learning to be humble and listen to people of other races, women, and those who live or have lived in poverty, I hope people with relatively low childhood trauma will make space to hear, acknowledge and graciously support those who grew up in much inescapable violence and panic.

The purpose in naming this is equally to bring comfort to those who feel unseen and unheard in how childhood trauma continues to affect them, and how they feel when looking on at others who don't have that particular challenge.

In naming a binary or spectrum, there is always the risk it will create a competitive conversation; one in which no one wants to identify as the privileged class and everyone instead fights to outdo one another with trauma stories. In some ways it's useful to have a reverse competition, only because it gets people speaking about their secret suffering and "competing" to have the worst trauma story, rather than competing to have things the most "together" as we seem to be doing in society now. And that competition to be the most "functional" seems to be creating a huge shadow of earthly destruction. Maybe if, instead, we were all competing to share our darkest and saddest trauma stories, we'd bee unearthing a whole lot of shame and secrecy to be healed, loved, and understood with open hearts.

A friend who experienced childhood trauma shared this hopeful conclusion:

Being a sensitive child growing up in a dysfunctional or abusive household just drives that wound and the challenges it makes even deeper. I have been given so many gifts lately to heal my wounds, and I'm so full of gratitude for the whole journey. It isn't about claiming you pulled yourself up by your own self-helping bootstraps with therapy, spirituality or hard work. It's just about showing up for the journey, and then receiving grace.

Saying No

I'm now advocating for saying 'No' whenever necessary and trusting that the right people and situations will stick around in your life even if you say 'No'–even if you say 'No' 1000 times!

Anyone who doesn't respect and accept a simple No, doesn't have space in my life! Charging money is also a boundary and can be a way of saying No. Not responding to a text/email/phone message is also a fine way to say "No thank you," to an offer or invitation.

Pressuring yourself to respond when you don't want to is another way of short circuiting your power to say 'No.'

People whose boundaries were respected more as children, who were less fearful as children, or who have undergone less trauma may have an easier time saying No. Perhaps those whose parents were more supported and didn't feel desperate for them to say 'Yes' all the time. I, on the other hand, often notice myself saying Yes to certain things without even thinking about it, and then later wondering why.

I also get anxious about how to say 'No' nicely, or I consider something I really have no interest in, forgetting that saying 'No' is even an option!

Saying 'No' is our birthright. It preserves our space and acknowledges our spirit. There is some talk and even valid theory on the practice of saying 'Yes' or phrasing all 'No's as 'Yes'es by expressing what you do want or are looking for. For me it can be a relief to simply say 'No,' even if I only say it in my own mind and not out loud.

Others can handle a 'No'-they aren't so fragile that my boundary will break them. I love the idea of saying No, over and over as many times as I need to, to practice remembering that I can, flexing, stretching and building my 'No' muscle.

People can sense your No muscle, and as you strengthen it, people might be a bit more hesitant around you-hesitant to assume "anything is okay" with you.

Yet, I often try to comfort others with reassurance that "anything is okay." This actually weakens my 'No' muscle, if it's not really okay with me, and I need to be really honest with myself about whether it's actually okay.

This is a power we don't always own. It is especially important to listen to our inner sense of Yes or No in the beginning of an endeavor/job/relationship. Often times people are very eager to start something and fail to express boundaries early on, which makes it harder to do later.

Saying 'No' when I initially said 'Yes' may still be necessary, but I feel I am learning to say 'No' sooner, so I am less likely to allow myself to be harmed or hurt.

I also respect when others say 'No,' trusting the Yes I need will come. Trusting a 'Yes' will come to the person I said No to. If it's a 'No' for me, it's a no for them, since there's only one of me! Every time someone has said 'No' to me, I later realized my answer was 'No' too (sometimes it took years for me to realize...). Ah the No. The No knows.

Having extreme allergies and other sensitivities has forced me to need to say 'No' a lot. There are many indoor places (with pets) I cannot go in without having an asthmatic reaction. I believe my extreme sensitivities in part came to me to teach me how to say 'No.'

Almost every time I get allergies, the situation is wrong for me anyway and the allergies signal the No. As an empathetic person, saying No can sometimes feel nearly impossible or doesn't even occur to me as an option.

As a healing person, I can easily merge with others energetically, feeling their feelings and healing them, or picking up their energy without always realizing it right away (though I'm getting better at realizing it).

This tendency to merge comes from being a healing spirit as well as from the child in me. There's a child in me that never wanted to grow up and individuate, a child that wanted/wants to be able to rely on others and feel safe, feel taken care of emotionally and even physically in ways I didn't always receive as a kid.

There's a part of me that feels I deserve to be taken care of by others since I wasn't always as a child...a part of me that longs desperately to merge, to find attached possessive parents who won't let me say 'No.' And another part of me that is terrified of that and keeps people at a distance, assuming they won't accept my 'No's, or I won't have access to the parts of me that can voice them.

This is all big stuff that takes a lot of unraveling but right now I'm starting with the basics life is presenting me with: practicing saying 'No' over and over. Trusting my 'Yes' will come in its own time and all the Nos are strengthening, ripening, seasoning and preparing me for the blessed Yes.

Saying No is a 1st and 2nd chakra endeavor. Yes is 4th and 5th chakra, so I see my 'No's as building a root system and a base-a stump- on which Yeses can branch out, leaf and flower.

It's like #1 we need safety, we need to keep harm away-so we have a home of some kind perhaps. An enclosed structure of any kind is basically a way of saying No. There's usually a lock on the door, which says No to anyone coming in uninvited.

Even the clothes we wear are ways of saying No. Our pants or skirts are often zipped up or buttoned-this says No, you may not see or touch these parts of my body without my permission/invitation.

From there we can move on to Yeses such as decorating our houses and clothing-but the No part is so fundamental, so basic, so important (and under-celebrated).

Let's have a No party! NoNoNoNoNo!

Achieving "Stability" Amidst Transience

(for those who have had a lot of change and moving around in their lives)

Stay in touch with friends. Reach out to friends/contacts/acquaintances wherever you currently are. Revisit old interests and affiliations in new places.

Keep a journal.

Drink tea.

Send emails. Chat online.

Throw/give things away when you no longer need them.

Keep a blog and share it on social media.

Find mentors.

Pursue income streams that appeal to you.

Cloud watch. Admire the moon. Walk near large bodies of water. Stretch.

Take baths.

Learn how to eat well on the go. Protein and vegetables makes a cheap and good meal at hot bars.

Talk to yourself/pray out loud.

Listen to your favorite old songs. Cry sometimes.

Collect scarves.

You'll lose all your hats.

Learn to love meeting new people. Learn to let go of friends who have gotten too busy (until they're free again). Keep calling people. Don't let loneliness get the best of you. Find other transient people to catastrophize with. Get massages at malls (or wherever you can).

Remember life is an adventure. It's supposed to be this way. Don't let anyone tell you you "should be more stable or settled down by now."

Lie down a lot.

Learn to cook in all different scenarios with all kinds of equipment and appliances.

Consider yourself versatile and resilient.

Learn from those around you.

Create art of some kind every single day.

The Need To Hide and Cocoon

Hiding is an important step in spiritual emergence. Sometimes it is how you can feel safe, while you build your creative ideas or rest in between projects.

Sometimes getting sick or having practical problems can be a way of hiding, or letting yourself hide. It's okay!

When you are working from a place outside the ego, you can hide and then come out again, knowing life is going in cycles and we are part of it, without needing to control it.

Let yourself hide out. Sometimes it's safer than being seen by a world that hasn't caught up yet. Hiding can also be a good way to stay safe when the methods of healing available to you seem too toxic, aggressive, forced or plain wrong.

In spiritual emergence, it's called the cocoon. Hiding is followed by a period of service where you spread your wings, or if you are a bunny rabbit, you hop off joyfully or chomp down on your carrot. And then you have an organic home grown carrot to share with others, which is so much better than the store bought ones.

Addressing Your Beliefs

Have you ever written a list of the disempowering things you tell yourself and then replaced it with a list of positive things people have actually said about you?

Here's mine if you need some inspiration.

Disempowering beliefs/things that were implanted into my brain by evil external forces over and over:
- not enough
- not valid
- not worth money
- Wrong
- Selfish
- don't do enough
- don't help enough
- Ineffective
- Unhealthy
- a failure
- not successful
- in danger of failing
- Concerning
- Lost
- Unrealistic
- needs and feelings are unattractive
- doing the wrong thing

Phew. Do you know how good it feels to admit all those things and get them out of your head?

Transforming negative beliefs.

Here are the empowering beliefs I've internalized from some awesome lucky sources and mostly life experience:
- faith in myself
- intuition/higher self will guide me
- will have what I need
- ideas will be well received
- I'm healing
- my presence is healing
- Psychic
- intuition is powerful
- I can trust myself/the Universe

Transforming negative beliefs. Here are some things trusted people have actually told me about myself (please please do at least this part for yourself!):

- You're so good at connecting with people
- You take such good care of yourself
- Being around you is healing
- You're worth being paid well
- You're very knowledgeable about your work
- You're helpful
- You're effective at connecting
- You've succeeded/are succeeding at your work/goals
- You're doing it
- I have total faith in you
- You have a clear purpose and direction
- You're doing the right thing
- Your needs and feelings are clarifying, healing and helpful to know

Now it's your turn.

Death and Medicine

We are all on the edge of death and of course fearful of that and our Western systems of medicine are based on that fear.

Of course while I am in this body I will do my best to take care of it and preserve it, but true medicine walks the life/death line. It always does.

True medicine is what lives beyond our bodies and attachments to ourselves. True medicine knows that someone will pick up where I leave off and healing happens in our souls and the Universe as a whole so there is nothing for an individual to fear about their health or state of mind or anything else.

True medicine is the medicine of the future.

Ironically, living is when we bring some of death into our lives and alchemize it so we are no longer so fearful. Then we feel fully embodied. Then we know our bodies alone aren't breathing, but the whole Universe on both sides of life is breathing through our personal lungs.

So find a way to add a dash of death to your medicine, whatever it may be. You can tell your doctor I recommended it, and yes, this is medical advice.

Workbook
Questions for reflection:

- Have you found any gifts in your trauma?
  _____
  _____

- What have they been?
  _____
  _____
  _____
  _____
  _____

- What talents have you developed as a result of trauma?
  _____
  _____
  _____
  _____
  _____

- Do you have a special healing power, knowledge, compassion, awareness or something else to offer others that came out of your trauma?
  _____
  _____
  _____

- Is there something mystical about it? Describe.
  _____
  _____
  _____

- Do you have a calling? Describe.

- Do you feel guided or as if you are on a "path"? Describe.

- Do you believe you have a destiny? Describe.

- Are there people who have served as models/mentors/symbols of your gifts born of trauma? Describe.

- How is your trauma directly linked to your ability to serve? Describe.

- Has your trauma helped you to learn self-care? Describe.

- Do you have support for taking good care of yourself while you use your gifts for others? Describe.

- Can you take care of yourself purely out of self love? Describe.

- Can you truly focus on yourself and release the need to be a savior for everyone else? Describe.

CHAPTER 8

SUPPORTING THE BODY

Damage From Psych Drugs

The damage to my kidneys, liver, adrenals and other organs was an issue when I came off those drugs at age 22/23 but I still had a young body. I still endured a week or so of semi-sleepless nights. It wasn't easy, but it was nowhere near as hard as it is for me now. Even one night of no sleep can have terrible results.

In one way, in theory, I believe most damage can be healed. Yet optimal conditions, (which hardly exist today) are required to achieve the healing of organ damage. And even then, it isn't usually easy.

Being disabled by psych drugs also led to years of "unemployment" or "underemployment" (not having a steady salary). This meant less money for healing resources. We know insurance covers virtually nothing (in most states) that serves to restore our internal organs to health after severe and acute injury from the drugs they do cover so readily.

I put unemployment and underemployment in quotes because even while I was too damaged by psych drugs to work at a job with a steady salary, I was still employed. In fact I was deeply, steadily and meaningfully employed writing, teaching and supporting others (often as a volunteer or for a small stipend). In hindsight, this may be one of the fastest ways to heal organ damage or overcome some of its devastating effects.

Still, with aging, and with the additional stresses in life, the organ damage and weakening of my already sensitive constitution that occurred when I was 20-23 and forced/coerced onto 7 psych drugs, makes things a lot more stressful.

I used to be able to take good care of my health and then feel healthy (before psych drugs). After the iatrogenic injury, I've consistently put a lot of effort into my health and only feel healthy sometimes.

I've increased my efforts many times over and still my energy and stamina have fluctuated. Some of this is a natural part of aging. Yet, I can't think of anyone my age who puts as much effort into their health for as little return on the investment.

Others I know (with the exception of some with Lyme or who are still on psych drugs) SEEM to have a lot more leeway to miss sleep, eat junk food, exert their bodies to their limit, smoke, get drunk, etc. without the instant backlash the next day.

Looks can be deceiving though. I don't know how healthy anyone is or feels, and this may be the other point.

Vata Dosha

In Ayurveda, I have the vata dosha constitution. This means I feel the health effects of my choices the next day. Others of other constitutions can tolerate more stress. However, the health effects build up and will show up years down the line as chronic conditions.

Vata is the immediate litmus test; it shows up right away. Vata is the first dosha to go out of balance in everyone, and psychiatric drugs tend to throw it out of whack.

Vata is considered the least desirable and least fortunate of the constitutions (except for spiritual growth which seems to arise from adversity) living in consistent anxiety, pain, aches and stress (but can also achieve deep meditative peace more easily and be highly creative).

Vata constitution is the least likely to tolerate psych drugs. I couldn't even tolerate a low dose of a single drug at the age of 20 without side effects. Anxiety, insomnia, panic attacks, severely compromised immunity, and social withdrawal were just a few. These are the effects I experienced RIGHT AWAY from taking the smallest dose of one drug.

So being an immediately intolerant, sensitive vata constitution (the thin, cold, anxious type) did perhaps keep me from being on a "maintenance" dose of drugs for many years. If I hadn't gotten off that drug cocktail, I know I wouldn't have lived much longer. That's how sick and incapacitated it made me.

Vata constitution has made it more difficult to heal all that organ damage. But I'm certainly not jealous of people who can tolerate psych drugs for years and years, only partly present and alive.

Because having more people who "tolerate" poison and toxicity for longer and longer periods of time is not helping our health as a society. In fact it is creating a society of half-alive half-zombies.

A society where being highly toxic and poisoned but being able to get by with some extra uppers and downers each day is the norm. However, underneath that is incredible suffering that is just barely glossed over. And yes, having a sensitive constitution, I feel that suffering emanating from almost everyone.

I recently had a personalized tincture made from an herbalist. It includes an essence, a subtle vibrational medicine that requires intention to work. The herbalist instructed me to take it each day with an intention.

Over a few weeks, I said intentions to myself as I took it. These included intentions such as "to receive the healing/guidance/wisdom of the plants" or "to restore my adrenals/energy".

One day I woke up feeling some adrenal restoration, after working on this actively for the past few weeks. This was following hitting a bottom of adrenal exhaustion and utter depletion from insane amounts of stress. When I took my tincture today, I said my intention. My intention was "to restore the health of the earth and myself together, to work with the earth in harmony."

Adrenal Fatigue

This below was posted in the Facebook group Adrenal Fatigue Recovery and everyone agreed and added more info. Not one person gave the usual defenses I see on here for the medical model of "mental illness" and most of them put it in quotes. So, yeah, there are groups of people doing their own research, taking back their power, taking their health back from pharma, and helping one another to heal.

I've actually been learning a lot about "alternative" health from some of these groups, and there's not much of the kind of hype and theoretical arguing as in the "mental health" groups.

Here's what was posted followed by a stream of supportive comments:

How many of you believe that a serotonin deficiency causes mental illness? Do any of you believe that it was made up by big pharma to sell drugs? Do you believe that most of the symptoms of so called depression are actually related to thyroid, Adrenal Fatigue, candida, gut issues, vitamin/mineral deficiencies? Maybe in some cases it's stressful life events which the body is responding to accordingly. Maybe it's stages of grief. I personally don't believe in the one chemical brain imbalance and I get so annoyed at the way society has viewed invisible illnesses. I am so sad about all the stories I have read on here for the last year about doctors just telling us all that we have depression or that we are crazy for believing or knowing that we have Adrenal Fatigue and other related conditions.

I've been following posts in this group as well as Magnesium and Iodine Facebook groups and have gotten some information that has been helping me heal my thyroid, adrenals and other health issues. Like all information online and elsewhere, it is necessary to be discerning, to listen to your own body and wisdom and sometimes to try things out slowly and carefully and see how they work for you.

I tend towards low thyroid, adrenal fatigue, coldness, low blood pressure and deficiency, so please keep these things in mind when you read my steps below.

The steps I've been taking recently that have helped have been:

-More seaweed (I eat dulse and nori straight, cook kombu and kelp with beans or vegetables and add kelp powder and dulse flakes to any meal as condiments)

-More himalayan sea salt/Real Salt or unrefined sea salt, including putting it in my water

-drinking well water as much as possible

-grass fed butter

-organic coconut oil

-pastured eggs

-extra Vitamin C

-Magnesium oil sprayed on my body as well as Magnesium supplements orally

-Getting sunlight as much as possible

-Going to bed early

Most of these are practices I have been doing for some time, so it can be hard to know what makes a difference and what is doing what, but I did notice adding in more seaweed and black foods made my thyroid feel stronger and I started to sleep through the night more often. For me, when my thyroid is stronger, I swallow more and my swallow feels stronger. Thyroid health is connected with adrenal health, and a lot of these things are interlinked.

These Facebook groups have been helpful for me because one of my biggest problems with health practices is that I do them for awhile and then forget and stop doing some things that were really working. So by joining these groups, I see little reminders and suggestions from other people in my Facebook feed and it has been helping me to stay on track with my health.

I know these things can be overwhelming and it can feel like there is too much to do and it's all so expensive. The cool thing about these groups is that people get that and are usually supportive and can sometimes have low cost or even free ideas. You can post your own questions or frustrations in them and some of the participants are truly knowledgeable.

Most of all I am excited about an era of community medicine, where we the people are educating, inspiring, encouraging and supporting one another with an abundance of ideas and options, all by personal choice (of course there is still the issue of access). I haven't gotten that in too many doctors offices.

How to Improve Memory (at any age)

I have a near photographic memory. Here are the things that work:

1. Daily writing longhand, 7 longhand pages per day, every single day.
2. Daily meditation-simply sitting quietly for at least 20 minutes per day.
3. Fish oil/cod liver oil.
4. Eating ample healthy fats like butter, coconut oil, olive oil.
5. Daily walking- at least 20 minutes per day, if possible. Physical activities that stimulate both sides.
6. Eating nutrient dense unprocessed foods as much as possible.
7. B Vitamins.

How to improve memory: In terms of recall at a later age, the sooner young people can start daily writing, the better. For people who dislike writing, daily drawing, photography or other creative activity can substitute. The sooner one starts, the more long term memories will be encoded.

Spending at least an hour a day doing a creative activity will improve memory. Passive activities such as scrolling online, watching TV etc. can atrophy the mind and memory if they aren't well balanced with mentally active ones.

How to improve memory for seniors

Mental games can help, such as computer games that require memory, especially to improve short term memory. But it is never too late for a senior to start writing, or taking photos, drawing, etc. Writing has the biggest impact on long term memory (or drawing images from the past for those who are more visual in their memory). The more one writes, the more they remember, and this can be activated at any age!

For seniors, limiting unnecessary pharmaceuticals helps with memory. Too many drugs interfere with memory and can contribute to dementia. Anti-depressants and other psychoactive pharmaceuticals are known for causing memory problems. If a senior prioritizes memory, such as if they are writing memoirs, it would be best to limit any unnecessary drugs.

Nutrition: Adding Things In

My ways with health and eating leans towards "adding things in", and reducing things, but rarely strictly eliminating anything.

There are several reasons for this, some more personal, others more general, which I will explain.

People eliminate soy, dairy, meat, fruit, sugar, gluten, eggs, grains, nightshades, nuts, fats, starches, alcohol, chocolate, cooked food, raw food, beans, basically everything. For every given food, there is a school of thought that warns against it (and I have probably tried eliminating it).

Eliminating certain foods makes some people feel better and healthier.

I need to eat a high almost everything diet: high protein, fat, vegetable, fruit, starch, calorie. So if I eliminated any source of protein, I end up eating more of others to make up for it, and I don't do well with too much meat/dairy/soy/beans/grains. This is why I don't eliminate dairy, soy, meat, or any other high protein source (even while they can all be mildly problematic for me both for my health and ideology), but rather eat them all in small to moderate amounts.

The only foods I eat a lot of on a daily basis are eggs, vegetables, and sometimes fruit or beans. Other than that, I rotate everything.

One issue for me is that I need to be an opportunivore because I have so much going on and I don't want to be isolated in my own little food-iverse, so if I'm out and someone offers me food, or cooks for me, I'll generally eat at least a little bit of what I'm given.

The only "food" I somewhat strictly limit is refined sugar, but I do eat a bit on occasion. I also limit dairy and refined flour, but do eat both of them a few times a week on average.

The other reason it's important to me not to strictly exclude any "food", including chemical preservatives (which I know are bad for me and do generally avoid) is that I have gone into states of food obsession that nearly killed me, primarily because I would lose my appetite and be unable to eat at all.

This was when I was 21 and perhaps a combination of parasites, digestive issues, trauma and spiritual emergence, which resulted in my being 5'8" and weighing about 80 lbs. Looking in the mirror at my naked body was scary and my period stopped for 6 months, where I've been completely regular in my periods at every other time in my life.

My loss of control over my life at that time was extreme, and it made me prey for psychiatry as well, with virtually no resources within myself to fight back or reclaim my autonomy.

While it has never gotten anywhere near that extreme since then (or before), I do still regularly need to be aware of tendencies I have to lose interest in food when I'm isolated, unhappy or stressed.

Almost every time I've had to move, I've gone a day or so without eating because I was anxious.

Sometimes on my period I go part of a day without eating, which I know many other women do as well, and is "normal", but since I have the tendency to stop eating due to any sort of stress, it's important for me not to have strict rules about foods that are off limits, especially since I have adrenal fatigue, so not eating when I need to exhausts my adrenals even more.

I realize many people are allergic or highly sensitive to certain foods and that eliminating them has been life changing for them, so I am not proposing my way is THE way, but yesterday I was feeling isolated and had my period, and the only thing that appealed to me to eat was this frozen box of pizza, pesto pizza.

I usually justify eating freshly cooked pizza on occasion as the bread cooked that day feels somewhat "healthy" to me compared with shelf stable bread of most kinds. I grew up eating both fresh (Brooklyn) pizza and (health food store) frozen pizza almost every single day, so this is a food my body is "used to".

Now I sometimes see pizza as a way to help me eat my greens.

I scanned the ingredients on the frozen pizza. The list was long and included preservatives and sugar. I popped it in the oven, topped it with a whole bunch of local organic baby chard, and ate the whole thing (minus the crusts). YUM.

And my day got better after that. It wasn't perhaps the best nourishment in the world, yet so much better than not eating at all, which felt like my alternative at that moment.

Do I do this often? No. Am I really really grateful I tossed those baby chard on there? Yes. Would I do it again? It just depends on circumstances so I never say never.

How Healthy Do You Intend to Be?

Finances and access are an issue (for many of us) but there are also always more resources around us we can take advantage of. Growing our own food, foraging wild foods and herbs, and doing our own research are just some of the ways we can better benefit from the resources around us.

We will absolutely never be "perfect" nor is that the goal.

Information out there can be conflicting and confusing, which is why a daily meditation/prayer/creative/reflective process is so crucial. Even if it is simply writing down your dreams or going for a walk by yourself. Lying in bed quietly for 5 minutes following your breath in and out, and stretching, can also prove necessary to strengthen your powers of discernment.

Health practices are practices; we need to practice them. While a lot of trial and error is required at first, we do improve our capacity to hear our body.

Eat Something Wild

This can be a challenge or no challenge at all depending on where you live and how much knowledge you have about wild foods.

Yet, if you are seeking to live a life with lots of energy, inspiration, deliciousness and freedom, you have no way around it: you must learn about wild foods! You must learn to identify some berries, greens and herbs you can eat and where it is safe to pick them.

For those of us who are committed to living free of dangerous pharmaceuticals, it is not enough to simply use store bought herbs and supplements. We must actually connect to the earth and the source of the medicine. We must taste the deliciousness of our medicine and become intimate with it. Our medicine was meant to be our lover, not our saboteur.

You probably have some berries ripening around you in summer, and those are the easiest for many to identify. Raspberry leaves make a nutritious tea. Most wild foods are healthiest when they are...in the the wild, far from cars, city pollution and houses or buildings which can pollute the soil with chemicals from their paint.

If you live in a city, there are still plenty of options for foraging such as parks, gardens and abandoned lots. Taking a trip out to the country for a day can be more valuable if you come home with bags of foraged greens, berries and herbs.

Here's another favorite. If you are lucky enough to find some nettle, this is an extremely nutritious herb/food and can be picked with gloves or a plastic bag to avoid getting stung.

There are infinite wild foods and herbs to learn about. I've learned mostly from friends and teachers in person, though there are also many books where you can fact check, and of course the good ol' internet for looking things up.

Most people who work in gardens know which weeds are edible (so you can ask them) and there are soooo many.

You may already know of a lot of great ones but just forget to eat them because we are conditioned to think food must always be bought or cultivated ourselves. Some of the most energizing meals I have ever eaten and the most nutritious teas I've ever drank have been from "weeds".

Eating weeds is also a way of affirming what we know about ourselves: just because some people or some parts of ourselves are considered weeds, does not mean they are less valuable. In fact they may be more valuable given the right conditions.

Take one step today to find wild edibles near you and most importantly: EAT THEM!

Turmeric

Turmeric has a slightly bitter flavor and I love scooping 1 or 2 generous teaspoons of it on eggs or dairy products like goat yogurt or cottage cheese (which I only eat occasionally). It you don't eat dairy or eggs, turmeric makes a good topping on bean dishes or even added to smoothies.

Adding freshly ground black pepper makes the turmeric compounds absorb better.

Organic or fresh turmeric should be dark deep orange. If it's lower quality, sometimes it doesn't have as strong of a color.

Turmeric has anti-inflammatory, anti-cancer and anti-tumor properties and it's good for the liver, which is so important given how much toxicity our bodies are coping with nowadays, especially when on or withdrawing from psychiatric drugs or other chemical substances.

Curcumin, an active compound in turmeric, has anti-oxidant and anti-aging properties and is good for the brain. It has also been called an anti-depressant.

Turmeric has also been shown to have preventative properties against dementia and alzheimers, both of which can be at least partially induced by psychiatric drugs.

The best place to get turmeric, aside from buying it fresh, local and organic, if you live in a region where that is possible, is to buy it organic in the bulk section of a health food store.

If you don't have access to a good health food store, or find it easier to shop online, there are high quality brands of organic turmeric.

If you eat one spice everyday, let it be this awesomely bitter, yet delicious bright orange baby.

Final Thoughts on Nutrition

Nutrition is one of the most important things that has allowed me to live free of psychiatric drugs and understand my body, my moods, and my energy levels.

Tip: if you tend to feel anxious and ungrounded, eat extra fat such as organic olive oil, organic coconut oil or pastured butter. When I started eating extra healthy fats, I felt so much more in control of my state of mind and even sleep. When I have insomnia I often consume a tablespoon of olive or coconut oil to put myself back to sleep. It almost always works. A high quality magnesium supplement and magnesium oil can help too, if your body resonates with those.

Note: Magnesium can have complications when on or withdrawing from psychiatric drugs as it can accelerate the detoxification process.

The main key for me has been to do a lot of research while consistently tuning in to what my body wants or doesn't want. There are days when I can take all of my supplements and days where I can't take any.

Workbook
Questions for reflection:

- What best supports your body?

_____

_____

_____

_____

- What do you need to do every day or several times a week for your body?

- What do you need to do weekly or every other week for maintenance?

- What do you need to do every month for maintenance?

- What activities and substances do you need to limit or eliminate to best care for your body?

- Which people in your life support and inspire you to take good care of your physical self?

- Which people and activities have a negative influence on your self-care?

- What activities, foods, herbs, supplements etc help you sleep?

- Which ones help you relax?

- Which help you feel grounded and focused?

- Does your physical body respond to life circumstances, emotions, and creativity?

- Do you have people (doctors, therapists, coaches/consultants) you can talk to about issues in your body who will listen? And those who will give helpful advice you can consider without coercion?

- Are there blogs/books/videos etc that inspire you in your physical health journey?

- What exercise do you love?

- What exercise is good for you but harder to do?

- What exercises do you need to be careful not to overdo?

- Are you getting enough rest?

- How much rest is ideal for you? (be generous!)

- How does your body respond to nature/cities/certain people/solitude/isolation?

- How do you keep the lines of communication with your body open?

- What self love and acceptance and body love/acceptance practices will you implement?

- Do you enjoy eating? What would make it more enjoyable?

- Do you like cooking? What inspires you to cook or incorporate new foods that support your body?

- Are you aware of fluctuations based on time of the year, time of the month, moon cycles (waxing/waning) and hormonal changes in your own life cycle?

CHAPTER 9

CONNECTING WITH THE WORLDWIDE MOVEMENT

-online
-in person
-by phone
-support groups
-blogs
-protests
-conferences/retreats
-videos

Northampton was where I was initiated into the psychiatric survivor community movement, where I came off psych drugs, organized with the Freedom Center, was involved with the Western Mass Recovery Learning Community, and pretty much lived as a psychiatric survivor community activist, writer and yoga teacher for nearly 10 years.

To my knowledge, Massachusetts as a state and Western MA in particular can't be rivaled (in the U.S.) in their psychiatric survivor community support and activist efforts as well as resources for those looking to escape, criticize and/or overcome the effects of psychiatry.

Without even realizing it, for a time when I moved to California, I was a bit lost, or rather, I had lost my passionate local activist psychiatric survivor community, which, even with its drama and in fighting, had been the foundation of my work and life for my entire adult life up until then.

I did meet some activists on the West coast and even reconnected with some I had already known in San Francisco and then Portland, both of which had their own small activist/psychiatric survivor community of sorts, but they were generally (with exceptions I'm sure) less rooted, less resourced, not quite off the ground and were more like budding communities of people who mostly didn't yet know each other very well. And perhaps it was me who was new and didn't know these communities very well yet.

After moving between San Francisco and Portland a couple of

times, back and forth, back and forth (not recommended, not for the faint of heart), I found myself longing to live in a small town again and following one friend and sublet opportunity, landed myself here in Olympia, Washington, where I'm finally in a longer term home.

It took me a few months to feel settled enough here to initiate something new. After moving over a dozen times in less than half a dozen years, I was very tired at times and needed to focus simply on the essentials of survival and maintenance.

There were a few individual psychiatric survivors and activists I knew here in Olympia, and I continued to meet more (it's mathematical), yet it seemed there was no actual psychiatric survivor community grassroots "movement" here, and my initial intention was to start one (not because Olympia is more ripe for this than any other college town, but because it's where I ended up).

Screening a Film

I knew very few people here and can be shy as often as bold, so my initial impulse was to screen Daniel Mackler's Coming Off Psych Drugs and start a discussion afterward, so the film could speak for me.

My friend and I had created a bare bones Olympia website and Facebook page, and I asked around about screening venues. A community cafe agreed to host our screening and I spread the word via a Facebook event and fliers around town, and through a woman I met who runs the yoga collective at Evergreen College.

Even though I've been to and organized countless events like this before, for this one I had no idea if 3 or 50 people would show up, since I had so few connections here. It ended up being 23. I brought all of the psychiatric survivor community literature I've held onto after so many moves in a single car up and down the coast, each time needing to downsize further (only 2 boxes worth).

The film was well received; the crowd felt like kindred spirits. Two organizers came all the way from Mindfreedom Seattle. So, in the end I felt very supported in this effort, but throughout the planning and organizing process I felt pretty alone and had no idea if many people would even show up. Still, I knew that this topic impacts so many people that it was at least worth a try to create a psychiatric survivor community (anywhere).

It made me realize that there are so many towns and cities out there without psychiatric survivor communities with survivors who feel alone, or like the only people who "get it" are online.

Just like there are psychiatrists offices and psychiatric wards in most every town and city, and many medicated people, there must be movements of psychiatric survivor community building activists in each of these places too.

I realize now how hard it is to start a movement "alone", but with the films and books we have available, we can feel less alone. Screening a film allows you to let the movement and other psychiatric survivor community activists in other places speak with you, and even for you, so I highly recommend that as an icebreaker and a way to initiate discussion (and am ever grateful to the filmmakers and their work!).

Budding Communities

Despite my initial doubts and insecurities, I can already feel a great group of people gathering to birth a psychiatric survivor community in Olympia, and have made some good friends now by taking the risk.

There must be at least one person like me in every city and town, who feels alone in their passion, who has a story to share, who's been connected to the psychiatric survivor community movement virtually for some time, and who can step forward to start a local psychiatric survivor community by screening a film, giving a talk or leading a discussion.

It always does help to have at least one or two collaborators, but isn't entirely necessary. If you have supporters online and in other locations, they can help you plan your events, and before you know it you will have people in your area to help. Bringing in speakers to visit or join by video chat is another way to collaborate in an area where there isn't a movement yet.

Most of us need local, face to face psychiatric survivor community, even while online connections can be valuable too, and of course some people are limited in their capacity to come to live events.

I truly believe, though, that when we talk about a grassroots movement, we need to cover as much of the actual grass as possible. We need to sit and stand and even hold hands and hug, in person, in our local geography.

Rather than allowing big pharma to divide and conquer us, we need to create united fronts of true connection, and we need them everywhere.

Here again is a list of alternatives to psychiatry Facebook groups to join for support.

Re-Occupy the Mind

Occupy Psychiatry Discussion Group

Psychiatric Revolution

NARPA

Coming Off Psych Drugs

Orange Dot

Life Beyond SSRI Antidepressants - Prozac, Effexor and many more

FREEDOM FROM PSYCH DRUGS

Women Envisioning Change

Mad Pride

Psychiatric Drugs destroy Life

ALL AGAINST PSYCHIATRIST ABUSES

MENTAL HEALTH ACTION REFORM GROUP AUSTRALIA (MHARG)

Stop the psychiatric drugging of the elderly

Free Thinking About Psychiatric Drugs

Repealing Mental Health Laws

Mad Pride India

Psychs

Speak Out Against Psychiatry

OccuPsy: Critical Psychology for Decolonization

Recovering our Stories

Un-Diagnosing Emotional Distress

Note: When you join alternatives to psychiatry Facebook groups, you may get a lot of notifications if you don't adjust the settings. You can choose to be notified of all posts, only your friends posts or not at all. Click on "Notifications" in the group to make your choice.

There is also a psychiatric drug withdrawal and recovery community on Twitter, which you can find by following psychiatric survivors and activists and then following the people who like and retweet their tweets.

Freedom From Psych Drugs Support Groups

Jennifer Bryant Roeder started a support group in Colorado for people coming off psychiatric drugs. Here is their preamble, which she offered to anyone to use if you'd like to start a group:

Welcome to 'Freedom From Psych Drugs' support group! We are a fellowship of men and women who share our experience, strength and hope with each other, that we may discuss our common issues

and help others to recover from the effects of psychiatric drugs. We have no affiliation with any medical establishments, political, religious or law enforcement organizations. We do not wish to engage in any controversy, nor do we endorse nor oppose any causes. Anyone may join us regardless of race, sexual identity, creed, or denomination. The only requirement for membership is a desire to be psychiatric drug-free. Our group is for those who are tapering psych drugs and also for those who are no longer taking them. Members must be 18 or older to join.

Our meetings begin with 'check-ins' while allowing new members to go first to qualify themselves. Each person shares for about 5-10 minutes about how they are doing in their tapering process, such as current withdrawal symptoms, improvements made, goals to achieve, helpful resources discovered, etc...while always keeping the focus on psych drug recovery. Questions are welcomed during shares, as long as the discussion returns to the person sharing. We speak for ourselves without imposing our tapering process onto others, always keeping in mind our different biological and personal histories. What works for one person might not work for another.

Tapering off psychiatric drugs can be disabling and even life-threatening for someone who comes off too fast or stops cold turkey. Psych drug-wise professionals suggest tapering 5-10% every 2-4 weeks, depending on symptoms and how one is able to tolerate them. There are many reliable sources available that offer safe tapering instructions and support, such as: survivingantidepressants.com for anti-depressants/other psych drugs, and benzobuddies.org for Benzodiazepines.

We also offer a list of additional resources to help.

We are each responsible for what we take from the meetings, how we use the information shared, and for our own tapering plan. We are not doctors or therapists, nor are we an advice forum. The opinions and experiences related here are not intended to be a substitute for professional medical advice, nor do we assert in any way to be qualified to act in this capacity. It is imperative that each and every person considering this approach solicit the professional opinion of their medical provider(s) regarding the potential benefits and risks of embarking upon this process.

We will incur no liability in regards to how each member chooses to utilize the resources offered through this group. For any medical emergencies, please call 911. For suicidal ideation, please call 1-800-784-2433.

Who you see here, what you hear here, when you leave here, let it *stay here.*

Workbook
Questions for Reflection:

- Which ways of connecting with the larger movement of psychiatric survivors appeal to you now?

　
　
　
　
　

- Which would you like to do sometime in the future?

　
　
　
　
　

- Which have you already tried?

- What benefits have they yielded in your life?

  _____
  _____
  _____
  _____
  _____
  _____

- What have the challenges been?

  _____
  _____
  _____
  _____
  _____
  _____
  _____

- Do you get inspiration from the movement or reading about the history of psychiatric resistance?

  _____
  _____
  _____
  _____
  _____
  _____

- Are you an inspiration to others? How?

- What's one thing you want to do next to feel more connected to the larger movement of psychiatric survivors?

CHAPTER 10

FINDING MEANINGFUL WORK (OR CREATING YOUR OWN)

Psychiatric Survivors In Business

Many psychiatric survivors have created a gift economy of sorts in offering peer support, and this is by no means to criticize those offering their best guidance freely to those who desperately need it.

In fact, the gift economy saved my life when it was threatened by psychiatric drugs. Most of us who have come off psychiatric pharmaceuticals relied on the generosity of other survivors who were operating in the gift. The more conventional economy alternative health systems sometime fail us and freely given peer support gives us something to be a part of, where we can give back right away, without any barriers to entry, financial or otherwise.

Yet, my entrepreneurial spirit, as chaotic and unsophisticated as it has been at times, has played a huge role in saving me from being a chronic mental patient with a chronic identity of "sick" or "failure" or "other". I still feel the weight of all three of these words at times, but my persistence in redefining myself and re-assigning value to what I offer others has allowed me to give the most back and escape psychiatry.

As a kid, I started my first entrepreneurial venture in fourth grade, selling handmade paper fans on the street with my friends. We hand colored regular paper with crayons in a checkered design, folded them into fans and stood out on the street offering them for a small amount of change, 10 cents, a quarter. When business got slow, I went to the corner store and bought a pack of gum to create a new deal, "Buy a fan get a free stick of gum!" For 10 cents, a 5 cent piece of gum and a paper fan that took about a half hour to make by a child, was in fact a great deal!

I wasn't selling these fans for pocket change, or even for something to do with my friends. I was selling them because I wanted to be somehow part of the flow of the economy; I wanted an adult with a pocketbook to value my "art" and pay me for it, in the currency they consider valuable. And a few did in fact buy our fans.

I bring this up because many psychiatric survivors may receive government funding or have a job in the system or get money from their family and not necessarily need to sell their art or services to sustain themselves (though let's face it, most are living in extreme poverty, and a higher income would make a huge difference in quality of life and "recovery" from trauma, abuse and psychiatric warfare). In either case, for most of us, there is a need to have our offerings valued by society, even if it starts out in very small ways. For people who work within the system, or elsewhere, at a J. O. B., great, I just happen to be more excited about the emergence of PSEs, Psychiatric Survivor Entrepreneurs.

Like many undervalued and oppressed groups such as women, immigrants, people of color, and differently abled people of all kinds, as psychiatric survivors we tend to downplay our offerings and have trouble expressing our worth in standard societal terms. After all, we were told that we not only didn't have value, but were a burden on the mainstream as our talents expressed themselves in sensitivity, extreme feelings and "anti-social" behaviors others didn't like or considered bizarre.

The same is true for many creative entrepreneurs, even the most successful ones, especially the most successful ones. It's an age old truth that our genius lies in our madness; I have met some of the smartest people, the wisest prophets and the greatest healers in my work with psychiatric survivors over the years. Many of these people are fairly unknown and undiscovered. The question is not whether we have value to contribute to society, though of course many stay stuck internalizing the psychiatric oppression that they don't for many years, or even their entire lives for those who over-identify as chronically mentally ill.

It breaks my heart to see so many in our community living in dire poverty, even those who clearly have copious amounts of value for others. I have seen this class/status/social standing piece divide the activist movement: those who have moved out of oppressive systems to a large degree, "above," and those for whom financial insecurity and lack contributes to depression, anxiety and despair, "below".

Psychiatric survivors who know they have important things to share with the world, in any capacity, need to GO FOR IT; participate in the mainstream economy and offer your gifts for a good amount. It may take awhile to transition off of SSI and food stamps, but I believe that is a good goal for those who aspire to it. My own transition was scary and at times overwhelming; I had days I was wrought with despair that I had so little money and financial security. It angered me from a very deep place that as a woman, "mad person", healer, intuitive, visionary, writer and artist, I was caught in a negative feedback loop of feeling unworthy, unappreciated and stuck hiding what I could give because it scared me so much to be seen. There are many millions of people out there like me who have been labeled useless by society, who have so much value for all of us.

Before that I also used government money as a "salary," though small, to support others in withdrawal, and for those doing the same, great, AND I'd like to see you making more money, being more integrated into "success culture," to fully and thoroughly leave behind the outcast identity.

The current economic system is not a great one, most of us can agree to that, but it is the one we have at the moment and as people labeled "mad", one of the best ways to integrate our vision into mainstream culture is to have them pay us for it. Because it isn't really about us and them; there's never been a certain group of crazy people and other normal people who are functioning better. This is a myth that is held in place by financial inequality. As people are valued financially and socially, the "crazy" identity no longer holds them down, and they are then able to give back to those most in need of the innovative ideas and ways that made them crazy in the first place (the genius in their madness).

The good news is you can move from "crazy weirdo living on the fringes" to valued visionary who connects the dots for others, bringing them relief, peace, joy, inspiration and magic, all of the things we humans value the most. I look forward to seeing a new category of consultants, coaches and healers emerge from the psychiatric survivor pool, who learn to offer their gifts in the mainstream economy, for an amount they can live well on, because we will be some of the most important game changers out there. We also have latent business skills many haven't discovered yet being trapped in "peer roles" for so long.

Don't get me wrong, I love the peer support model. I love friendship, community and free giving and receiving from fellow humans, but I think many of us are too good at that, at the expense of our own health and thriving, and at the expense of making a larger difference in the world by being more visible in the standard mainstream economy. We do need money, the great majority of us, especially to heal from psychiatric abuse, and I'm excited to see us step into professional roles where we are visible to more people.

Being visible can be terrifying. Saying I am charging money for something that challenges the pharmaceutical industry can make me feel not only vulnerable to criticism and ridicule, but scared for my life. I got this comment on reddit yesterday: "Dude she is an anti-med herb healer whose endorsed by an esthetician with some kind of PhD. If you want some non-med ways to fight psychosis there are some good ones by science professors with schizophrenia," (and wanted to correct their grammar-it's who's not whose).

The witch hunt still exists as a consciousness within most of us. Offering healing and guidance that isn't backed yet by corporate "science" is scary; we have been killed for it, we could easily be ostracized for redefining science, for snatching it back as what it originally meant, from the Latin, scire and then scientia: to know, assurance of knowledge, certitude, certainty. Not to guess and present hypothesis as fact, but to know. I've always felt an affinity with the word science, and hurt by how it is misused, because what do we know? We know what we know, knowledge is mystical and mysterious more than it is based on measurable phenomenon. Perhaps we don't truly know anything and "science" is a moving target that each person must define for themselves, in each moment, incorporating every part of reality they have access to, including the intuitive and ineffable. Science incorporates a lot more feeling and sensing than "modern science" would like to allow for, and it's this type of knowing that has helped me most as a psychiatric survivor, entrepreneur and business owner.

Where I Sit Between Worlds

I realized this in the shower:
I can "be myself",
meaning, I can do what I feel drawn to
and skip what doesn't work for me,
and there will be people who need me as me.
I can present myself authentically,
with all of my sensitivities, trauma, in-process things, health concerns,
and there will still be people who need me
and they will find me more easily when I present myself honestly.
Isn't that amazing?
I just want to write forever!
People say you can't make money that way,
imply that's not a service or a job or work
yet the more I keep "indulging" myself,
and allowing myself to write forever,
the more I attract people who do need me,
either who need my writing, my inspiration, or who I am as a result of writing,
which satisfies, grounds and interests me like nothing else.
It excites me,
when I write;

I'm on the edge of my own seat as to what I'll write next
and it can feel like listening to a great song.
 Today the sun shines down on me and I'm up and outside writing
more and earlier than usual.
The wind gently blows grass blades which are still wet with morning dew
and my hair still wet from my morning shower,
and when the wind settles,
the sun settles on me,
warming my legs and cheek and the back of my ear.
 It's like the winds blow through my ear, telling me things,
telling you things,
knowing what's next, what to worry about, what not to.
It's my earth and air and fire and water,
my blue sky and garden flowers,
hawks squawking whenever they want to,
breeze blowing the heat of the sun off my cheek and shoulder,
as if to remove the weights that have been put on me,
or that I've held onto.
 It's been this way from a young age.
This pen, this notebook,
the spider's web weaving around me,
only seen when the wind blows it from the shade into the sunlight,
and then it disappears again,
and smaller birds are tweeting,
nibbling out their sounds just like they do every morning.
 This is where I sit between worlds,
my favorite place to be,
singing like a canary,
smelling like a rose,
swimming while only moving one hand,
breathing so much air while the peckers have their own tunes.
 How do we know, how are we so sure we aren't here to wake up
each day and make music,
and listen for our songs
and be still sometimes like tomato vines,
and exist like the rest of creation,
flying in circles and spirals,
singing out in spurts?
How are we so sure?
How are we so sure?

   If you are starting your own business, or have one, don't demand the Universe pay you in money. The Universe WILL pay you when you follow your life mission, no question, but that payment can look like a wide variety of things: free stuff, free housing, luxurious travel gifted to you, money for your services, money from other channels and sources. Stay open to how the world wants to pay you, and you will always live in abundance.

Let go of any sense that you should be a slave or that you "have to work for your money" or your "living." Work should be enjoyable, meaningful, healing (for you as well as others) and empowering. If you believe work needs to be hard, painful and drudgery, just watch the world intervene and teach you how to let go and play.

Choose freedom. bliss and enjoyment without guilt. You should never feel guilty for being happy, lucky or prosperous, nor should you limit where that joy or prosperity can come from. If you demand only to be paid in money, you will severely limit your prosperity, and it will be coming from your ego.

Yes we are living in a world where, for many of us, money is necessary for living, but we are also living in a world of tremendous abundance to be gleaned and had outside the money realm entirely. Be humble. By receiving some of your income from sources other than money, you are almost surely saving a piece of the earth. You are almost definitely minimizing pain in others and preventing the WASTING of time, labor and resources, which money has mastered.

The amazing thing about taking some of your business outside of the money realm is that you end up feeling more connected. You give your gifts that connect you and receive others' gifts that connect them. Here's how to do it:

1 Follow your Bliss.

Spend most of your waking and working hours doing things you would do for free (or are doing for free). Don't spend more than 10% of your day doing something for money that you hate to do or would never do otherwise. At least have this as your long term goal, if you can't do it right away.

2 Stay awake to "payment" in all its forms.

Receive well. Accept the abundance of free stuff that is available. Connect with the ever increasing networks of clothing and stuff swaps, food rescuing, DIY learning, sharing, potlucks, crowd funding, free-cycling, donations and gifts of all kinds. The other day I found $40 on the street! If resources are what you need, open up to creative ways of receiving them in abundance.

3 Continue to create no matter what.

Commit to the creative practices you love. Don't let any notion of lack stop you. Creativity has a certain "Don't mess with me" undercurrent (even while expressing vulnerability) that you will tap into and strengthen every time you take action.

My Own Work Transition

On New Year's Day, 2013, I woke up crying and angry. I was emerging from a 3 week long cough which finally ended when I broke up with the guy I'd been seeing. I'd gotten this horrible cough (which landed me in the emergency room due to asthma) while working a new job at a Montessori day care, which, despite everyone's enthusiasm about Montessori, clearly didn't have my name on it. I knew I had a different mission in 2013.

Someone I'd been dating had been on a mood stabilizer for about 10 years after addiction, alcoholism and other things resulted in him being labeled and identifying as bipolar. I didn't know any of this when I met him. He was a math professor, a gym junkie and one of the most charismatic people I had met in awhile. I adored him and will never know whether or to what extent the mood stabilizer was the cause of certain things he experienced or didn't experience, despite being a sensitive, intelligent, attractive and spiritually focused person. There were things about him I knew pretty well were caused by the drug to some degree, which he was the first to bring up, yet to him there was no safety in going off the drug.

I say all this about him to illustrate the nuances of psychiatric drug harm. Most of us would agree that those on 7 drugs who are basically incapacitated would be better off without them or on far less of them. We probably also all know at least one somebody who is on just one mood stabilizer or antidepressant who says the drug helps them and they can't live without it. I've been in love with individuals in both camps. And who are we to tell someone what to do or even what we think of their choice if they haven't asked? This question isn't as easy as it seems if you love someone and they are taking substances that nearly killed you and have killed others you loved. Still, the humble part of me knows I can never ultimately declare what is best for someone else, what will save their life, what will kill them.

It's amazing how much life or death conversation and thinking psych drugs inspire. In a way this seems to miss the point since our lives are obviously about something far more profound than weird chemical combinations that we don't understand. Yet they are what our first-world society has in place to respond to the life or death existential (and holy) questions and crises people tackle.

There's something about life or death existential crises that interest me like nothing else. They are like nuts that need to be cracked open, that have good food and nectar inside if we don't fear them. Of course we do fear them. Yet shying away from any question out of fear eventually leads us to despair.

So after this relationship, this 3 week long cough, this failed attempt to work in preschool for 40 hours a week for $9/hour, I knew I needed to devote 2013 to what mattered most to me-moving towards these questions with others equally interested. I knew there were many people who wanted to live without psych drugs, or with less of them, and to come closer to the questions that provide us with nourishment if we can brave them in supportive community. I knew I wanted to be a resource for all of those people. My tremendous suffering from my own existential holy despair was designed to go to good use.

Up until January 1, 2013, I had done most of my "mental health" work under men who had started groundbreaking organizations. These men had helped so many people with their courage, intelligence, vulnerability and willingness to share their lived experience of breaking free of the mental health system, creating support networks and finding holistic health alternatives and other resources. They had inspired me, believed in me, given me opportunities, taught me a lot and in some cases been role models. Yet working "under" them or for them had gotten harder and harder for me, and eventually became intolerable.

Working under them and being paid by them meant I could hardly ever execute my own ideas without running them by these leaders. In December 2012, I fell into a pit of near suicidal despair at being *told* what to do rather than consulted and by January 2013 I finally knew what I needed to do to get out of it. I needed to start my own teaching and coaching business, which I'd had as a side project for several years but never fully invested in.

Working as my own leader and guide that year, I was able to offer certain services that I never would have had the confidence to express in my own words if I still had to answer to an older, more experienced, more educated man. I am quite susceptible to second guessing myself (as well as being second guessed) when I am in that position. I dreamed of bringing my intuitive and healing gifts and skills into supporting those who are choosing to come off or stay off psych drugs.

My dreams that came true that year showed me so much about being a psychiatric survivor, a leader and a voice of change. They showed me how important taking action on our dreams really is, how I will never believe I can do something until I do it first, and that anything is possible.

They showed me how our biggest offerings to others often lie tangled up in what the mental health system would call our illness. They showed me how important it is to never ever stop dreaming and envisioning life as I'd like to see it. I probably touched several thousand people that first year alone year in some way with my writing, speaking, classes, website and coaching (none of which I could have done without the help of many others).

This is such a small amount in the grand scheme of things, and how many people have lost all hope in the hands of psychiatry, or who's self perception has been severely cropped and limited by a label. I also know that no dream I have is mine alone and I could not have had any of my successes without the help and support of others, which was abundant, and which I believe will always be abundant when we follow our dreams.

As I sit here, writing at a desk, as I do every morning with a cup of tea, I glance over at the label on the tea bag, which says, "dream." Amidst all of the oppression we face, I would like to keep coming back to that word.

The testimonials I received are evidence to me that every once in awhile our dreams come true. Every now and again believing in our dreams, against all odds and all conventional thought, can work. Having belief in ourselves from that all knowing place that is stronger than any opinion, label or judgment is sometimes all we have. And all we need. Until we find ourselves among those who see us, know us at our essence, and believe in us, once again.

Disability Identity

Has American culture cornered artists and healers into identifying as "disabled"? Is a diagnosis and the benefits that come with it one of the best strategies for being funded? Is a disability manifestation of a need for money and time as an artist or healer?

I find myself asking these questions because, let's face it, only the most business-savvy artists and healers can get by on their work and gifts alone. That's why many of them choose, consciously or unconsciously, to accept a disability diagnosis. Being sick seems the only socially acceptable excuse, especially as a young person who is not yet established, for living one's life as an artist or healer.

While some can play the game, compromise, and fit their art/gifts into corporate America, many cannot and I'd venture to guess that's why we're losing some of the most valuable members of society to illness. Now that "mental illness" is diagnosed so readily and often arbitrarily based on who has the prescription pad (if I had one I'd diagnose almost all psychiatrists), being abled or disabled is clearly a matter of perspective. This is a controversial way of framing disability,

I am aware, but please bear with me as I continue to explain why ability and disability are culturally defined and far from easily determined.

Let's start with the question of value, which I believe is an important place to start when discussing mental health (or anything for that matter). Do we want a world that values what is essential to us? Or will we continue to play along with the idea that warfare and patriarchal politics, medicine and education are working for us? You may say "I'm not playing along with those notions," but if you believe in mental illness, you actually are, without even realizing it.

If there were funding for arts would "ability" suddenly spike and disability fall? The only problem would be a simultaneous fall in drug company profits, so let's not talk about that.

When I hear people talk about disability rights and access, I have mixed feelings. On one hand, I'm deeply relieved that being differently-abled can be spoken of. I certainly don't function highly as a cog in the American machine and if I were told I had to I would become quickly disabled. Yet with the paradigm shift of diverse-ability, I believe no one is disabled, at least not as a primary identity. Dis-abled means lacking in abilities and we all have abilities (as well as things we cannot do, of course). Moreover, we all have exactly the abilities we need to fulfill our unique life purpose.

People who are considered the highest functioning in American culture such as politicians, lawyers, medical doctors (including psychiatrists), major league sport players, etc., all lack certain abilities that I possess (and, of course, vice-versa). Are their abilities actually the real ones and mine "soft," surreal, abstract, inaccessible and useless? With due humility, I must say no. I must defend that my abilities and yours, and all of ours, are either of equal, greater or immeasurable merit and value.

Is imagination a soft skill and major league baseball a hard human need? Is love useless and war necessary? Is beauty an indulgence and and punishment a requirement for the survival of our species? Is mental expansion woo woo and corrupt data funded by pharmaceutical companies the science that is saving our lives? Is peace extravagant but complex, abstract computer simulations sophisticated and worthy of funding?

It all comes down to worth and who is determining worth and who has been determining it for as long as we can remember. In order to redefine health, we must redefine worth. Are you sure the "abled" are able to accomplish what you value? Are you sure the "disabled" aren't more able to heal the world?

Since there is quite a bit more funding in America for those diagnosed disabled than for those who call themselves artists and healers, we need to look at our value system. Of course it is important to put value on supporting those who are sick, injured or otherwise suffering. Many of us seem to agree on that as a basic premise, but have we ever asked ourselves why this is a value we share? The easy answer is, out of sympathy, empathy and compassion for our brothers and sisters. But is that the only answer?

I'd like to propose a balancing addition to that answer, which is healthy self-interest and concern for the evolution of our species. To become disabled is to-at least temporarily-take a break from business as usual. Some religions and traditions consider illness or disability a blessing and an opportunity for healing. True healing is not only healing of one's own body and mind, but healing of the interconnected web of humanity, healing of how we relate with one another.

So I venture to guess that the underlying motive in supporting those with disabilities that render them "less useful" in current culture is to pave the way for progress. And if it isn't it should be. Charity alone, without believing in the potential of those receiving the charity, is useless. We must be giving "handouts" because we believe in the abilities of those receiving them. We believe they do or will have something to offer and it is worth helping them stay alive. If this fundamental belief isn't recognized, charity can become an ego boosting mechanism of the "abled," who are projecting their own insecurities about their ever so important corporate and business savvy abilities onto those with abilities they don't understand.

Ironically these overlooked abilities are necessary if we are to survive (and thrive) as humanity.

When I was 21 I took a year off from my expensive liberal arts college to enter the mental health system against my will. Being on psych drugs (up to 7 at a a time) disabled me by almost all possible conventional standards. I was a classic case of dysfunctionality, unable to walk, read, communicate or think clearly. (Ironically some of my best poetry and songs came to me at that time). It was at this time that my mom applied for Social Security disability income for me, incumbent upon the fact that I was without a doubt "clinically" disabled. I started to receive payments of around $700 per month, plus free health insurance, which covered therapy (until I quit) and doctors' visits, and enabled me to live without receiving money from my parents after a while.

I slowly withdrew from the drug cocktail and, at about the same pace, regained a lot of abilities. In a few years I was writing and self-publishing books, teaching yoga, fundraising, dancing, hiking, traveling around the country presenting at conferences, doing childcare, singing, acting in plays, entering into relatively healthy romantic relationships and friendships, and making side money equal to and then greater than the amount I was receiving from Social Security.

At what point was I no longer "disabled?" Since the only disability that seemed real to me was that caused by the "medicine" doctors gave me, I had a conundrum. It was important to me not to identify as disabled, yet I was still the person I always have been: able to do some things very well, other things so-so and other things not at all.

The SSI checks I received each month brought up feelings of embarrassment and secrecy, while at the same time substantially supported me to live my dreams, develop talents and hobbies, spend less hours working for money and still save a considerable amount, living a simple life.

I believe all artists, healers and teachers deserve these things. In fact I believe all people deserve this luxury. "Do what you love and the money will follow" became so true for me -yet I saw my amazing artist and healer friends who didn't receive $700 extra per month struggling financially in ways I didn't have to worry about. I was concerned about receiving this money, concerned it would limit me, but the main thing about it that limited me was asking myself if I deserved it.

Returning to the abled/disabled discussion, there were and are many many things I was and am unable to do. I have less strength and stamina for physical labor than most people I know. Yet I taught 5 yoga classes a week for awhile, some pretty vigorous. Being in nearly any kind of 9-5 office environment is not possible for me. I have extreme allergies that keep me from being in a variety of locations. If I'm not doing something I love, I get more tired more quickly than many others.

I don't have the ability to work with other people all day. I can't work in a noisy environment much. Keeping to a schedule that isn't entirely self-designed is almost impossible for me. I can't work in environments that contain cigarette smoke. I have many dis-abilities.

I also write more than almost anyone I know and write things that move many people regularly. I am highly intuitive and tell people things about themselves and the world that are just the very things they need to hear to move forward with confidence in their purpose. I have a healing presence and many people feel calmed, eased, and inspired when they come to my classes, listen to be speak, or read my writing. I have many more great abilities, but rather than continue to toot my own horn, I'll say I'm incredibly grateful to have had "disability" income. It enabled me to nurture and expand these abilities when I was young, impressionable, and didn't have the confidence to share these offerings in ways that would have brought me abundant money for them directly.

About 9 years ago as of this writing, I decided to go off of SSI. I had a meeting at the Social Security office in San Francisco where I had just moved. The worker asked me if I'm still disabled and I said, "I don't know." I knew of my abilities and disabilities as mentioned above. I knew I have the kind of ability/disability scorecard that doesn't always make it easy to live in this world financially. Yet, I wanted to be honest, and part of me was tired of living with this secret money. I decided to have faith in being honest.

That decision not only lost me my monthly check, but resulted in Social Security claiming I owed them $12,000 for saving more than $2,000 in my bank account. I'd had more than $2,000 in my bank account for nearly 10 years, but they had never noticed. My credit score went from almost 800 to under 600 over the next couple of years as I couldn't afford to pay back the $12,000, or really anything between my San Francisco rents and my full time job relocating to Arizona (while I stayed in California).

I was not especially more abled or disabled. I did feel good about having come clean and it has been a struggle to not have that support. I haven't had health insurance or travel money in several years, but life has given me incredible donation based alternative health resources and some good travel opportunities that were funded. I have had nights of tension, tears and fear about money. It has been harder to relate with the wealthy people in my family who don't know what it's like.

In the end, I feel some satisfaction in putting myself out into the world more, offering my gifts and having faith that the money and/or resources will follow. I would like to see a world that supports diverse-ability. I would like funding to go to artists, healers and other peacemakers so we can all identify as "able" and have the abundant resources we all deserve!

In the meantime, I accept and respect all people who receive SSI, as it is one of the few areas of funding provided by the government that generally does more good than harm, I believe, giving those of us with unique abilities resources to stay alive. I still hope for a way to offer this money and more to people, without requiring them to identify with what they can't do.

Creative Blocks

My work with many clients has showed me that creative blocks often get diagnosed as mental illness so being able to recognize and break through them can be life saving. It can even keep people from suicide.

Something important is consistency, having a daily creative practice that is done no matter what. Mine is daily writing every morning.

Daily meditation and walks are helpful. I've had years of creative blocks but when you do daily creative practices no matter what, all of a sudden, the brilliant aha moment will come.

It's important for creative people not to pressure themselves too much or push too hard, because ironically, trying too hard or getting impatient can lead to creative blocks. But most truly creative people know that the good stuff will come through when it does and we mostly need to be there with a net to catch it.

The most important secret to releasing creative blocks is to take care of yourself: your body, mind and spirit. Then the universe will know you are ready for more inspiration and art to come through.

Cleaning and organizing can help. Every time I clean my car or my closet or basement, new creative inspiration happens. Looking the other way from the creative work is absolutely essential to breaking through.

Eating well, spending time with friends, even getting extra sleep can really help. Creativity doesn't exist in a vacuum, so blocks must be seen holistically. They are sometimes there because you need time to percolate or discuss the matter with someone else.

The people with the most creative blocks are the perfectionists who will never share their creativity or even create anything because it isn't "perfect". By practicing your creativity a little every single day, totally imperfectly, purely out of your own need to, you will set yourself up to beat any creative blocks, and more importantly, have faith while you are blocked, because you have proven to yourself that you will prevail against all odds.

On Being a Healer

What is healing? How do we respond when someone says they are sick or implies they have a problem in need of healing?

Gosh these questions have disturbed me since I was a child and the answer was a spoonful of pink sugary amoxicillin or some pill to swallow, amidst still unhappy circumstances.

What is healing? How is it we can have entire medical systems that fail to answer, or even ask, this fundamental question?

Is healing even our goal? And what does it look like?

From dictionary.com:
adjective
1. curing or curative; prescribed or helping to heal.
2. growing sound; getting well; mending.
noun

3. the act or process of regaining health:

a new drug to accelerate healing.

Healing is also a verb. We are in the process of healing, perhaps, though many people do not feel they are healing, but rather becoming more fragmented, hidden, fearful, resentful, alienated, in pain, etc. as they move through the world, as the years go by and there's more burden on the organs in their bodies and the systems that function (or fail to) outside of themselves.

Does it make sense to have entire systems of medicine, government, education, and even religion of people who don't have common mindsets, goals or even definitions of basic words like "healing"?

I can hardly remember a time when I trusted the general population or even most of those around me, instinctively. I've felt levels of trust for individuals, and even more so at times for mt life path, or life itself, but this has required a certain, often large, level of retreat from the "outside world".

Healing is not simple, or linear. To demand healing happen in a linear fashion is to be as aggressive as what caused the injury.

Anger implies caring, it implies investment in the world, a relationship, something.

Apathy, on the other hand, implies detachment, disinterest, not caring, not investing, and perhaps there is a well of anger underneath, anger that has lost hope, anger that has been lost, drifted away at sea, let go of, because the world doesn't seem worth investing in. Because things are too far gone: relationships are beyond repair, health problems are beyond reversibility, the earth has been too disregarded, the feminine has no voice, the child no space or place or protection or freedom. There's no real "help" anywhere.

Now, I'm one who has long said, "Anything's possible." This has been my *healing* mantra, if you will. I still believe it when I contemplate deeply; I still believe that with proper intentions, belief and healing, relationships, the earth, our bodies, society can all be transformed and restored.

But as time goes on, as I grow in years and life experiences, some possibilities seem so unlikely to me that I naturally discount their potential. We all do this everyday and call it sanity, though it is only half sane and only a limited idea of what sanity could be.

Ultimately it becomes less and less sane if less and less seems possible and we are severely limited by what we think our own and other's potential is on a daily basis.

If "healing" means fitting in or blending with a social order I hate, I will resist healing, I will choose to be sick. In fact I would prefer to be home "sick" many days over out there in our current culture.

Sick or healthy or *healing* I often prefer solitude or very specific gatherings to the random chaos of life in an aggressive society I despise. (Yes, I am using words like hate and despise more freely than I have before.)

My body reflects this hatred, this lack of trust, this feeling unsafe, this sense of limitation, this feeling of aloneness, this growing apathy inside of me.

My face reflects something else.

Often when I look at my face, I'm surprised to see it looks quite nice, like a "healing" person, like a healer, like someone with medicine.

The body doesn't lie in either case. I am distraught and beyond hope or anger or investment in this world most of the time, which I feel in my body, and I do transform this disconnection into a mysterious medicine every day, which my face shows.

Part of "being" medicine (a.k.a healing) is that you offer something beautiful because you have composted a lot of pain, a lot of falsity, a lot of bullshit, aggression, apathy, power imbalances, and so much more. You've sifted through it all daily.

You've sat with it, mixed it all up in your mixing bowl and now it's food, it's pretty, it's nourishing even to look at because you've made space for the medicine.

I don't know if what I do could rightfully be called "inner work"; I think of it more like retreating and making space for medicine to manufacture through me, inside of me.

So I make medicine and I am a healer, not exactly out of any process of formal education, but straight from the source of medicine- the working through of what disturbs me most, the alchemizing of my hatred, apathy, disinterest, even victimization, sense of being abused, oppressed and unfairly judged.

I do carry a certain healing frequency at times, a lightness, a holding of complexity, an open channel, a clear seeing awareness. This is simultaneously the hardest and easiest thing about being me: a kind medicinal face with insides that are often collapsing with agony.

Enter at your own risk. Heal in your own way. Make your own medicine; healers need healing too.

How to Get Money If You're Poor, How to Get Soul if You're Rich

Due to inequality in the world, if you have a lot of money and resources, others have parts of your soul. If you don't have money, property or assets, you have parts of other people's souls they need to pay you for.

Same with health. If you are very healthy, people who are sick have parts of your soul you can retrieve by helping them. If you are sick, you have parts of healthy people that they need and can get by helping you, healing you.

We need to use our money, if we have it, to buy our soul back as much as possible, so, to buy the soul offerings of others, especially others in need of money. This will create balance in society.

Workbook
Questions for Reflection:

- Do you have a business idea?

　

- What type of work feels most meaningful to you (there is no right or wrong answer here)?

　

- Do you prefer variety/consistency?

- Being your own boss or being told what to do?

- What are the qualities that make work meaningful to you?

- What qualities make work enjoyable and possible for you?

- Working mostly alone or with others?

- On a predictable schedule or more flexible one?

- If you were to create your ideal work, what would it look like?

  _____
  _____
  _____
  _____

- How would you help others?

  _____
  _____
  _____
  _____

- What would they get out of it?

  _____
  _____
  _____
  _____
  _____

- How would you feel?

  _____
  _____
  _____
  _____
  _____

- What does your intuition tell you about how to bring in or attract the money and resources you need?

- Do you have old stories of unworthiness or that you don't deserve money or to live well?

- Do you believe you can "have your cake and eat it too"? Can you do work you love AND have your needs met?

CHAPTER 11

GOING PUBLIC, BEING KNOWN

Writing and Blogging

Sharing my writing with the world has been a lifelong dream and process. In elementary school I remember asking an author who came to our school for a visit how they felt when they got their first book published. My heart glowed with anticipation as I asked this, knowing, perhaps, at the age of 7 or so, that one day I would publish my own books and writing.

I also remember how exciting computers were, and later the internet. If you are a writer, artist or one who has something important to express, even if you don't know quite what form it will take yet, I encourage you to explore the many publishing opportunities on the web. They are so much faster, more democratic and more efficient, in most cases, than print publishing (which I have also done some of via self-publishing and grants). You can start by sharing your words/work with a select group of friends/colleagues on social media or by email.

I started by creating blogs on wordpress, live journal, and gather.com. You can find some of my older writings on those sites. Then I made my website and started to share my writing on Facebook.

When I wrote about the suicide of my lifelong friend Michael, Bob Whitaker invited me to publish it on Mad In America. I had a sleeping dream soon after that of becoming a regular blogger on that site. My writings were already reaching many of my friends and colleagues via facebook and my blogs and website, but blogging on Mad In America has expanded my reach substantially. As a writer who spends a great deal of time in solitude, I must say there is little more satisfying to me than knowing my words are reaching many people.

I began sending my writing to other blogs. I looked at who was publishing my friends' writing first and sent my essays to those blogs after reading their submission guidelines.

Similarly to when I used to send my poetry to magazines for submission, I felt a huge rush when my words were accepted. It reminded me of being a child and getting a good grade or finding out I got into a school. But it felt so much more real, like this success was from the ground up. It started in my spiral notebook and came directly from the source of my being and now has wings to fly to many many others. This is one of the greatest miracles I have experienced in recent days.

Privacy

When I first started blogging, people asked me if they could share my blogs on their social media pages. These are blogs I have on my website with social media sharing buttons underneath them and that I post on facebook, twitter, google plus and others on the public setting and post publicly in facebook groups full of people I don't know. Yet the people who've asked me to share them don't know me and the blogs contain personal, vulnerable information about myself that many people wouldn't feel comfortable sharing.

Some express concern about revealing publicly that they've received a mental health label or been on psychiatric drugs since a future (or current) employer, professor, or even friend or family member could see it and disafford them of an opportunity. I respect that. Some of us have a path working within systems of oppression and making a difference from inside where a certain kind of reputation may be important for a time.

I also question how much and for how long we can serve one another while simultaneously concealing our own life experiences.

This isn't a matter of judging anyone who values their privacy and personal information. There are parts of society that are so entrenched in oppression that this guarding of personal traumas, challenges and vulnerabilities is a wise decision, and one I certainly make at times, when I am enmeshed in an oppressive structure I feel dependent on for one reason or another, for a time. Still I hold to the vision of liberation, of a world where revealing is healing.

When I first emerged from the mental health system and the clutches of psychiatry, I was more careful about sharing my experiences at times as I was aware that some people would stigmatize me and see me as "other." Ironically the more I told my story publicly, the less of a concern this became. Looking back I realize this revealing was an expression of an internal commitment.

Commitment

We need to ask ourselves what we are committed to. (This will guard us from being duped by psychiatry's lies.) I wasn't even aware of how committed I was to being public and "out" about my life (and there are many things I'd like to be further "out" about). What I did know and have known since my experiences with psychiatry is that I am 100% committed to the flow of words coming through me and committed to sharing them publicly as long as it feels safe to do so.

This goes hand in hand with my commitment to "right work," which for me meant starting my own venture. And when I started it I wasn't toe dipping. It wasn't a one year experiment or a "start up" that may or may not succeed.

It succeeded from Day 1 because it was directly connected to higher guidance and a sense of knowing that it was what the world asked of me and needed of me. It's an incredible thing to know you are needed for something (which we all are), and to know it within even before anyone expresses appreciation or validation.

So without even considering it, I have had few fears of revealing myself publicly. Uncertainties and insecurities have popped up in other ways and I have an almost incessant fear/self consciousness of being judged, disliked or criticized by others doing similar work as me.

Faith

But the amazing thing about working and writing from this place is that it is a Rock. The religious phrase, "The Lord is my Rock and my Redeemer" comes to mind. It isn't about whether or not you call yourself "religious" (a word with just as complicated and corrupted connotations as "bipolar" or "schizophrenic"), but about where you find your own religion, your own Rock and Redemption, and following that. The word "Lord" can be replaced with whatever your Lord is.

Sometimes "Lord" sounds to me like an evil, destructive, commanding, punishing patriarch in a black cloak, but, letting go of those associations, my Lord is whatever guides me.

The problem with psychiatry is that it has lost sight of this truth-that we all have a Rock and Redeemer, that we are all solid in our purpose and essence and can be redeemed by our life's work whenever we lose sight of it. Instead psychiatry plays with tinsel on the margins of our real lives. It discusses less relevant things like personality traits, moods, "disorders" and matters of the ego and persona, which as humans we can all get distracted by. If you are on a path towards "redemption," or whatever you want to call being true to yourself, psychiatry, as our world conceives of it, is distracting.

Some Buddhists practice meditation and mindfulness to remember who we are. The teacher Pema Chodron says, "We forget and remember, forget and remember. That's why it's called practice." Psychiatric jargon is the forgetting of who we really are and why we are here and the best path away from psychiatric oppression and psychiatric drugs is the path of right work. You know and grow familiar with this work because it is your Rock and your Redeemer. It is unconditionally part of you. No one else can tell you what it is or isn't or who you are or aren't. This can only be determined by your own personal "Lord" who you will uncloak, de-robe and come to know more and more over time.

Story Medicine

When I was a senior in high school, my poetry class had sharing day every Friday. We were all writing poetry from our own experience, and I thought, Wow, what if all of life was like this? Heaven on Earth.

Now we have that, to some extent. That's why I'm somewhat addicted to Facebook and personal blogs. I want what I always wanted: to know you, and now I can have it with the touch of a finger, anytime, anywhere, many ones, any topic.

For real? Is this real? My 16 year old's dream come true?

Is life an open mic now? No wonder I can't scrape myself from my iPhone at night, reading all your tidbits as my bedtime stories.

Maybe it's time to accept it: we're in a phase of story excitement; we're hearing stories and perspectives we never had access to before. We're absorbing new perspectives, famished for them; we gobble them up like candy, like pasta, like soup, we are starving; we need these written accounts, they are changing us and escorting us into the new world.

We don't know what this world will be, but all of the information, stories, ideas, personal accounts of life on the margins we are devouring like hungry beasts are preparing us for it. They are showing us what's under the rocks, who people are in their homes, under their clothes and blankets.

It's a messy time; the old stories still reign, they still hold weight over us at times, but those of us who are choosing liberation are gradually but without a doubt ushering in a brand new look at humanity, at animals, at plants, at every aspect of consciousness.

None of it can continue to go invisible or mute. Everything has a voice now; it's your turn. It's our turn, and as we accept our turn, the world is turned; we will not recognize it when we are through speaking our minds for it to hear.

A lot of trauma gets stuck in our voices, and even makes it hard for us to think clearly and function if we don't speak out somehow, so blogging can be written words, audio, video, images, etc.

Whatever form it takes, we are all liberating each other. I recently wrote a blog in which I talk about how important it is for every one of us to tell our story because our stories are all wound up in everyone else's stories.

There are still some stories I don't share, mostly about my family and childhood, where I feel most silenced and by not sharing those, I'm limiting my own and other's potential.

Many of my friends are terrified to share anything at all publicly and many people haven't caught on fully to our current responsibility to make media. Blogging connects us to others, builds our movement, helps us make offerings from our pain that connect us with others and helps us find support too.

I can't say enough about the potential we have as media makers.

The thing is, we all need to do it ESPECIALLY those who are most scared. We need to take ourselves more seriously than Facebook posts; by having blogs, and eventually books, we create lasting content that others can link to, refer back to and reference later on.

The Mad In America blog site has clearly been a game changer for our movement, yet it has a certain slant and some psychiatric survivors express not feeling safe there, so we need to create our own blogs as well.

Coming Out Of Hiding

Some people associate wanting to be famous with their ego, but for me hiding is the preference of my ego. Being seen and exposed and vulnerable to the masses are purifying and healthy for me. And coincidentally they are my highest form of service to others. Being known. Because everyone who knows me in the utterly authentic way I put myself out there is likely to feel less alone.

Being known is a gift I give freely and publicly, which many do not, but it is my preference to live this way. It is my form of practicing the gift economy, to be exposed and honest, to tell others freely how my life works, so they can pick and choose which of my methods and ways resonate with them.

This revealing, I believe, is one of the biggest gifts we can offer others. I'd almost always rather hear the authentic experience of another than receive their advice. Why is this? Reading or hearing an experience makes me feel connected, and that's what brings fulfillment in life. Advice can help, but often when we're feeling connected we don't need any advice at all. We realize in these moments we aren't perfect and don't need to be. This fosters self-acceptance and acceptance of others, which just may be the starting point of the new world we are creating, as well as the antithesis of most problems in the world.

If all people accepted themselves and others, just as we are, there would be no need for psychiatric drugs or other forms of warfare. Rather, we'd be busy revealing and expressing ourselves in satisfying ways.

How is revealing healing for you? What would the world look like if we all revealed ourselves?

Not writing and owning our own story in some way wreaks havoc on those around us. We are silently killing ourselves and them, too – the part of them that is awake and listening and wants to hear from our hidden parts. This silent killing is akin to what happens when taking psychiatric drugs.

Divulging is a gift; hiding is thievery and holding back oxygen. When I am hiding or sense someone close to me is hiding, it can be hard to even breathe.

Psychiatric drugs are tools for hiding – they inhibit our breath and rob us of our healing potential and power to heal others. Any wound or darkness gives us that much more power to witness and assist in healing others. Perhaps I needed to be wounded by psychiatric pharmaceuticals, enter that darkness, in order to greater witness others.

Writing and reading are witnessing practices. I knew so when I read my friend's story at 2am and felt like a master witness. Witnessing myself so much through writing so much makes it possible to witness others when they bring forth secrets from their places of fear. I know what that's like – I recognize it. I feel the importance of liberating one's self through words, through telling, through recreating life story.

Recreating life story is so necessary as the original story we tell ourselves has to be incomplete. It has to be influenced heavily by corporate media and advertising unless we and all of our ancestors have lived under a rock. It is the story we made up based on the limitations in the minds of our family, friends and society. It is not ours until we make it ours by retelling it. Any holes we leave in our own storytelling are holes in which industries such as the mental health system can enter. Telling our own story protects us from that invasion, making it easier to see clearly when someone tries to make up a story to sell us something (i.e. a pill).

Even those with a story that looks powerful and free because they have a high social status (or for whatever reason) are bound by their untold story if they haven't recreated it, or simply told it in their own words. High status stories and low status stories are two sides of the same coin. The real story we need to tell can only be told by us. We can liberate ourselves from being status pawns in a game we imagine really exists, but doesn't except in our collective imagination.

Someone I work with once asked me, "Who am I to write/put myself out there?" At first I was stumped as to the nature of the question. In retrospect, it sounds like internalized oppression (when societal oppression enters our psyche and we use it against ourselves, sometimes without realizing it). Imagine asking a child, "Who do you think you are to sing/play/draw a picture/speak?" This would be emotionally abusive, if asked the way she asked this of herself.

It makes me wonder who asked her, directly or indirectly, "Who do you think you are?" Who implied she should have to justify her existence and right to expression? Who did they think THEY were? If someone silenced you, it's time to interrogate them. We are living in a lot of fear that is keeping our mouths shut, many of us.

I for one, have a lot to say. I've written and published a lot, but the amount I have to express and share feels endless. In my blood and veins and arteries, I hold eons of silenced women, ostracized mystics and "crazy folk." They all want to speak too. Most of us have less overt excuses than ever to write and publish and be heard. In a sense, the world wide web is at our disposal 24/7. In another sense, we may have more fear than ever, not only our own fear, but all those eons of fear, others' fear we are holding for them. I hold my parents fear, and probably their parents fear etc.

Counting Yourself

When I pick up a pen, I put down my fear. Sorry, they don't both fit into my hand at once. Meditation teachers often say the hardest part is getting to the cushion. The hardest part of writing is probably picking up the pen. So, pick up a pen, I dare you. Write even if you think no one will read it, even if you don't want anyone to read it.

Recently a woman expressed ambivalence to me about sharing her personal story of successfully coming off of benzos after being on them for about 40 years. "Who will listen?" she asked. "No one listens to me," she said. "No one listens to me either," I said and laughed because I feel truly desperate to be heard. "That's why I write."

It may seem redundant to tell one's story. We may ask ourselves, "Why bother?" or "Who will listen/read it?" It is important to make a choice – a conscious choice – about what story to tell. The mental health care crisis (and the whole health care crisis for that matter) is in large part due to lack of creativity and suppression of voice. Only suppressed creativity and a morbidly silenced voice would "choose" by default to listen to the stories of the psycho-pharmaceutical industry. This is sad. You can do your part in recreating our collective fantasy by retelling the story of your very own life. The story your soul came to tell, knowing it would liberate others.

I got validation as a writer early on-some-but it was passion and long term steady habits that gave me confidence, and eventually more consistent validation over a longer period of time.

Now the sky is clear where the rainbow was big and bright 5 minutes ago. It's like that with sexual abuse. One minute it's happening and the next it's not-the sky is clear-and you remember it so vividly but no one else can see it if you don't describe it to them. And describing a terrible thing is just as hard as describing a wonderful thing-you need photos, you need video, or you need to be a writer with the very right words, but even then they are your words, so they only count if they are counted.

Writing has always given me a place to count myself first, even if I didn't count to anyone else.

If I was known and knew I counted for who I was, I probably never would have bothered to start writing so much, to bring notebooks with me everywhere as a kid, teenager, young adult, now adult.

I've decided to count my own voice and it's made every bit of difference in my life, is one of the few things that has, consistently.

Nothing counts more than a dream except a memory-because memories birth dreams-we remember what has happened and dream of what could be.

Mastery

Though many times the words write me, like life breathes through me and paints through artists and sings through the chorus. The best is when nothing else matters-when the dream, the memory, and the moment of connecting them are one, like a union. I think this is what we call a state of "genius" or "mastery" but it only comes through facing what we were told not to face, what we were told faded 5 minutes ago and therefore may not have happened.

It only comes when we team up with the colors of the rainbow and tell all of the stories, of the things that have happened to the diversity of us.

It only comes when there's a pathway for it to be received, and a receptacle of some kind.

It only comes when its memory is stimulated in the right fashion, with the framework to hold its outpouring without shame.

It only comes when there's a pot of gold at the end of the rainbow for the gold to gather.

This is why we are all telling stories, telling stories, painting the rainbow with our multifaceted lives.

This is why we are eager to shoot across space in our splendor, in a huge arc that encompasses our whole field of vision. We've seen it behind our eyelids long enough-we need it to be vivid out there

once again. We need our boldness seen, even if we lost it long ago. It still lives as potential where the sun and the rain can meet, and proudly share what happens when they do.

None of this is abstract really. Life hands us something tangible, like clay in the palm of our hand. We pinch it.

We scream, even if silently 99% of the time.

A slimy thing arrives suddenly, like a salamander-it moves fast-darts around and wakes up parts of us we'd forgotten, and it's in those places our dreams too have gotten folded up, put at the bottom of some drawer we rarely look at the back of.

We don't swim around everywhere, but when we find a dark spot, or a bunch of little nails and tacks in that drawer, it's time to nail something to the wall, something new or old or whatever.

It doesn't matter. What matters is we found it back there-we looked-

We had the courage to move a few things aside, and next to all those things, a hammer-exactly what we needed. The wall, once pounded with our nail, never looked the same again. And we each have those stories, we each have those nails, we each have those hammers. We each have those long unopened drawers. The sound of people working in unison never sounded so good.

Each hashtag is a nail. Each story is a hammer. Each rainbow is a sign we are visible, connected, remembering, speaking, in unison.

Workbook
Questions for reflection:

- How have the public stories of others affected your life?

　

- Have you shared any of your life story publicly?

　

- What are your fears?

- Can you share any of your story publicly in a way that feels safe?

- Do you have a blog or would you like one (can be under a pseudonym)?

- Do you prefer to share publicly through writing/speaking/art/music/theater/fiction/other?

- Is it worth the criticism that you will inevitably receive?

- What's the worst case scenario of sharing your story publicly?

- What might the benefits be?

CHAPTER 12

SUICIDAL THOUGHTS AND FEELINGS

Until the night before I wrote this, the only time I ever came close to having a suicide plan was when I was 21 and on a cocktail of 7 psychiatric drugs. I had visions of hanging myself out my window with a rope that I'd never had before and have never had since. I've spent precious little of my life being actively suicidal and even those visions seemed more like haunting images than actual plans or intentions.

I've been lucky enough not to make a plan to kill myself despite a growing mass of time feeling suicidal. Since my lifelong friend Michael Bloom's death by suicide 2 years ago, it has been a default state of mind for me to feel suicidal when I feel broken. As naive as this may sound to some, last night was the first time I ever went towards a plan in my mind.

After having a recurring stomach flu that felt intertwined with a lot of feelings of separation and alienation from many people I have considered family (including my birth family) and losing my appetite on and off for a week, the thought of downing a bunch of pills went through my mind. When I lose my appetite (for emotional or physical reasons), I almost always feel suicidal, due in large part to the deficiency and lack of reserve from not eating. The combination of physical and emotional loss of appetite this week put me over the edge to finally approaching the loss of my suicidal-plan-virginity.

The ironic thing was when I played out the prospect of downing a bunch of pills, I had the realization I wouldn't die anyway. I would go through another trial of the body and I wouldn't die. I can't explain how I knew this or why some people die and others don't, but I can say I know it's not my time to die. Many people survive suicide attempts and other near death experiences "against all odds" (while of course many, like my dear friend Michael, do not and I have no explanation for this).

This might sound like a torturous thought to someone feeling suicidal and at loose ends, but rather it was the opposite. After playing out this scenario, and having the realization that I simply am not gong to die anytime soon no matter what I do, I felt relieved. I felt light hearted. A sense of optimism returned to me. I recalled something a friend wrote to me almost 15 years ago when I was losing faith as I was last night. "You are woven into a fabric that holds you and loves you and will not let you fall." This phrase came back to me and rang true in a new way.

I feel most at ease and safe when I know I have no choice. This is strange to many people, I am aware, but it has been true for me for as long as I can remember. I like to feel that the Universe is guiding me and I am basically going along for the ride. Perhaps someday I'll grow into a more willful and self-directed approach to life, or maybe I'll continue to move toward surrender and feeling protected by something bigger than myself. What I know right now is that surrendering to something bigger than myself has thus far been the only option that works for me and it is what keeps me alive.

Knowing there is a purpose and plan for my life that is stubborn, relentless, unwavering and unwilling to die (just yet) is a relief. When I share suicidal feelings with others, I usually say, "I don't have a plan." Now I have numerous friends I don't need a disclaimer with. They know by now I don't have a plan. And now even if I do I have another disclaimer: I'm here for a reason. It's not my time to die. I have more to do even if these things terrify me. I have a purpose. The Universe has dreams for me and holds them solidly even when I can't. Especially when I can't.

Sometimes every day feels like a suicide attempt, a stomach pump, a near death experience and the combination of feeling further damaged and a stronger sense of purpose. Since I go through this cycle regularly, a suicide attempt seems frivolous. The only point would be to indicate to others how much I'm suffering, how real it is.

This brings me to the humble task of communicating, telling people emphatically how much I am suffering at times, asking for reassurance that my dear ones love and care about me and sense my purpose. This may sound self indulgent, and it may be, but it is also a preventative measure, harm reduction and what keeps me from addiction and suicide. Haven't most of us had moments of wanting to die so others would finally value us, notice how much pain we're in, name our special qualities, express how much they loved us, regret their behavior that hurt us? Isn't it humbling to admit we need our loved ones to tell us how much we mean to them sometimes, how much they care?

My vulnerability and brokenness in this regard may make me unpopular with some who pride themselves on being "more together," yet it also fosters the intimacy, closeness and trust I feel with so many. And because of it, I don't need to ask myself if anyone will care if I die.

I can experience that reassurance while I'm alive if I have the humility to ask for it, and keep asking until my soul is met with other souls who genuinely care. That experience humbles me greatly and somehow makes all of my brokenness feel like love and open heartedness. Against all odds.

Disclaimer: I am not suicidal, nor did I have a plan for suicide when I wrote this piece. And Gosh I wish disclaimers like this didn't feel so necessary. Gosh I wish the psychiatric pharmaceutical industrial complex police state could not monitor my written medicine even one iota.

Feeling Alone

I'm so alone in this world-yet I am a writer-I have that, and that is often all I have; it's me when no one else can be a balm or salve or comfort.

It's me in the wee hours of the morning devouring my own essence from myself, terrified of all things except this, because at least I can be honest.

I get so enraged that so many are not honest with themselves, not telling the truth. I cry so hard at how alone this makes me, and in a way it improves my self worth to know that when I write it's for everyone; the lift out of despair is so heavy and suddenly my muscle seems strong.

I just know when I do this for myself I'm doing it for you too and I can't live without doing it-I mean that seriously.

The images that go through my mind would terrify those who love me, yet in those moments, no one really loves or cares about me-they only would if I were to no longer exist and the images themselves, which are so dangerous to speak of, remind me that I won't be entirely alone once I'm gone.

In fact, once I'm gone I won't be so alone at all, yet right then I am hot and there-there-not gone-not merged with anyone or anything and I think of Michael Bloom, my friend who killed himself, wondering if any thoughts like this crossed his mind.

And I remember something simple, like I could take my vitamins, and I think of people who drink alone in hours like these-so grateful I have a small stock of pens and paper but no whiskey or rum in my bedroom.

And, for what it's worth I have some different vitamins, teas, and I know how to stretch my body, but none of those things will save me and I won't be able to swallow any of those pills or move those body parts until I've found a way through what could be called my madness.

In fact I hadn't put out many red flags at all; in fact I seemed quite well and normal those days, to some degree, and I was living in San Francisco where everyone was too busy to care or concern themselves with others to that level. And no one came into my room, so no one was bound to read my journal or these words, unless I shared them.

I will share them mostly because they have brought me back to some semblance of "sanity" and because the world right now, even in the best of places, at the best picnics and dinners, doesn't feel right to me, and as a writer maybe never will, but I do find my suffering can create a medicine of sorts for myself and others, when I write things down to describe it, since we are all suffering so bad and sometimes even the prettiest of scenes looks unfortunate and even the ugliest of things looks alive.

Talking About Suicide with Teenagers

At the end of an hour long discussion with high school students at a Western Massachusetts high school, I was grasping quarter page slips of folded paper as it they were sheets of gold. On these slips of paper were questions the students asked me, as well as their answers to my questions, "What can you do to make yourself feel happier as an alternative to psychiatric drugs?" and "How do you get through hard times?"

To some of them these answers may have been flippant, including things like Mrs. Rivera's humor, Batman music, tumblr, and biting my nails. They also included love, eating, snuggling, my boyfriend, my girlfriend, green tea, good friends, drawing, playing guitar, a new book, flowers, fluffy things (pandas), writing, music, talking to friends, not isolating myself and sex novels.

After my workshop on coming off psych drugs, a guidance counselor from Holyoke High School asked me if I'd speak at his weekly open support group about my experiences in the mental health system. After telling the group of teenagers a few things about my experiences, we gave them the option to write a secret question or comment on an anonymous slip of paper to be put in a box and read at random. The first question read was, "Have you ever tried committing suicide?"

I said I had never tried to commit suicide but I threatened to once and was locked up and drugged against my will. I added, "I've thought about suicide a lot, though." When prompted to share more about their experiences, one girl raised her hand and asked, "Will we get in trouble?" I laughed, "You won't get in trouble with me." I looked at the guidance counselor. "I don't think you'll get in trouble with him." We smiled, and he confirmed that they would not.

The second reader of these anonymous pieces of paper picked one out of the box, unfolded it and said, "Same question." We all figured the first question paper had accidentally stayed in the box-but no, it was a different person's question, this time phrased, "Have you ever attempted suicide?"

The third question was, "Did you ever want to die?" At least half the students admitted to having attempted suicide numerous times. One smiling vivacious girl said the third time was a turning point for her. Her mom caught her and asked her loudly in Spanish, "Don't you know people care about you?" It was then it hit her what she was doing, she said; it was a turning point and she hasn't attempted suicide since. Most of them who had tried to kill themselves had either taken lots of pills or cut themselves in their attempts.

At this point I told them that doctors have a higher rate of suicidality and depression than the general population. I mentioned the article, "Could Your Doctor Be Mentally Ill or Suicidal?" recently posted on Mad In America. Quite a few of them laughed and one girl suggested a reverse diagnostic process, bringing in a checklist of symptoms to use to assess your doctors' mental health.

In one hour we touched on many topics and I was exposed to an incredible amount of firsthand witnessing that was brand new for me. Only one person in the group said he takes psych drugs (antidepressants). One boy said he used to take stimulants for an ADHD diagnosis but they made him sad, anxious and unable to sleep so he stopped taking them. At first he held them in his mouth when his mom gave him the pills and spit them out when she wasn't looking. Eventually she stopped giving them to him. He was a freshman. It impressed me that a boy under 14 did this, knowing the drugs were causing him harm, knowing outright refusal might not be safe.

I was impressed with the awareness these kids had about how the drugs were affecting them and their friends and family members. One girl said she took antidepressants for awhile but they made her feel like a zombie so she stopped. She said it made her have a fake smile on her face all the time.

I took the very queer friendly environment (which included a recently out trans person scheduled to share his story the following week) to mention that homosexuality used to be a "mental illness" in the DSM. They were horrified and looked lovingly and sympathetically at two of their friends, an adorable gay couple with arms around each other on the love seat.

This led in to the topic of gender identity disorder and other obviously questionable diagnoses. In a very queer friendly high school with 5 out transgender people who are accepted, these diagnoses, which have come and gone, and the new diagnosable behaviors I mentioned, led one girl to ask, "So is it possible for them to tell you you have something and for them to be wrong?" I could see her comprehending the whole thing when I said, "Yes, of course-and these diagnoses are all created with large influence from pharmaceutical companies and insurance companies who are profiting from the drugs sales."

One girl said she wanted to take anti-depressants but was scared to. For one thing, her therapist said "No," which, to my surprise was a common experience. A number of kids had asked for psych drugs but were turned down. Phew. The reason for her fear, though, was that her dad takes psych drugs and her mom thinks he's crazy, "but he's isn't," she said. "And I don't want people to think I'm crazy."

I validated hers and other fears of taking meds, letting them know they have never been tested on people their age and there are real dangers in taking a mind altering drug everyday while their brains are still developing. Most of them nodded, totally getting it. I was again impressed with their intelligence, and I added, "These drugs have only been tested in short trials and are primarily tested on healthy white men in their 20s." A girl exclaimed, "That's so racist!" We all nodded in agreement and added sexist, ageist and health discriminatory to the list.

The girl who wanted to take antidepressants but was too scared asked, "I don't mean this in a depressing way-I really don't mean this in a depressing way- but what is the point of life? I don't see what the point is if you don't get to save anything you do since you die at the end anyway."

I told her I feel a sense of purpose in writing or speaking about things I feel I have a unique perspective on or am angry about so that I can hopefully make a difference in people's lives even after I die. A girl who had been quiet most of the session said she finds meaning in writing and typing her thoughts with the hope that others will take action on her ideas.

Before we got into any of this, the group started with a check-in. The counselor asked for a topic, and a girl suggested, "What you love about unicorns," which he modified to, "How you feel about unicorns." About half of us said we like unicorns because they're magical. The other half said they don't like unicorns because they aren't real. I believe in magic, I like magic, but I don't like things that aren't real, like psych labels, so perhaps that odd seeming check-in topic had some relevance after all.

Walking down the hallway after the session, the counselor and I ran in to another school social worker. The two of them casually chatted about how 2 new people had come out as transgender in the past week, both with the same new name. I thought of how different things are now than when I was a teenager, even though my high school was in New York City and very queer friendly.

On our way out, the counselor told me the psychiatrist at the school is very nice, but is a medication dispenser. She gives everyone drugs if they go to her. Having a psychiatrist in the school is another phenomenon that was foreign to me. Why would a school need a psychiatrist?

He's only referred one student to her, ever. He doesn't know enough about psychiatric drugs to feel comfortable talking about them or making that decision for anyone, he said (but clearly he has a strong feeling about the topic and wants to learn more since he invited me to speak).

He then asked me a question I get a lot, that usually, quite frankly, makes me yawn: "So do you think medication can ever be helpful in the short term?" This question bores and annoys me, for it indicates how effective the overt and covert advertising from pharmaceutical companies is, despite how obviously dishonest it is. It causes intelligent thoughtful people to ask themselves whether something they would never consider otherwise, should be used as the first line of "treatment" for social problems.

I was surprised that I finally came up with a unique counter-question that didn't bore me to ask.

I started by reflecting on my own experiences of taking Prozac for about a year as a teenager. I tried to open myself up to the question anew, pretend I had never thought about it before. I told him taking Prozac as a teen may have made me fit in more socially for a little while, but it didn't help me learn how to be me in the world. It made me more extroverted but stole time from me that could have been better spent learning how to live with my introversion and get the most out of it. It made me a people pleaser but didn't help strengthen me and it put a damper in my ability to learn about myself and the world in a genuine way.

So I posed this question: "What about asking a gay person to try being straight for just a year?"

Workbook
Questions for reflection:

- Do you have people you can talk to safely about suicidal feelings and thoughts?

- Can you ask those in your life for help when you feel suicidal?

- Can you ask for what you most need and do not need when you feel this way?

- Have you explored you own suicidal feelings or impulses?

- What are they telling you?

- What IS your purpose in living?

- What have others told you they value about you?

- What self care and care from others do you most need when you feel this way?

CHAPTER 13

SURVIVING THE SUICIDE OF A LOVED ONE

Michael

As a preteen he had a big hairy mole on his neck and that was the first thing I noticed about him, though he had it removed early on. In his earlier years he was on the chubby side and in his later years on the skinny side but what remained the same was he made everyone laugh. He told me when he was skinny and quiet girls liked him more because he was more mysterious than when he was heavier and talked a lot. In my earliest memories of him on the office porch or waterfront steps at Sandy Island, he was laughing about something, making fun of something, and that something usually included himself. He liked to make fun of Jews, which we both were, and of course our families. I can still hear him making fun of Mama Bloom and "Mama Grossberg" as well as "Papa Grossberg".

As teenagers Michael and I both primarily had "friend" status with the opposite sex. I thought I was too skinny, he may have thought he was too chubby. There were other reasons, far more complex than body type for why we both remained virgins until college. To the girls, he was the one we most wanted to talk to, but least wanted to kiss. He had his crushes on most of us, but none seemed too serious, and perhaps, like me, he enjoyed "friend status" where conversations were often more interesting and everything felt a bit more sane at that age. I'm not sure which came first, his nickname Sugabear or his "perverted gesture" which was basically lifting up his arms and thrusting his pelvis. We girls would ask him to do it over and over, never getting enough of it, cracking up every time. Finally he refused to do it every time we asked for fear it would lose its novelty, but I'm not sure it ever did.

It was August of the summer before my first year at college so he was 19 and I was 17 when he came into my cabin and woke me up to watch the sunrise. His idea the night before, others were supposed to be woken up too, but no one else would get out of bed, so it was just me and Michael Bloom. Silent except for lightly crashing waves of Lake Winnipesaukee and morning ducks, we sat on the wooden waterfront chairs resting our arms on the arm rests as the sun bounced off the lake and hit us in our faces. Late August in New Hampshire the sun was warm even at 5AM, 6AM...by 7AM we could hear the sounds of kids being ushered to the bathrooms by parents mildly hustling to get everyone's teeth brushed amidst Daddy Longlegs and muddy boot trackings on the bathroom floor, which could only stay clean for the first family.

But hours before the hubbub, Michael and I only saw the gleam of Lake Winnipesaukee, only heard the light waves, vocal ducks and each others voices talking about what it was like to go to college a virgin and feel like the only one. The warmth of the sun on our faces made everything okay. The fact that it was silent except for us, the only 2 who followed the plan to wake up before sunrise since it was our only week together all year and though the days were long, filled with time to roam, the week was never long enough and before we knew it it would be over. We'd be back to our ordinary (or not so ordinary) lives where different rules applied and there wasn't a perfectly quiet lake to sit by with a friend we'd seen every summer for as long as we could remember summers.

Michael valued Sandy Island above all else, for it was where there was time to dream, meander, cry, have adventures...all in a timeless bubble, yet it seemed to create a time capsule by being repeated each year....a thread woven through our lives. It was just one week a year, or two for some families, yet one week on an island can feel like eternity-until it ends. It can feel like a timeless place where what you discuss floats along the tide, the lake whispers things to you. You may not know just who it is you are talking to or what they wear in their everyday world, but you know for the moment you are lifelong friends, you know this is important, to carve out time away from everything else to ponder mysteries, act out rebellions, make up jokes, give everyone a strange nickname, and laugh as the sun bubbles up.

In college at Rutgers, Michael met Andrea who he called "The Big A" and developed a romance with. Their connection was strong enough that she tried to contact him in recent years, nearly 15 years later! Sometime in his first few years at Rutgers, Michael had some experiences ranging from joyful ecstasy for his new connections with people to utter despair at the state of the world. These were on the continuum of what many young adults touch upon as they come to know the freedoms and burdens of adulthood, yet he experienced them in a more extreme way than some do. Or perhaps he just had the courage to admit it. I certainly had my own extreme states of awakening and despair at a similar age, and similarly experienced them in heightened way.

I visited him at Rutgers where he was sociable and excited about connecting with just about everyone we passed in the hall. This was different from high school where he had a small group of friends and didn't socialize much outside of it. In college he seemed high on life, on meeting new people and engaging with everyone he could. These states were sometimes followed by states of despair at the state of the world, which led to a suicide attempt and landed him in the hospital.

"Life on Lithium is totally boring," he told me after that, "but it saved my life and I may need to be on a small dose of it for the rest of my life." He said many times that without it he could become suicidal again, which clearly was not a risk he was willing to take and it was hard to argue with that. "On Lithium, I don't feel the highs and excitement I used to feel, but I don't feel the lows as much, so it's keeping me alive." In the years to come whenever I suggested the Lithium could be causing some of his problems (apathy, boredom, constant unhappiness, being disinterested in everything and sometimes unable to connect with people), he would come emphatically back to this exclamation, "Lithium saved my life," angry that I didn't seem to get how true that was for him. Despite that we were both raised by East Coast Jews who put Western medicine on a pedestal, we took very different paths to address our "mental health" and sometimes seemed to have opposing views.

Michael's mom was a nurse and his father a professor of science or history (I forget which). My mom was a math teacher and social worker and my father a dentist. My parents had a hair more skepticism of psychiatry, for my father became a dentist rather than another type of doctor in part so he'd be less influenced by pharmaceutical company corruption and my mother was trained as a therapist before the Prozac-is-aspirin years. She had an uneasiness about drugging mental distress from the first time my therapist referred me to an expensive psychiatrist when I was 15.

I steered away from allopathic doctors, not trusting them and I was a seeker of the alternative early on. In my teens I became vegetarian, practiced yoga and meditation (which I first learned from books, then classes) and stopped taking the Prozac my therapist recommended. In college, I studied herbalism, nutrition and everything I could get my hands on about alternative healing and spirituality. From a young age, my spirituality was connected to my body, my breath, what I ate or consumed, what surrounded me.

Michael's interests and path were entirely different, though not incompatible with mine for he had a passion for art and philosophy and was one of the biggest dreamers I knew. Yet, over the next 10 years, he seemed to gradually decline in energy levels, happiness, aliveness and functionality. I saw him at least a handful of times in these years, for his brother went to school in the same town as me, and he visited us every so often.

On one nighttime visit when I was still in college we walked around the cemetery in Amherst, MA, where Emily Dickinson was buried and he asked me if I'd marry him someday, if we were both single when we were 30, or something like that . We were disagreeing and debating and he commented that we sounded like a married couple-a married East Coast Jewish couple like our parents, anyway.

On another visit he came to a Freedom Center Northampton meeting with me. At this time I was withdrawing from the cocktail of psychiatric drugs I'd been put on the previous year and having insomnia. He asked skeptical questions about the Freedom Center, how people "like us" lived without psychiatric drugs, and we had many debates on the phone about mental health diagnoses, the pharmaceutical industry, what we believed. These disagreements were both meaningful and frustrating for me. Michael said that he had bipolar and a lot of people were pressuring him to just get a job or go out, get out of his own mind, but they didn't get that he had a real illness that actually limited him the same way a physical illness can.

Although this was not exactly my explanation of him (I saw him as a sensitive, hilarious genius with unlimited potential stuck in a rut due to Lithium, an indoctrinated limiting view, a sick society which upset him, not enough support and a number of other factors), it was when he tried to define me in a similar framework that I could not stay silent. Mike frequently asked me what my diagnosis was and whether I was taking anything, which was bait for the fat fish of my own story.

At around the same time as Lithium was credited with saving his life, the drugs I was on (Risperdal, Buspar, Effexor, Ambien, Prozac and Xanex) nearly killed me and rendered me unable to think, function, or even move much of the time. I told Michael this many times, along with sharing my lack of belief in diagnoses, how they never helped me understand myself or the world better, and emphasized diagnoses were created to sell drugs, which he couldn't argue with. Sometimes once we got that far in the conversation, he seemed humbled a bit and perhaps relieved.

Still, I was the only person in his entire world who believed the Lithium was harming him or even questioned its efficacy. He told me sometimes all he could do was chain smoke and watch movies, but there also came a time when movies no longer did it for him and there was nothing. He lived in Hawaii for a few years, but hated it and returned to live with his father in West Newton, MA until his suicide in 2012. He had various jobs over the years from being a mailman (which was one of his childhood dreams!) to working in the census office, and in Hawaii he volunteered at a museum. In the few years leading up to his death, he went to DBSA meetings (Depression Bipolar Support Alliance which is a pet of Big Pharma that "supports" the medical model view and unquestioned psychiatric labeling) but felt no one there was smart enough for him and they were too entrenched in the system. I imagine they were highly drugged, more so than Michael.

When he returned from Hawaii, which was several years before his suicide, his mom developed tinnitus, ringing in the ears, that was unbearable to her, Michael told me. This led to her suicide in 2008. I couldn't help but wonder if she had been psychiatrically diagnosed and drugged and if the drugs had been a contributing factor, or even the primary cause of, her suicide. I was still living in Northampton, MA (sister town to Amherst) at the time without a car, so when I got the call about Mama Bloom I booked a bus ticket to Boston right away. Michael and I hadn't seen each other since before he had moved to Hawaii, so it had been quite a few years and he had been hard to reach by phone that summer.

When I saw him at the funeral my heart rushed open and I cried; we both cried as we embraced, my heart so full of love for my old friend. He looked and felt better than I'd expected him to and he later told me how good it was to have family and friends around but how hard it was when they went back to their busy lives weeks later. Michael's younger brother read something Michael had written about their mom at the funeral, which made me so proud of who he was. I realized also that he was surprised and moved that I had come as I was the only non-relative who traveled from outside the Boston area to come, although I was only 2 hours away. It was that moment when we hugged under the canopy, next to the rabbi, that I felt the true meaning of friendship-of being part of someone's heart and knowing your presence does in fact make a difference. And what a difference that made to me!

Michael held friendship as one of the highest values in life, higher than work or even marriage, it seemed. He frequently told me how disturbed he was by our society being so isolated into couples and not staying loyal to friends much of the time. Though there were a couple of times he expressed interest in being more than friends with me I never felt that get in the way of our friendship as it seems to with many others. I never felt awkward or like he needed more.

Over the years following Mama Bloom's death, Michael seemed to sink deeper into despair and then apathy. Frequently his phone messages were in a flat tone and said, "I hope you are okay." He could no longer say "I hope you are good." for being good, or anything beyond okay was no longer in his frame of reference. There were countless messages from him saying he hoped I was "okay," and the way he said "okay," I knew he was striving for just that.

He also told me the shrinks were changing around his drugs and adding more. They added an antidepressant or two to the Lithium and increased doses and eventually he seemed to have very little life left in him. Our phone calls became trying for he was so down, practically dead sounding a lot of the time, and I felt unable to do anything or say anything to make a difference. To even try felt futile and I wondered if talking to me at all was becoming the burden of yet another person he couldn't connect with.

In the early years, he liked to think of us as being in the same boat, both "mentally ill", since I'd also had a meltdown and I also am extremely sensitive. But as the years went by, especially towards the end, I seemed to be in the ever growing "other" camp in his eyes, which meant I was yet another person who didn't get what it was like to be him. And at that point I can confirm I did not, and perhaps did not want to.

When Mike's brother, called me one morning and left a voice mail saying there's something he needed to tell me, I was on a walk and on the other line talking to my friend and coworker Jenny. Since he doesn't call me ordinarily I knew it couldn't be good news. I had called him once several years earlier when I was concerned about Mike, after we had a big argument-perhaps our biggest ever. It had to do with his time in Hawaii and I was at Sunset Beach in San Francisco feeling lonely. Michael had yelled at me and gotten enraged about how horrible Hawaii was. He compared California to Hawaii and said he hated that culture, hated the people on the West Coast and kept asking when I was coming back to the East Coast, when I was coming back to my real home. I had no intention of coming back to live on the East coast again, ever, once I moved to the West Coast. I got angry that he asked me that every single time we talked, since I was lonely and wanted to talk about other things, like what was actually going on in my life, and his.

Something in me knew what he was going to say. When we got off the phone (all I had said was "Oh My God" over and over-like the opposite of an orgasm) my pulse was racing as I walked through the Whole Foods parking lot back to my car. I had an acupuncture appointment, should I go? The idea of being physically alone was too daunting so I went. Katie said my pulse was rapid and it had never been rapid before in our 5 months of weekly sessions. I cried on the table and finally blurted it out, "One of my closest lifelong friends just committed suicide. And I just found out." The small room seemed filled with his spirit and I swung between feeling the despair he must have felt and the joy and liberation he must have felt. I saw him dancing on clouds with kiddie-boppers (his endearing term for children) and I saw him cutting his wrists in his basement.

When I got home that day I didn't leave my house for 2 whole days. I texted everyone I could think of and asked friends to come visit me the next day since I couldn't bring myself to go out and I could not be physically alone. All night the image of bloody wrists haunted me. Bobo had asked if I was sure I wanted to know how he did it and I'd said yes- I knew I had to know. That night I called my mom around 1am, 4am her time in New York. I cried and told her over and over how freaked out I was. She said she had to get off the phone, asked me if I had a Valium I could take to get to sleep but I said "NO, I need you to listen to me." Strangely, she didn't remember Michael, though they met in New York when he visited and she had made an impression on him, with her thick Bronx accent, which he carried with him and mimicked from time to time.

The following day was Friday and Jenny and Nina (my oldest friend, who I have known since I was a few weeks old) came over with pastries and coffee. We sat in my yard in the sun and I talked about everything I could remember about him: tidbits of memories like his favorite song (America by Simon and Garfunkel), his favorite line in it (about the New Jersey Turnpike) and the Billy Joel song that played in the car the last time I saw him (You May Be Right) and how I used that song to defend myself when he made fun of my personality. "You may be right, I may be crazy, but it just may be a lunatic you're looking for."

Later CJ came over. We said a prayer holding hands and spoke to his spirit. After that I felt more ease and eventually he came to me in a waking dream state and told me death is like an airport-you go into different terminals and resolve things, come to understandings with all of the people in your life and you fly to different places. Gradually the tormented feelings I'd had faded, as did the "high" feelings, where I experienced the world as he did in his most passionate moments.

I told Michael I loved him once or twice and he responded, "Do I have to say I love you too?" I said no, and didn't feel hurt. On a walk the other day, I thought of the cliché, "It's better to have loved and lost than to have never loved at all," and decided it was true. I actually had to think about it, considering how painful loss can be, but nonetheless it must be true.

The following was written when I heard of the suicide of a 28 year old woman living in Northampton, Massachusetts. I didn't know her well, but she came to two of my workshops on coming off psychiatric drugs, and she was brilliant, well spoken, passionate and had well earned wisdom that many of us psychiatric survivors have about how the system works. She had been on and off psych drugs for years (since childhood) and, if I remember correctly, she had gotten off of most of them but was still on a psych drug or few and several drugs for other health conditions.

Sara

Hearing about her suicide last week brought me into a deeply silent and reflective place, in part because the few things I knew and saw about her reminded me of myself when I was 22 and a Windhorse client, though there are many differences as well. She was a Windhorse client and, like me, had been going through a lot of run around between psychiatry and general medicine.

Like me, she had digestive issues, though hers were much more severe. She had also been on psychiatric drugs starting from an earlier age, and for a longer time. Still, her death had a flavor of reminding me of "what could have happened to me" if I hadn't been lucky enough to get off of a 7 drug cocktail and connect with a freer life. Reading Sara's Facebook wall after her death, it is clear that she had many admirers and was very well loved.

Here's what I wrote right after I heard of her passing:

Her death is a lot like what would have happened to me if I hadn't found the Freedom Center 10.5 years ago, if it weren't for Will Hall, Oryx Cohen, and the others at those support groups who listened, validated, believed in me and understood. Ten years ago, in December of 2004, I completed my process of coming off of Ambien, which was the final psych drug in my cocktail. I was still on a thyroid drug, which I had never needed, and Prevacid, which caused me more stomach acid problems. I got off of both of these a few months later.

When I was entirely off of the neuroleptic, benzo, SSRI, SNRI, sleeping drug, azapirone (had to look that one up-it's the class of drug Buspar falls in) cocktail, I sent out an email to the Freedom Center list and right away got back messages of congratulations. After spending 2 years mostly bedridden and taking those years off from college, I was back at Hampshire to complete my degree. The semester had been difficult and it was hard for me to write and think clearly until I was off of the drugs.

It was such a disorienting and lost time for me, while on the other hand I felt a spirit pulling me along. I was still in an altered state from the psych drugs a lot of the time. I still felt very disconnected from the Earth. I often went into states of being in another plane entirely, feeling as if I were dead-not in a negative way per se, but completely disconnected and non-attached to things in this world. I wasn't hungry for anything. It seemed like some form of enlightenment and utter transcendence that I hadn't even been trying to achieve, that was so far away from any kind of ordinary reality I had ever experienced.

Looking back, I can see that these few years of being sick on psych drugs, I was going into this altered state all the time. I imagine it is a state similar to states of being of people who are old and dying as their bodies gradually stop functioning well enough to live. I didn't care about anything; I was floating on clouds. Writing about this 10 years later with a pretty healthy body here in San Francisco, I feel connected to that state of "being" again. It feels like some part of myself I will connect to once I do die and depart from this body.

Hearing about her death gave me the chills. She was a client at Windhorse, and similar to me, going through so many hoops of doctors, medical care, physical illness, psych drugs, other pharmaceuticals. I was a young person on a whole cocktail of things who no longer had the ability to manage my own life, and I wonder if this was, in part, true for her too.

This musing clearly does no justice to her life story, (and isn't intended to speculate on the causes of her death) which I know little about, and hope to learn more of. May her memory be a blessing to all who loved her, and may it inspire us to create more support structures, outside the mental health system, for those who are suffering.

Workbook
Questions For Reflection:

- If you've lost people to suicide, how has it affected you?

- Has it made you think about suicide more yourself?

- Have you had ample opportunity to process and talk about those people?

- Can you connect with their other loved ones to talk about them and your feelings?

- Do you still have unresolved feelings about their suicide(s) years later? Describe.

- Do you feel their presence in your life/dreams? Describe.

- What were the qualities of these people that inspired you? Describe.

- What do you wish had been different in their lives?

- What kind of support and resources do you wish they'd had?

　

- Who do you see they could have been with better circumstances?

　

- How can you use this awareness to access better circumstances for yourself without questioning your worthiness?

CHAPTER 14

SURVIVING DEATHS OF COMRADES

Everything Leaves

The process of dying is so colorful
the plight of falling
the journey of change
from new to crumbling
from fresh, green and shining
to a skeleton
The process of dying is more beautiful
even than birth
in its variety of colors
its seasons of wilting
its times of being bright with agony
speckled with the unknown
always in process
dying
bright and beautiful
sad, willing to journey away from perfection,
away from the pure self
to the collage of idiosyncrasies
the melting pot of disasters, tragedies, celebrations, successes
in the name of a life headed towards death
lush green ever transforming to bare bones
and branches
that have their own story to tell
that never went anywhere, all along,
whispering their reason for existence
without moving or changing
while being a skeleton for the myriad of colors,
tears, raindrops, snow shelves,
everything.
The dark green of things
is painful as it shifts, reminding us ever so slowly

of what care is
reminding us of the constancy of all things
whether life or death,
whether being born or dying,
there is always a color of some kind
there is always something speaking its own language
there is always a dream
in everything
always something too beautiful to grasp with a
pair of eyes
always something going by unseen,
something being missed
but everything that dies was once born
everything old and tired
was once young and fresh and fertile with brightness
as its own beauty passed it by,
too much to see all at once
with such young eyes
such a young heart
it is only as we age we can see and feel this changing,
this weight of difference,
this sadness at missing some things
in order to preserve others
this sacrifice we must make
of releasing moments gone by to be present
for even one second
as life pours gifts all over us
and opens up space for just that second
and opens our hearts to everything sometimes
so we can see the changing of colors
and remember everything leaves.

Leonard Roy Frank

    The December I was about to turn 24 and living in Northampton, Massachusetts, I took a week long trip to visit my cousin in San Francisco. This was my first time on an airplane, or really on any excursion out of Western Massachusetts, in over 3 years, since I had been bedridden on 7 pharmaceuticals (mostly psychiatric drugs) for the greater part of my 21st and 22nd years.

    I had been off of the drugs and involved with the Freedom Center in Northampton for a year, and had finally graduated college. I was just emerging into the land of the living and a more "normal" life after those years of complete isolation and brain fog.

    My cousin was living in the Inner Sunset with several of his college friends. They lived in a large apartment with a large poster on the wall about things to do before you turn 30 (they were all 28).

I hadn't seen the ocean in over 4 years, so I walked there one day, a couple of miles in a city I was unfamiliar with, without looking up directions; I sniffed and sensed my way there, smelling the sea getting closer to me as I walked. I sat there for a long time looking at the ocean. It was a cool foggy day and I was the only one on the beach. I texted a friend from the Freedom Center who I had started a writing group with and sent him a photo of the Pacific.

Getting to the ocean, a whole year after getting off psych drugs, was a marker of my liberation from psychiatry and all the limits and loneliness it preserved in my life those few years. In my year after getting off those seven drugs, I was scared to travel and was on a restricted diet due to blood sugar problems Risperdal had caused me. In order to control my life, I ate certain foods at certain times and primarily ate them alone those few years. When I went out, I brought food with me in tupperware, no matter what, since I had to know what I was eating.

My eating habits were isolating but I was scared to give them up because it was food and eating problems that had caused me the most instability in my life right before I started taking psychiatric drugs.

Eating a specific diet was something I clung to for dear life, until it was time to loosen my grip. It took me about a year to feel "normal" about food again.

There I was, a year out of the system, on the beach, certain I'd reached a milestone that only the ocean waves could mirror back.

This is a poem I had written while I was on 7 drugs and in quite a trance:

A Wrap, A Wash

Now things are well.
They want to know about my journey.
Were there rocks?
Were there diamonds?
How did you sleep on the slants of hills?"
All I have in my pockets is quiet, I say
and open my hand to their ear, to their footsteps.
They want to eat chocolate with me,
and dance.
They don't know what these things
mean to me.
If you step on a rock, get a degree in diamonds,
You must hold their weight strong in your ear, in your footsteps.

The world is full of brown and retreat,
purple and history,
clear and mystery.
The world is full of Snickers bars and ballerinas,
hospital potatoes, wheelchairs,
writing and waiting
and watching people work
with the wonton of
Want.
It's been called a wrestle
and wonderful.
I haven't been waiting.
I haven't been watching.
I wrinkle at the wonders,
which has been called a withdrawal.
I call it a wrap, a wash.

   A friend from the Freedom Center had suggested I meet Leonard Frank in San Francisco, so I called him and later that week accepted his invitation to come to his studio apartment in Pacific Heights and to go out for lunch at La Mediterranee, his favorite restaurant. My cousin seemed somewhat baffled as to why I would be going to meet a man in his 70's I didn't know, for no apparent reason.

   I explained that he was a survivor of forced electroshock and my friend had suggested I meet him. He responded with surprise that forced electroshock ever happened, and seemed to be under the common impression that it was an outdated, hardly used practice.

   I got directions from him and headed off on the bus to meet Leonard. When I arrived at his apartment, I instantly felt a sense of peace and holiness in his presence. His apartment was full of tall bookshelves, books covering the wall space, and his desk with a large computer.

   He told me about his experiences as a young adult, being force shocked over and over at the age of 30, and how, upon exiting the mental health system, he had huge gaps in his memory from his life before 30. He couldn't remember a lot of his childhood and a lot of things he had learned over his life, but he was determined to relearn as much as he could, and build back his mind.

   Leonard spent most of his time, for decades, reading. In order to help himself remember, retain and synthesize information, he kept a database of quotes and passages that were relevant to him. For days and days, years and years, Leonard collected these lines and paragraphs.

   He eventually put together a Quotationary, a dictionary of these lines, published by Webster. He said there was still quite a bit of his memory he never recovered, and I could tell he had deep grief about this, this permanent loss. When I offered the idea that anything is possible, implying that it might be possible for his memory to come back, or for anything at all to happen, really, he insisted I was wrong. We a had a moment of holy disagreement where I said anything is always possible and he stood strong that some things are permanently lost, nothing can bring them back.

He was a literary soul, he wanted to remember his life.

Psychiatry for a literary soul misses the mark. This is why so many who escape psychiatry have a passion for words, memories, storytelling, blogging, writing books, reading. We have this awareness that so much of life is in the telling and that storytelling can limit us forever, or it can freshly liberate us in each passing moment.

Leonard didn't merely spend all of his time reading, writing and walking around his neighborhood because those were his favorite things to do. Perhaps they were, but he was also liberating himself from psychiatry everyday. His simple life of reading and finding the truths that were true for him was a stand he took for his spirit, for the spirit of so many of us.

I think of Leonard as a monastic; he never owned a car, was vegetarian his entire life and spent almost all of his time studying, contemplating and collecting deep truths. Like a monk, you could feel this in his presence. He was spacious to be around, it was easy to breathe while talking to him.

As a literary soul myself, who spends hours a day writing and walking around my neighborhood, wherever I may live, it's clear to me that literature is cornerstone in resisting oppression of all kinds. By reading and writing, we keep our minds agile and able to see things from different angles and labeling ourselves or others has very little, if any, place. A literary soul will naturally discard psychiatry with its oversimplifications and attempts to "cure" our complex genius, always hiding underneath any madness.

Leonard was a mad genius in the very best sense-he was devoted to truth and justice, a maddening pursuit, but one that always leaves a legacy, always leaves people remembering and crying when the "madman" is gone.

When I returned to my cousin's place that evening, he asked about my day and I didn't say much. On the wall was still the list of things to do before you turn 30.

Workbook
Questions for Reflection:

- How have the deaths of comrades or mentors influenced you?

- Have you ever felt you are continuing another's legacy or mission?

- Do you feel supported by those who have passed on?

- Have you studied their lives and works for inspiration?

- Have they gone through any similar struggles as you?

- Have you written or spoken or otherwise expressed your memories of them?

CHAPTER 15

SUPPORTING OTHERS WITHOUT INTERFERING, ACCEPTING OTHERS WHERE THEY ARE, AND LEADING BY EXAMPLE

5 Tasks if Your Child is Diagnosed with a Mental Illness

When I teach workshops or lead discussions on coming off psychiatric drugs and alternatives, there are invariably parents present who are at loose ends. They want to know what to do for their children, how to help them best, and how it can be possible for their child to live without medication given all they have been through. Oftentimes there have been violence, suicide threats/attempts, substance abuse/addiction, and a long history of diagnoses and psychiatric drugs that haven't worked but to sedate their child. Most of the time, the child (who may be an adult) is on numerous psychiatric drugs and lacks motivation and energy. Here are 5 ideas:

1. Forget about the label. Yes, your child is suffering. Yes, your offspring has something to bring to the world that hasn't been understood or effectively supported. Space hasn't been made for it... yet.

2. Find their gifts and support them in those. If your daughter/son has great gifts that society doesn't acknowledge so much, let them know! As their parent you can see them more clearly sometimes (less others). Find out more about their gifts from those who admire them and see the best in them.

3. Don't take responsibility for the label. Instead take responsibility for yourself. Don't call yourself a bad parent. Do call yourself a traumatized person yourself. Do write and speak of your own trauma, in whatever ways feel best, with your community. Do share your own life story with your children (when/if they are in a place to hear it) and the world. Do create. Do have fun. Do sup-

port your child as much as possible. Don't stop focusing on your own life. Your child is picking up where you left off, so the more secrets you unearth about your own trauma, the less burden your daughter/son has to hold. Write your story and share it with the world, or find another way to express it artistically. In your story, focus on yourself. Don't focus on your child or share things about them without their permission. Keep gossiping about your child in check. It's very socially acceptable for parents to talk solely about their children and to do so without respecting their confidentiality. Challenge yourself to keep the focus of your conversations on your own feelings and experiences.

4 Don't use your child's challenges to distract from your own. This is easy for parents to do. Your children are used to being an energetic dumping ground for your anxieties and fears. They receive them no matter how hard you try to protect them or keep secrets. They are likely to benefit if you address your own challenges.

5 Keep coming back to yourself. Are you lonely? Do you need more connection with friends? Do you have enough creative outlets? Are you sharing your creativity with the world? Do you have a form of meditation that you practice daily? Are you taking out your relationship challenges on your children? Take care of your own body and health. Do all the things you want your children to do to take care of themselves.

Finally, be open to learning something new from your child. Be willing to admit you don't know everything and you child may be your greatest teacher. Be loving, kind and compassionate with yourself. Sure, you weren't a perfect parent. Maybe you had so much stress and trauma of your own that you abused your children emotionally or physically. If this is the case, acknowledge that you are a hurt child underneath too. Seek out support groups, mediation, friends, artistic expression, and whatever else helps you own your own life experiences and respect and forgive yourself.

Most parents have been abusive in some way. And most have an incredible amount of shame about this. Most parents were also abused themselves. Ask yourself what you need to do to reconcile this. Apologize to your child maybe? Apologize to yourself, surely. Share your traumas with a professional if needed/desired. Eventually move into sharing with friends, your wider community and/or the public with some form of artistic expression.

Disclaimer: I am not a parent so I offer this with due humility that I do not know what it is like. These are things I would have liked someone to say to my own parents when I was in turmoil, and things I'd like to say to other parents as well.

Routine Lab Work

It started out as an ordinary visit to Quest Diagnostics to get routine lab work. I was 15 minutes late. The receptionist, who was also the office manager and medical technician, told me she loves my freckles. Well, that wasn't entirely ordinary.

When she sat me down to draw my blood she asked me if I'd ever had my blood drawn before. "Hello. I just told you my full birthday. I'm 33..." I thought, but I answered a simple, "Yes."

I realized it had been awhile though, and I didn't want to look while she filled the tubes from my elbow crease so I looked the other way.

"Do you have any plans for the weekend?" she asked, to distract me.

"I'm hoping to get outside and see some friends," I said. "I've spent the past couple of days indoors working."

Her: What do you do for work?

Me: I do coaching and teaching, mostly from home, so I'm looking forward to getting outside a bit.

Her: Coaching in any particular field?

Me: Mental health, alternatives to mainstream mental health.

Her: So is that like psychology?

Me: Well, I do coaching and teaching about alternatives to psychiatric drugs for people who want to come off of them.

Her: Oh, my partner might be interested in that at some point down the line. She experienced agoraphobia and couldn't leave the house, but she'd like to go off the drugs eventually. Do you have a card?

I wrote down my website and email address for her and told her some of the people I work with aren't ready to come off yet, and it's very individual. Coming off can be very difficult and I would never tell someone they are or aren't ready; it's up to them to know. I don't give medical advice.

Her: So how did you get into this line of work?

Me: I was on psychiatric drugs myself and they had a negative effect and were hard to come off of, so I wanted to support others who were coming off.

Her: I was put on drugs as a kid, Lithium and Depakote. When I was hospitalized they told me I'd never amount to anything in life because I was bipolar and I'd need to stay on these drugs forever. When I wanted to come off, my doctor got angry at me and wouldn't support me, so I went off on my own. It was very hard; I was sick for about a year afterward.

Me: Oh, you had intense withdrawal?

Her: Yes, but now I'm 37 and I'm the manager of this office, a medical technician and I'm getting a masters in Psychology.

She was proud and triumphant. My appointment was over. I rolled down my sleeve over the taped gauze with a tiny blood stain. She showed me to the bathroom. When I got out I was turned around and couldn't find my way out of the office. Seeing me going out the wrong door she said, "It's like a maze in here," and showed me the way out. I dropped my water cup in the blue recycling bin. It ended as an ordinary visit to Quest Diagnostics to get routine lab work done.

Med Free Solutions Certificate Course

If You've Broken Free From Psychiatry

If you've broken free from psychiatry or any other type of oppression or form of injustice, leaving a trail marker for others to be guided by is crucial.

There are many ways to leave trail marks. You can tell your story to people you meet, write it down, audio record it and share it online, let someone interview you, make a video, write a book or even write it under a pseudonym if anonymity is a concern.

You can choose to make a difference in a few people's lives or many.

The path to liberation from psychiatric harm runs on word of mouth. Most of us who are helping one another have little else to work with. We aren't major corporations who can pay for a lot of advertising (and most of us are gentle souls who don't want to tell others how to live their lives), we don't have great political clout in most cases. We have our voices, our words, our stories, the power of our soul's urges to make a difference, to spare others some of the hassle, disillusionment, pain and torture we went through ourselves.

While hiking on the land here in Olympia I came across several of these trail marker flags and couldn't help but wonder how long ago they'd been tied up. Were they tied by someone I knew who lived on this land?

Leave a trail mark behind you for you never know who might find it and when they will need it.

You may be scared, but imagine where you'd be (or wouldn't be) if others hadn't taken the courage to whisper their secrets to you, or share them publicly.

When you find something important, leave a teaching or sign post or trail marker behind so someone else might find it too. You're walking with everyone who came before and will come after you.

Our Stories Are Connected

My story is your story even though you don't know. Your story is my story even though I may never know the details.

I may see them in your face, the way your jaw slants, hear them in your voice, how it's hard for you to speak at times; I may sense your story as it screams out of you no matter how hard you try to keep it silent, but only because it's my story too and we always recognize ourselves in the mirror, no matter where we are, no matter how far from home or what time it is or how much or little we've slept.

I will always know my own story when I hear it, so I want you to tell it, even if you have no clue how, even if you hate the sound of your voice, you MUST remember it's my voice too and just like you never wanted to be silent about what mattered to you, I never wanted my words to go unread or my voice to fall on deaf ears, or tired ears, so exhausted from the absence of our stories that they can no longer listen to, or hear, anything true.

Truth is what I live for, even if it is a moving target, even if it doesn't exist for more than a moment or a breath at a time, even if I'm living in an illusion which I call truth just because its tune sounds good to my ears and I see myself in its facial expressions.

The truth is...all over the place everywhere, yet sometimes nearly impossible to find like a single green pea under many mattresses and feather beds, pillows and sheets, blankets and foam cushions and love and clothes and equipment and makeup and grooming and terror and pain and fear and regret and temptation, all rolled up like a sleeping bag in the closet with so much potential yet currently in a state of stagnation, hiding, uselessness.

Someday it will come out, someone will invite you on a camping trip and something in you will require that you say yes, even though it's been so long since you've thought about that sleeping bag, all rolled up in the back of the closet with everything, and covering that green pea you forgot about.

And when you say yes, someone inside you will leap up, ready to speak, ready to say everything you've always thought you'd say someday. Someday. Someday.

And someday became your mantra until you started to pray to make someday today, to make someday today, and today again and again TODAY, not another day, not some other time and you started to tell yourself how much you love you, only it wasn't like you were saying it, it was like someone outside you loved you so much, like a parent or a child, and you didn't know who but you didn't care either.

You didn't mind not knowing because this love was so strong and this love knew who you were and loved you no matter what; this voice was the realest thing you'd ever known and nothing or no one could drown it out or be too loud or oppressive for you to hear it.

The love was more than anything you'd known before, so strong, so reassuring, so safe and solid, the security and stability you'd always dreamed of like a big slate rock in the woods, in the woods of your mind, your essence, which could get so clouded and uncomfortable and hardly even alive at times.

Yet, once this voice of Love told you your story, you knew something else, even in your pajamas, even in the middle of sleepless nights, even after difficult times with family or times you wondered if others thought poorly of you or if you'd perhaps done something really awful because you are so human and have such weird habits sometimes, that don't make sense, yet you can't stop them, you can't help yourself from looking the other way and hiding under your own hood because it's too much sometimes and you just can't deal you can't deal you can't...No No No NO, get me out of here no.

I don't know, logic can't always explain our vague morals and logical morals can lead us astray in such an unjust world; justice is so much more confusing that any of us can admit or even come to terms with within ourselves or-

If it's simple we're doing even worse crimes, the very worst, yet the easiest: lying to ourselves.

It's the very easiest felony; no one is innocent, no one will be innocent until justice has weathered us all and who can even begin to imagine how long that will take?

Not you, not I, not anyone you can think of, so you settle for love, you settle to be loved anyway; you settle for being human and looking in this mirror, sometimes foggy, sometimes clear, sometimes steamed up and the window needs to be opened.

But even if you don't, even if you don't do anything, the voice is there when you listen, reminding you you are loved. Really no matter what at all, no matter what, or what or anything, nothing at all makes any difference at all when you hear the whisper, "I love you so much."

Workbook
Questions for Reflection:

- How have you interfered in others' lives by offering advice that wasn't asked for?

- How has your tendency to want to solve others' problems distracted you from improving your own life?

- Can you trust that focusing on your own self care will in turn inspire others?

- How can you best be a support to others without sacrificing your own well being?

- What is your line? Are there certain emergencies in which it feels right to put your own needs aside for a loved one?

- Are you able to be clear about your boundaries and take good care of yourself in the process?

- If you are aspiring to support another, have you asked them clearly what they do and don't find helpful?

- Can you let yourself off the hook from feeling responsible for the outcomes in others' lives?

CHAPTER 16

THERAPY?

Ever since I recovered from pharmaceutical abuse that nearly killed me over a decade ago, I hadn't used mental health services. There were many reasons for this and I can't say I was always decidedly against them for myself, or entirely convinced I couldn't be helped by a good therapist.

Therapy had benefited me a lot as a kid, teenager and young adult (not because I had an illness and needed to be fixed, but because I had trauma and needed to be listened to).

There were many obstacles to going to therapy though: lack of therapists I could trust, times of not having health insurance, and times of being so busy that making another appointment sounded more stressful than just taking an extra nap.

There were times I had more social connection and support and therapy seemed superfluous, draining even.

There were times I longed for someone I could talk to in that one sided way, where most of the listening and attention was on me, but I never felt safe with therapists I interviewed who believed in diagnoses or psych drugs, and of course most do.

As for coaches or counselors outside of the mental health system who did not rely on diagnostic criteria for insurance purposes, I often couldn't afford them, or if I could I was working full time and didn't have space in my schedule. As an introvert, a few hours alone in my day is essential and I probably wouldn't be able to give it up and retain my sanity even if I were talking to my favorite person in the world.

So, maybe you've figured out the punch line by now. After 10 years of vacillating between not believing in therapy and not having the time or money for it, I found myself in a new town, after dozens of moves, and with almost no social support. I have state health insurance, which covers therapy, and after 10 months of finding only providers who won't take my insurance or aren't accepting new clients, I stumbled upon a goldmine.

I'm writing about this publicly not to tout the virtues of the mental health system, which arguably there are few that are often overridden by its shortcomings, but because many psychiatric survivors who don't have strong social networks or family ties, or money for private services, might be encouraged to keep looking for the needle in the haystack (if they want to).

In my case, I got incredibly lucky.

I walked into a clinic in the next town over, where I'd heard the director is relatively anti-psych drugs and for alternative approaches. I filled out the paperwork and the receptionist made me an appointment with "Caren". I had no choice of providers, though there were interns available if it wasn't a good fit. She had no information about Caren, who was new to this clinic, except that she was very experienced and "everyone loves her".

Google had little information about Caren either, so I went in for my first appointment having little idea what to expect, but for some reason the anxiety I'd had in the past about walking into a therapist's office wasn't there. After a decade of ambivalence, I was feeling more optimistic (AKA desperate) to see a therapist.

Caren told me she'd need to ask me questions for the insurance paperwork (oh trust me, I knew) to determine my "medical need" and she made quotes with her fingers when she said "medical need". Phew. I felt at ease right away.

Okay, I felt more than at ease. I felt something like salvation. We quickly established that neither of us believe in diagnoses (she asserted that view first) and after the questions, she let me know she put me down for "adjustment disorder" and explained the things I already knew about how the system requires a diagnosis to pay for therapy.

She also told me she's anti-drugs, after I mentioned I wasn't interested in them as part of my answer to one of the insurance questions.

So...once all that was out of the way, she became someone I could talk to each week, someone compassionate and wise, not who would tell me what to do or take any of my agency away, but who would listen and be supportive and occasionally give suggestions, or relate from her own experiences. So far, she has never been intrusive, invasive, assuming or condescending.

I know how rare this is. It took me 10 years to come across such a person, and in this case it was almost sheer luck.

I share this because, yes, we need to fight against the atrocities of the mental health system, and yes we need to be very careful, and yes, many times friends are far more what we want than professionals, AND because there are those of us who, for a time and a reason may need focused support from someone and may not have friends with the time and energy to be that for us consistently.

In theory, I love the idea of the state funding people to provide emotional support, listening, encouragement and kindness. That's my idea of good therapy. As we say in the psychiatric survivor or "peer" movement, the best way to support someone is often to be authentic and use common sense.

Of course capitalism has its awful flaws and the system has its major problems and I hope someday both will be eradicated in favor of more compassionate and humane systems, but in the meantime, they are basically the systems we have on the material plane.

Having this support has enabled me to feel less completely alone with my problems, which, yes, are socio-political, economic, rooted in systemic oppression and all the rest, but knowing that can only go so far when a person is lacking the social capital, health and material resources to act on that knowledge in ways that result in change.

It's not an either or. I'm thrilled for those who have the resources to be completely independent from all of the corporate healthcare systems that are damaging many of our lives.

I share my story, though, because finding the right resources within a corrupt system can be harm reduction that can help someone feel less alone and debilitated. That's what it has done for me, after 10 years of sifting through hay, or turning away from it, sure there was no needle in there.

Do you want your therapist to be honest with you about their triggers or not?

(I recognize that many readers have had negative experiences in therapy or fundamentally don't believe in it, yet the question can be for any sort of mentor, practitioner, healer, teacher or even doctor.)

When juxtaposed with psychiatry and its capacity to damage our bodies and even kill us, therapy can seem like a gentler beast, even an opportunity for healing, self-understanding and growth. Yet, similar to psychiatry, therapy started as a way to medicalize human suffering that was clearly based on social, political and economic injustice at large.

The original therapy setting: a male "doctor" who analyzed "hysterical" women who couldn't quietly tolerate their marriages or their place in society. Instead of giving women opportunities to have more meaningful, free and powerful roles in society, we gave dissatisfied women the opportunity to "talk about it" behind closed doors, safe from causing a fuss in their families.

This talking about it may have had a sophisticated quality, and may have helped some women express their feelings.

But the premise itself, that the woman was mentally sick, hysterical or otherwise, was a lie. The benefits the therapist earned from that relationship and the role as doctor "outside" of the social system the woman was contexted in, were largely accepted and ignored.

Therapy may have been helpful in some way because it gave women (and now anyone), the opportunity to talk about their feelings (this in itself was hugely revolutionary not too long ago!) without having to take into account the other person's feelings.

People know the difference between being listened to because someone genuinely wants to and cares, versus there being an ulterior motive or financial incentive. These two can overlap, but a therapy client — and even a therapist if they are honest with themselves — is likely to feel some conflict and burden around this at some point.

Based on my own experiences, I'm pretty sure that therapy isn't a long-term path for me, but I have experienced it being useful and even lifesaving at times. Perhaps I feel it's on a spectrum with psychiatric drugs? Only for emergencies (but lesser ones) and if sustainable organic support is truly unavailable? Unlike drugs, it has resulted in healing and self understanding for me at times, just not as a long term "solution."

Whether or not therapy is something I can benefit from or whether it's "for me" has been a question I've grappled with for a long time (as well as spending plenty of time not considering it an option at all).

Most of my experiences in therapy were as a child and very young adult, and I've only had one experience of therapy recently (in the last 10 years or so). As a younger person, I was too new and naïve to therapy and how the mental health system operates — let alone how it originated — to know any better, so I got the "ignorance is bliss" type of therapy, which did land me on Prozac as a teenager but otherwise had some therapeutic effect. Without having to think about or concern myself with my therapist's feelings, I could focus on my own.

This can be incredibly healing for some of us because it is something hard for us to do naturally without judging ourselves as entitled or bratty. Does this go all the way back to the woman's role as emotional caretaker? (For men who feel this way, does it go back to their role as warrior, worker, soldier, provider?)

My make-up and family conditioning correlated with me becoming an empath early on, too aware of others' feelings and triggers for my own good.

In my dream recently I have a male therapist, only a couple of years older than me. He refers to me "acting entitled" in a situation between the two of us.

The issue is a familiar trauma trigger for me and we talk about it over and over, looping back around the same storyline for clarity, in a way that feels fruitful regardless of whether a conclusion is reached.

Then I ask him what it is about HIM that calls me entitled in that situation. He looks uncomfortable, then admits he does have personal triggers around the topic. He seems emotional, vulnerable, and childlike for a moment.

I tell him I'd rather he open up about it than simply act stoic and accuse me of being entitled. We keep discussing it. He tells me about his lifestyle. At the end of our session, I have a full bar of dark chocolate, and one square of coffee-colored chocolate in my hair. He takes the full bar as if to say I'm a spoiled brat "entitled child," and walks out without any niceties or even a goodbye. I pull the coffee-colored square out of my hair, which is in knots.

By not revealing his vulnerability, he leaves whole and with a larger treat. I'm left with knotted hair and only a small treat. What a metaphor for how therapy can be sometimes.

Being able to be heard by a professional when we talk about our feelings certainly is a small treat, but having a socially valued role and the power that comes with that is perhaps a larger one.

Coming back to my original question: Do you want your therapist to be honest with you about their triggers or not? If a therapist is honest about their triggers, they risk equalizing the power imbalance. They risk being on the same plane as their client. They risk losing their precious socially valued role as a needed professional. If the therapist has triggers too, they may end up being as "bad" as the client's, and then what? Then who is the healer?

If they try to hide and cover up their triggers to remain professional, a sensitive client will pick up on it somehow.

One reason I developed empathic skills as a child was that I could sense the truth if someone was lying to me or trying to cover up their feelings, and I only felt safe knowing the full truth. I saw how hiding feelings resulted in others being manipulative to try to cover up their dishonesty. And then there would be some kind of blowup or retaliation, a backlash that I would feel responsible for.

My parents were a therapist and a doctor respectively, so they may have had some training in this type of role playing, which made me into a natural skeptic of those power imbalances.

Dishonesty and covering up triggers can bring seductive social rewards.

Any stuffing of feelings or dishonesty has always made me palpably uneasy, like I can't stay in my own skin. In close bonds, when someone is deceptive or withholds information relevant to me, I've become violently ill on many occasions. Sometimes it has taken years for me to figure out that I'd been lied to and that correlated with that three-week worst cough of my life.

This is why I grapple with therapy, because I can bliss out for a while, "looking the other way" and letting the sessions be "all about me," and that is healing and helpful to me, to a point.

But what about when something comes up that triggers the therapist? And they maintain professional boundaries?

Here's what happened with the therapist I finally found last year, who I loved. She was the therapist of my dreams: smart, socially aware, completely disbelieving of the medical model. She was a therapy professor herself and taught Bob Whittaker's books in her classes. After opening up to her weekly for about 6 months, I went in one day with a lot on my heart that I wanted to outpour... but she had something to tell me.

The clinic she worked at would no longer be taking my insurance.

This is an instance where the bliss bubble and illusion I was in suddenly popped. Even though I knew in my mind what I was doing, that I was talking to someone who was being paid by my medical insurance to listen to me, I convinced myself that our relationship had some reality to it. I convinced myself, without realizing it, that she cared about me and that we had a real connection, that we were almost like friends.

I got a lot of small treats out of letting myself go along with this dynamic. I got to talk about all kinds of problems each week and basically control the conversation to my liking, switch the topic whenever I wanted to, express my vulnerability and be in all other ways the "client," a role I had resisted for many years, skeptical and ambivalent.

When she gave me this news I felt like I was being dumped or personally rejected. She had a stone cold look on her face and didn't show any emotion for most of the hour while I cried hard.

As I emoted, she seemed to solidify in self protection, perhaps because I expressed that I felt embarrassed that I had fallen for the therapy trap — that I had trusted her, and a situation that I should have known better than to trust.

That may have been why she looked so unfeeling, or maybe she actually was detached (and there's the view that a professional should be).

It did feel quite like heartbreak to me — like the feeling of disillusionment I've had after a relationship ending, even if I knew very well from the beginning that it was destined to "fail."

Similarly, therapy is a relationship that must be opened to fairly fully in order to "work," and yet is fundamentally limited to a professional setting and many laws that can be devastating (or even dangerous, such as forced incarceration/drugging) when real triggers come up.

I told her I felt like she didn't care about me. She replied, "I care about all of my clients," but still with no feeling. I judged myself more and more as a desperate, pathetic fool for even being there, like I had been duped all this time into thinking she cared about me.

I did ask her if this was bringing things up for her, if she was triggered, and she admitted she was upset that the clinic told her of their insurance policy changes without warning and she had no say. She admitted she wanted to go into private practice so she could see people on a sliding scale.

I sensed, though, that there was more to her trigger that she wasn't telling me. She had never looked stone cold like that before. This became, as it was and is always destined to be, about the systems we were in rather than about two people.

Her honesty brought only a small amount of relief and I cried and cried, and did get sick that week. My intuition told me I needed to cancel my remaining appointments with her (I had a month before the insurance cutoff) and once I did I felt better.

Once again it felt like accepting the end of a romantic relationship and the relief and liberation that follows the sadness, when you accept that you can't talk to or see this person for awhile. (Similarly, some of the heartbreak we experience in romance is sociopolitical rather than entirely personal in nature.)

Do other people have an easier time with therapy? Can they compartmentalize better than I can?

Do psychiatric drugs make it easier to continue the therapy system, making people a little (or a lot) more complacent and less questioning?

Anything that strips us of our health and power makes us more vulnerable to getting trapped in unequal and unrealistic relationships that we come to feel dependent on. One dependency (psych drugs) can increase another (needing a therapist to talk to) by taking a bit of our agency and self awareness away.

What led me to therapy last year was having been stripped of a lot of other things in my life that had, up until then, provided natural social support. Without that support, a therapist tasted like the meal

I was starving for. The sudden loss of that "food" felt like I was being robbed and might starve again emotionally.

A friend was in a similar situation where she lost the insurance her therapist accepted, and she became obsessed with her ex-therapist. She went as far as finding her home address, going to her home, meeting her daughter, learning as much as possible about her personal life and practically stalking her.

Many people get attached to that one person who listens to them go on and on because it's their professional role. Perhaps I've had the sense that therapy may not be for me because I do get so attached. Not knowing what triggers are going on for the therapist makes it easier to idealize them, which plays into the attachment.

Yet, if they did share their triggers all the time, therapy might not be as therapeutic, and might be more like a conversation between two people on equal ground.

My ex-therapist said something else that fateful session. She said that this is her calling, her gift, that she's not in it for the money, and I believed her 100%. She does have a gift and uses it in the system, which I suppose could be said of all of us, even those who work independently but within the money system somehow.

This leads me to the belief that therapy, when it does have a place in our lives, is (like all relationships and endeavors) more of a mystery than it is a science.

A Society Where Therapy Isn't Needed

My friend posted on Twitter: "Imagine living in a society that you don't need therapy to recover from". It got 399 likes and 101 retweets. It inspired me to write this.

A world we don't need therapy to recover from is one where everyone is living close to their soul.

Everyone is listening deeply to themselves and others, everyone is an artist practicing their art daily, everyone exercises their imagination, makes music and expresses life poetically.

Every situation is viewed and addressed soulfully, all bodies are fully embodied and being around any other person or living being is a reminder of our soul's freedom, of how connected we are, how loved and safe we are, and who we are.

Everyone's face feels like family; we are all living enough of our soul's purpose to be recognized by others and to recognize ourselves in others, and therefore to recognize others as the individuals they are, also interwoven and interconnected with ourselves.

In a society you don't need therapy to recover from, life is dreamy and poetic and there is space to listen to and act out shadow characters asking to be heard, seen, witnessed.

The integration is palpable and rather than feeling the need to prove ourselves to others as adequate/enough/good enough/anything else, we view one another as opportunities to embody and repossess more and more of our spirits and souls.

Then our beings feel light, full, strong and heartful, like nothing is missing; there are no screws loose, we don't have to cover up our playful authenticity (which is unique and free to explore in each moment) for the sake of straight jacketing conformity that is "comfortable" but doesn't feed us the full meals we need to stay willfully alive.

We are truly alive with the vitality that comes when we are free to play, experiment, imagine and at all times do what is interesting to us.

In a society you don't need therapy to recover from, the potency of passion is free to explore, to listen to deeply in oneself and others. It naturally flows in the direction it is welcomed and connects in a mutual ecstasy, spontaneous and always free to deviate from any presumed script in its own way.

The levels of vulnerability and connectedness are so high amongst the masses that people are free from clinging. Fights are not destructive, but opportunities to voice and integrate anything more. Speaking our truth is so common that big blow ups and certainly wars are unnecessary. Each soul naturally cares about the wellbeing of the others and the natural inclination is to have all needs met for all.

A society you don't need therapy to recover from.

I'm not sure if this gives a complete or concrete answer to what a society you don't need therapy to recover from would look like or how we would get there, but this is my answer for now. What is your answer?

Note: I am currently seeing a therapist and am benefiting from it a lot. I will write about this in the future.

Workbook
Questions For Reflection:

- Have you tried therapy? Did you find it helpful or harmful or a combination and why?

  _____
  _____
  _____
  _____
  _____
  _____

- What is your criteria for a therapist?

  _____
  _____
  _____
  _____
  _____
  _____
  _____
  _____

- What are some red flags for therapists?

  _____
  _____
  _____
  _____
  _____
  _____
  _____

- Does therapy have a place in your life?

- Are there alternatives to therapy you have tried or would like to try such as co-counseling, support groups or peer mentorship?

CHAPTER 17

HAVING FUN AGAIN

One of the most healing times in my life was when I lived in Northampton in my twenties and felt free and encouraged to try lots of kinds of art I hadn't thought I was good enough to do before. I experimented with dance, singing, theater, piano, visual art, performance poetry, film and a lot of other things that I would say I'm not naturally all that "good" at.

In my early life, I grew up in a competitive New York City culture where I didn't feel encouraged to try new types of art, especially ones I wasn't already good at (even though my parents encouraged me, the rest of my world seemed so cut throat and competitive).

It's so strange that we put way too much emphasis on being "good" at things rather than just doing them!

Realistic visual art was never my forte, or interest, so I was surprised that I decided to try this still life painting of some flowers a couple weeks ago at an art meetup in Portland. Usually, if I do visual art at all it will be collage or abstract mish mosh.

Creative Tip: Spend an hour every day doing some form of art, and once in awhile try new things.

Drama

The drama is not the problem. It's the gift when you find the places for it.

Even if you don't think you have drama, you do; we all do, it's the nature of being alive in an f-ed up world.

When I see housing ads seeking, "peaceful, mindful, drama-free roommates," I chuckle inside. Those peaceful, mindful zen folk are fantasy robots. They don't exist! No one has ever lived with one!

If you think you know any, you've never lived with them.

The tarot and all ancient traditions and practices of integration or even religion, recognize that being human is a drama filled affair.

Drama exists in all of us because we have many parts, and the current state of the world asks us to fragment ourselves and put our parts in neat boxes. And we can't.

So we have huge raging monsters inside.

We have rebellious catatonic mutes who are unwilling to speak. We have babies who are crying all day.

We have the homicidal, suicidal, escapist, rapist, confrontational, all within us.

Rather than shut it all down and show up for "work" like society asks us to, I recommend you find some outlets, some stages, pages and playgrounds to enact all these dramatic characters.

Humans love drama, just not in their kitchens. They want it safely on a screen, in the pages of a book, in a live performance. So go create that art, where you can use all your craziness to expose the underbelly you're being told is a mental illness.

Ideas for where to keep the drama:

1. laughter yoga (just tried this, wow it really works)
2. improv
3. writing
4. painting
5. theater
6. vocal improv
7. ecstatic dance
8. board games
9. Sports

See? All of our favorite "fun" activities give us an arena for our drama, to fight, to have a "safe" space to defy normality, to escape mental conformity.

Unfortunately, more people sit on their couches watching sports or movies or listening to music, rather than using outlets for their own drama. There's nothing wrong with being an audience member for drama, but don't forget you have your OWN drama.

And if you don't find a stage or page or playground, it will show up in your life. Which is fine, if that's what you prefer. But, even if you want a dramatic personal life (which may be inescapable-darn it), the more drama you can discharge elsewhere, the less you will need to bring into your "real life" arenas unnecessarily.

Dreams are another arena for drama. More evidence that we all have it, we're all crazy, no matter how normal.

I took all the photos in this post while lying down laughing, after my first laughter yoga group. If the clouds are doing this, I thought, we are meant to have some drama (and fun) too.

P.S. There are times when life forces us to face drama in our actual lives, no doubt.

Post-Pharma Party Cocktail

    May psychiatry fall into its own trap
    May its karmic destiny finally come
    May it become disabled and disenfranchised
    as it has made me and my people
    May it like all things have its day
    May its sun set in the heavens
    the post psychiatry mystics and seers
    shining and glowing in the night
    alongside moons and stars
    untouched by Pharma's chemical personality adjustments
    May all beings wear cloaks of protection
    heavy and padded
    and learn to spot criminal
    in party lines and eyeglass rims
    until then
    And until then may we look for each other
    underneath cocktails of wrong things
    May we cast aside anything anyone has ever told us
    about the mentally ill and mentally healthy
    and look someone in the eye
    deep in the eye
    and breathe
    and ask ourselves, for as long as we need to,
    until we find an answer we can trust,
    "What is this about?"
    Yes, find the answer while looking into their eyes and breathing.
    Find the answer beneath all contrived illnesses you've been told
    about or come to believe in
    as though they exist
    as though they exist
    as though they exist
    When you breathe and meet eyes with another being,
    ask yourself, "Where are these illnesses?"
    ask yourself, "Where did they go?"
    ask yourself what you need to reconstruct to resurrect them
    and ask yourself if that's necessary,
    if that's absolutely needed

if it's worth the price of
a life well lived
if it's worth the dignity of those you love
if you'd want that dignity robbed from you
ever
ever
EVER
under any circumstance
in any social construct
would you give life over
to an outright evidence based
lie?
Or would you rather boot the lie and its industry
to the next curb
with steel toes and power kicks
ready for the party that follows?

Workbook
Questions for reflection:

- What is most fun for you?

\

- What was most fun for you as a kid or in the past?

- Are there new things you'd like to try?

- Did psychiatry or a diagnosis inhibit your ability to have fun and trust your instincts?

- Do you enjoy things you aren't necessarily "good" at?

- Are there fun ways you can work through traumas? Ways that feel liberating? Finding spaces to yell or express anger and outrage if you weren't allowed to?

- Do you make time specifically for things you enjoy?

- Do you stretch your capacities for fun and freedom?

- How can more of your life be fun and free?

CHAPTER 18

FREEDOM FROM PSYCHIATRIC DRUGS WORKBOOK

Alongside this book, I created a workbook and meditation for coming off psych meds. The workbook asks questions to help get at what the fears are, but more importantly, what the vision is on a deeper level.

This isn't a WRAP (Working Recovery Action Plan) type of workbook, though I do recommend WRAP to some of my clients and friends. The purpose of the workbook and meditation for coming off psych meds isn't crisis aversion or symptom management, but rather to delve into any deeper blocks to psychiatric drug freedom that might exist.

These are the intentions of this workbook and meditation for coming off psych meds. To see who you are once you are off of psych drugs, and who you were before. The questions in the Workbook for Psychiatric Drug Freedom are designed to help get to the essence of what this freedom means and looks like for you as an individual. It's different for everyone.

After I wrote this workbook, it sat as a Word document on my hard drive for many months. Then one day, Sheryl Sitts, podcaster at Journey of Possibilities contacted me about doing a collaboration. She had interviewed me for her podcast several years earlier and we'd talked about psychiatric drugs and the possibility of freedom from them on her show.

I told her about the workbook I'd made and she suggested creating a companion audio meditation that folks could listen to. We worked to create a script for her that would be most effective in guiding the listener through a process of envisioning themselves free of psych drugs.

I tweaked and re-tweaked it and got feedback from other psychiatric drug survivor comrades and Mad In America readers, who helped us make it more effective. We thought about what prompts would and wouldn't be interesting, useful and digestible to those in withdrawal.

Sheryl recorded (and re-recorded) a beautiful meditation to envision yourself free from psychiatric drugs.

Both the workbook and meditation for coming off psych meds are designed to be able to be used repeatedly. The workbook questions can be revisited monthly and the meditation can be listened to as often as desired, even daily. For those who connect with audio mediation and guided visualization, practicing the daily meditation will be a great tool for reprogramming the mind and consciousness to open to greater possibilities.

Of course these tools are best used in companion with other peer supports, sound medical advice, nutritional and naturopathic counseling and careful tapering plans. The workbook and audio are in no way designed as a substitute for any other support, medical or otherwise. Rather, they are a supplement, and a powerful one.

I made this workbook and meditation for coming off psych meds because, for me and many of my comrades, it was in part my soul strength that got me through the hardest times in life, especially breaking free from psychiatry. It was something other than tapering protocols and supplement plans that was at the core of my ability to break free, though all pieces of the picture were and are important.

In addition to the workbook questions, there are mixed media art pieces by Jessica Charity Wachtman which illustrate the document. It comes as a fillable PDF, which you can type in or print out.

I'm planning, as well, to create some online and telephone support groups for those using the workbook and meditation and will write about those once they are established. Feel free to join my newsletter to be the first to hear and get the lowest prices - you'll get a free e-book on alternatives to psychiatry when you join!

My goal with this workbook has been to create something affordable that is also useful and will connect people with their own deeper longings and those of others. Creating ways to connect those who are using these tools will be the next step.

Please visit my website for more info on accessing the workbook: www.chayagrossberg.com.

See Chayagrossberg.com for info on the

Med Free Solutions Certificate Course

ABOUT THE AUTHOR

Author, Chaya Grossberg is a consultant working with people seeking creative and nutritional alternatives to psychiatric drugs.

Chaya has been working as an activist for change in the "mental health" system and provided holistic mental health alternatives for the past 15 years, starting as a Freedom Center organizer for six years in Northampton, Massachusetts. She has worked with the Western Massachusetts Recovery Learning Community, Massachusetts Protection and Advocacy council, Windhorse Associates, Alternative to Meds Center, the Mental Health Association of Portland, Portland Hearing Voices and the Mental Health Association of San Francisco.

Chaya currently lives in Olympia, Washington where she spends her time writing, drinking herbal infusions and living life imperfectly to the best of her ability.

If you enjoyed this book, we would so appreciate it if you reviewed it on Amazon so it will reach others!

Thank you so much!